BATTLEFIELD

The skills of modern war

BATTLEFIELD

The skills of modern war

David Miller

MALLARD PRESS

First published in the United States
of America in 1990 by the Mallard Press
An imprint of BDD Promotional
Book Company, Inc.
666 Fifth Avenue
New York, N.Y. 10103

Copyright © 1990 Brian Trodd Publishing
House Limited

ISBN 0-792-45396-4

Printed in Italy

CONTENTS

INTRODUCTION

Wars and rumours of war have abounded since peace theoretically returned 45 years ago and every continent, with the sole exception of the Antarctic, has been the scene of some form of armed conflict. Even the waters under the Arctic ice-cap have become naval testing grounds as ever more powerful nuclear-propelled submarines grope their way around the oceans' depths. Space, too, 'the final frontier', has become the scene of military activities as hundreds of communications, photographic, electronic and other 'spy' satellites circle the Earth in support of military activities below. Space also provides potential passage for nuclear-armed re-entry vehicles as they fly from one continent to another, should nuclear war ever come.

There are, however, indications that some nations feel that the process has gone far enough. In the latter half of the 1980s there have been a number of encouraging signs that, in some areas at least, nations are prepared to step back from the brink on which they seem to have been poised for so long. The SALT 1 and ABM treaties set limits on certain types of weapon and prevented some future production, but the INF Treaty actually removed a whole existing class of weapons from the inventories of both Superpowers. There are encouraging signs that that process may be extended.

Numerous, seemingly intransigent problems have been resolved, or are well on their way to resolution. Over a relatively short period the Soviet war in Afghanistan has ended, an armistice has been signed in the Gulf War, the Vietnamese have begun to withdraw from Cambodia and the Cubans are withdrawing from southern Africa. There have been momentous political changes in Eastern Europe, and the sight of Soviets observing exercises in Britain or of US inspectors watching missiles being broken up in the USSR – unthinkable ten years ago – has now become almost commonplace.

These signs are indeed welcome, but the world has seen similar episodes before. Treaties are signed in an atmosphere of euphoria and with total sincerity, but a change of leadership in one country or another, the collapse of a currency, a series of bad harvests, or sometimes the unexpected interference of a third party, have suddenly changed the whole situation.

Further, while the process of building confidence in Europe appears to be progressing well and the first tentative steps in force reduction are taking place, the situation elsewhere is by no means so rosy. The Iran–Iraq war is suspended, but while it lasted it proved how horrible 'conventional' war can be and also showed that weapons supposedly deplored by the majority of the civilized world – chemical agents – can be used with little real reaction from outside. In some areas, too, national armed forces are actually increasing in size and capability; perhaps with little evil intent today, but conferring the means for a change in intention tomorrow.

Below: Admiral William J. Crowe, Jr., Chairman of the US Joint Chiefs–of Staff, greets his Soviet opposite number in the Pentagon on 10 December 1987, a scene unthinkable ten years earlier.

The Size of Armed Forces

There are two possible indicators of the importance which countries place on defence. The first is the amount of money they spend, but it is virtually impossible to obtain accurate and generally accepted figures. The second is manpower, where a more accurate estimate is possible, even though some countries are always in the process of changing the size of their armed forces; some in Europe are reducing while others, notably in Asia and Latin America, are increasing. There is also the complication of whether or not to count reservists, paramilitary forces, armed police, and so on. However, recognizing these problems and using the reputable *The Military Balance: 1988–1989* published by the International Institute for Strategic Studies in London, the number of full-time servicemen currently on active duty (i.e. including navies, armies and air forces, but excluding reservists and paramilitaries) is of the order of:

Warsaw Pact	6,435,900 (USSR 5,226,000)
NATO	5,512,100 (USA 2,158,000)
Other Europe	459,100 (Yugoslavia 213,500)
Middle East	3,168,200 (Iraq 1,000,000)
Africa	936,900 (Ethiopia 320,000)
Asia	8,409,400 (China 3,200,000)
	(India 1,262,000)
	(Vietnam 1,252,000)
Latin America	1,378,500 (Brazil 283,400)
TOTAL	**28,930,600**

Below: In Asia there are many potential conflagrations, where one false move could spark off a major incident or even an all-out war. Here US Army and Republic of Korea infantrymen watch at the border with North Korea, a border which has never been quiet since the 1953 Armistice.

Above: The military tension in Central Europe reduced dramatically in the late 1980s, but the situation in Latin America remained very tense. At Christmas 1989 US forces invaded Panama, while elsewhere other trouble spots remained. Here, US officers lecture Honduran soldiers.

This is a massive total and even though three Superpowers account for some 40 per cent of the grand total it suggests that even the smallest and poorest countries still devote a large part of their resources to 'defence'. The largest armed forces in each area are noted in the column on the right. It will be seen that in Asia there are three countries with armed forces over one million strong, with the two Koreas only marginally behind: 838,000 in the north and 629,000 in the south. In South America there are three countries with armed forces greater than 100,000 strong: Brazil – 295,700; Mexico – 134,500; and Peru – 113,000. In the Caribbean Cuba has by far the strongest forces – 175,500.

Naval and air forces are, of course, of great importance in any conflict and may make significant contributions to the outcome, but it is in the land battles that the most bitter fighting takes place and where the ultimate decision in any war is reached. The crucial importance of land warfare is underlined by the fact that, in the virtually ceaseless conflicts since 1945, naval and air superiority have not, of themselves, been the major factors affecting the outcome in any of them. Indeed, in many of the wars won by anti-colonial movements the side that lost had virtually total naval and air supremacy, for example in Indochina and Afghanistan.

Types of Modern Warfare

The many wars fought and prepared for over the past 45 years suggest that modern military possibilities fall into three broad categories:

General War: a global conflict between the Superpowers and their alliances. It is assumed that such a conflict, were it to take place, would be fought with few, if any, limits other than crossing the nuclear threshold. The threat of nuclear war would remain a possibility at all stages and once the first nuclear weapon had been fired, there might be a short pause and possibly a halt, but thereafter there would probably be no restrictions whatsoever.

Limited War: a conflict fought within some form of implicitly agreed restrictions, both as to participation and geographical extent. The possibility of extending the conflict and the danger of escalation exists in all such wars, but has so far been avoided.

Counter-Terrorist Operations: military and police activities in dealing with terrorism, which may vary from individual acts, such as bombing, to coordinated group activities over an extended period, such as the IRA in Northern Ireland and ETA in Spain.

The First and Second World Wars were, as their names suggest, global conflicts, although Europe shared importance with the Far East as the two critical theatres in the latter. However, since 1945, Europe has been the major area of confrontation between the Superpowers and it has, by common consent, been the area where the next global conflict would most probably start. Further, the conflict having started, it would be events in Europe which would most probably be the cause of escalation to nuclear war.

The Central Front

Viewed from a global perspective, Europe seems to be a cohesive mass stretching from Norway in the North to the Mediterranean in the South. Indeed, from a Soviet perspective, too, the potential European battlefield is a homogenous geographical entity, certainly in military terms, since they have a land border stretching over the entire area from Norway to Turkey. However, although the Scandinavian and Mediterranean areas are of great importance, it is on the

Above: Guerrilla fighters have achieved some spectacular successes, even against modern Western armies.

Central Front that the most crucial battles in a future conflict are likely to take place. The Central Front is also the place where the most sophisticated and powerful war-fighting machines that have ever existed face each other and have faced each other for the past 40 years.

Although accurate figures are impossible to come by (and whichever source is taken there will always be someone who will disagree with it) the British Statement on Defence Policy 1989–1990 states that the in-place forces stationed on the Central Front are:

NATO		Warsaw Pact
3,100,000	Personnel	4,100,000
14,500	Artillery	43,400
16,400	Tanks	51,500
3,000	Helicopters	4,000
5,300	Aircraft	8,900

These figures are just those currently stationed in Europe and European USSR west of the Urals and exclude the reservists who would be mobilized in the countries in the area, plus the reinforcements which would come from North America and the USSR east of the Urals. Thus, within just a few weeks, perhaps even days, there would be well over 10 million men and women under arms.

Other Scenarios

The most intense preparation for war, the highest states of readiness and the most sophisticated armed forces have existed in Europe over the past 40 years. But the actual fighting – and there has been a lot of it – has taken place elsewhere. There have been limited wars in the Middle East, Africa, Asia and Southern America, and there have been counter-guerrilla wars on all continents. Further, the new scourge of terrorism has struck across the world, giving certain elements of the armed forces a new role in the exceptionally difficult task of countering this new threat to the fabric of society. Thus, the threat which most modern land and air forces have to confront ranges from global nuclear warfare through limited warfare in the classical style to dealing with a group of two or three terrorists holed up with their hostages.

Organization for Fighting

All armies use similar terminology to describe their units and formations, but different tactical requirements and historical factors lead to differences beneath the surface. All have the battalion as the largest unit with an autonomous existence and a coherent, single-arm, composition. Thus, in all armies an infantry battalion consists almost entirely of infantrymen, apart from a few specialists attached from other arms, such as armourers, radio technicians and vehicle mechanics. Further, the infantry battalion consists of three or four infantry companies, supported by a heavy weapons company with mortars, machine-guns and anti-tank weapons, and a headquarters company to give logistic support. However, the size varies and in some armies the infantry battalion is about 400 strong and commanded by a major, while in others it is about 650 strong and commanded by a lieutenant-colonel. Most armies have a number of different types of infantry battalion: mechanized, which are equipped with APC/IFVs; light, for limited war operations and either foot-, helicopter- or lorry–borne; and parachute, for use in the parachute assault role.

All armies also have tank battalions, equipped with between 30 and about 50 tanks. Tank platoons can vary in size between three and five tanks. Like infantry battalions, a tank battalion consists of three or four tank companies, a support company and a headquarters company. In some armies with a strong cavalry tradition, tank companies are called squadrons and tank platoons, troops.

At the next level, units of different arms are brought together into a fighting formation known variously as a brigade (US, FRG and UK) or a regiment (France, USSR, etc.). These are commanded by a brigadier-general (US, FRG), brigadier (UK), or a colonel (France, USSR). It should be appreciated, however, that in some armies a brigade or regiment is permanently constituted (as in the British and Soviet armies), while in others (such as the US Army) a brigade simply exists as a staff headquarters until such time as the divisional commander allocates it a task and the assets (i.e. tank, infantry, artillery units, etc.) to complete that task.

Such formations are normally the smallest combat bodies which can undertake

Below: British Royal Marines advance across typical Falkland Islands countryside in their 1982 campaign to eject the invading Argentine forces.

an independent role, as they are the first level where sufficient and balanced elements of combat arms (infantry, tanks), and combat support (artillery, engineers, aviation) exist, together with service support units (i.e. medical, transportation, supply, etc.). Such brigades and regiments normally include in their title an indication of which is the predominant combat arm: thus, an armoured or tank brigade would have (say) three tank battalions and an infantry (motor rifle) battalion, while a mechanized infantry (motor rifle) brigade would have three infantry and one tank battalion.

A further complication, but one with substantial benefits, is that brigades/regiments will frequently 'group' and 'regroup' to suit the tactical situation. This means that they form 'battle groups' (UK) or 'task forces' (US) in which the commander balances the units in order to carry out the mission. Thus, a British 'armour heavy battle group' would consist of a tank battalion headquarters, two or three tank companies and a mechanized infantry company, while in a 'mechanized battle group' the balance would be reversed; i.e. an infantry headquarters, three infantry companies and a tank company. The high mobility of modern units and their extensive scale of radios mean that such groups can be formed and reformed on the battlefield, a manoeuvre which is practised regularly in peacetime.

The next step up is a division, commanded by a major-general, which is made up of a number of brigades or

Above: Two British Royal Armoured Corps officers discuss the tactical situation during an exercise in Germany. Such exercises have brought European armies to a very high stage of training, but civil communities now question their necessity.

Below: A column of West German Marder APCs and an M113 ambulance on exercise. The harvest has been gathered and the crops will not have been harmed, but such exercises still leave their mark on the countryside, as the track marks show.

regiments, normally three or four. There are also a host of divisional troops, including artillery, engineer, aviation and logistics units, the resources of which are controlled and allocated by the divisional headquarters.

In published force comparisons (for example, between NATO and the Warsaw Pact) the normal level at which such comparisons are made is the division. However, great care must be exercised in interpreting the results of such statistics since divisions can vary markedly in actual size. Thus, for example, a Soviet motor rifle division contains some 12,000 men and a Soviet tank division 9,439 men, but a US division in Europe is some 17,000 strong: quantities of major equipment such as tanks, APC/IFV, artillery pieces, helicopters, etc., vary dramatically also.

A number of divisions are grouped into a corps (NATO) or an army (Warsaw Pact), and these again have, in addition to the divisions, a number of corps/army-controlled troops, whose resources are allocated as decided by the commander. As an example, a Soviet army might comprise:

– Between three and seven motor rifle or tank divisions, the balance depending upon the tactical mission.
– One surface-to-surface missile (SSM) brigade.
– Two to four artillery regiments.
– A number of specialized, independent, anti-tank and air defence (gun and missile) units.
– A signal regiment for army-level communications.
– A number of combat engineer units, including those equipped for assault river crossings and bridging.
– Transport units.
– Supply, storage and petrol units.
– Medical units and field hospitals.
– Equipment recovery and repair units.

In NATO, the corps is the largest *national* formation and the title always includes the national designator; e.g. 3 (US) Corps, 1 (BR) Corps, 1 (NL) Corps (Note: BR = British; NL = Netherlands). Above this level, NATO corps are formed into army groups, which are international; for example, Northern Army Group (NORTHAG), Central Army Group (CENTAG) etc.

In the Warsaw Pact the army is the

Above: For military forces in NATO and the Warsaw Pact multinational operations are routine. Here troops of five NATO nations watch an exercise in Norway.

highest peacetime tactical grouping. The next echelon of command in the Soviet Army in peace is the 'group of forces'; for example, all Soviet forces in peacetime in the German Democratic Republic are subordinated to the newly redesignated 'Western Group of Forces (WGF)'. There is no direct equivalent for the non-Soviet Warsaw Pact forces, who are simply subordinated to their national ministries of defence. In war, however, the Warsaw Pact forces would all come under the command of *Front* headquarters (roughly equivalent to a NATO army group), with fronts coming under a Theatre of Military Operations (*teatr voyennkh deystivy* (TVD). TVD HQs are believed to exist in peacetime with the Western TVD HQ being at Legnica in Poland. All front and TVD commanders would be officers of the Soviet Army.

What Would War Be Like?

There is an interesting underlying train of thought in many debates in the West about defence, where it seems to be assumed that conventional war would somehow be a less harmful and therefore more acceptable alternative to nuclear war. It is, of course, perfectly true that unrestrained nuclear war would be cataclysmic in its consequences, causing – at the very least – many millions (possibly hundreds of millions) of deaths and rendering huge areas of the Earth uninhabitable for generations. However, while nuclear weapons have introduced a new level of destruction and increased in power since their only use in 1945, conventional weapons have also increased dramatically in their destructive capability as well as in their general availability.

Indeed, it is worth mentioning that during the Second World War the two most devastating air bombardments were not the atomic bomb attacks on Hiroshima and Nagasaki, but the conventional bomb attacks on Dresden and Tokyo. The Dresden attack (13–14 February 1945) consisted of two raids, one at night by the RAF and the second the following morning by the USAAF; German casualties were at least 100,000 killed. The most severe of the attacks on Tokyo (9–10 March 1945) totally destroyed 15 square miles of the city and killed over 83,000 people, with a further 100,000 injured. In contrast, the Hiroshima raid (6 August 1945) killed 78,150, with a further 70,000 seriously injured, while that at Nagasaki (9 August 1945) killed some 40,000, with 25,000 injured. However, the atomic bomb attacks introduced a new scale of economy of effort, since each involved only one bombing aircraft to drop a bomb with a yield equivalent to 13,000 tons of TNT (13kT), whereas the conventional raids all needed hundreds of aircraft; the Tokyo raid, for example, needed 334 aircraft to drop 1,667 tons of conventional bombs.

It must be remembered that the First and Second World Wars have had massive consequences in terms of military and civilian deaths and casualties, as Tables 1 and 2 show.

It is difficult to compare the human cost of the post-1945 conflicts directly with either of the two World Wars. Perhaps the nearest to a conventional war

Below right: The city of Hiroshima in Japan virtually ceased to exist after just one 20kT atomic bomb was dropped on 6 August 1945.

TABLE 1: FIRST WORLD WAR

Country	Total Force Mobilized	Military Battle Deaths	Military Wounded	Civilian Dead
USA	4,350,000	50,585	205,690	–
Russia	12,000,000	1,700,000	4,950,000	2,000,000
UK (incl. Empire)	8,904,467	908,371	2,090,212	30,633
France	8,410,000	1,357,800	4,266,000	40,000
Germany	11,000,000	1,808,546	4,247,143	760,000
Austria-Hungary	7,800,000	922,500	3,620,000	300,000
Others	12,574,343	1,272,978	1,849,768	3,512,000
TOTALS	**65,038,810**	**8,020,780**	**21,228,813**	**6,642,633**

[Source: The Encyclopedia of Military History, Dupuy & Dupuy, Jane's, London, 1980, p 900]

TABLE 2: SECOND WORLD WAR

Country	Total Force Mobilized	Military Battle Deaths	Military Wounded	Civilian Dead
USA	14,900,000	292,100	571,822	–
USSR	20,000,000	7,500,000	14,012,000	10–15,000,000
UK (including Commonwealth)	6,200,000	397,762	475,000	65,000
France	6,000,000	210,671	400,000	108,000
Germany	12,500,000	2,850,000	7,250,000	500,000
Japan	7,400,000	1,506,000	500,000	300,000
China	6–10,000,000	500,000	1,700,000	1,000,000
Italy	4,500,000	77,500	120,000	40–100,000
Others	20,000,000	1,500,000	Not known	14–17,000,000
TOTALS	**100,000,000**	**15,000,000**	**c.25,000,000**	**26–34,000,000**

[Source: ibid, p 1198]

Left: The damage wrought by conventional weapons in the Second World War has been largely forgotten, but the town of Cleve in Germany was devastated in February 1945.

was the Korean War (1950–53), although this was fought with essentially Second World War weapons, apart from jet aircraft and the threat of the use of atomic weapons. However, even though limited to the Korean peninsula and the immediately adjacent waters, it was a costly conflict. There were 118,515 deaths on the UN side (33,629 of them US), which does not include the South Korean military, of whom an estimated 70,000 died. On the other (Communist) side there were some 1,600,000 battle casualties, 60 per cent of them Chinese. A particular feature of this war was the high number of prisoners taken by the Communists (92,987) and the very large proportion who died in the POW camps; for example, of 10,218 US captured, 21 refused to return and only 3,746 remained alive to be repatriated after the signing of the Armistice, the remainder (6,451) having died in Communist hands. The number of civilians in South and North Korea who died as a consequence of the war has never been determined, but assuredly ran into many hundreds of thousands.

The next large-scale protracted conflict was the Vietnam War. In this the casualties were also very high (see Table 3).

The list of post-1945 conflicts is too long to record here, but it seems not unreasonable to suppose that a total of some 10 million have died as a direct result of these wars. Thus, although the Hiroshima and Nagasaki bombs show that atomic and nuclear weapons give high casualties for little effort, conventional air attacks against Dresden and Tokyo, and operations in post-1945 wars (e.g. Vietnam, Cambodia, Afghanistan) show that modern conventional weapons can cause casualties and devastation on a truly horrifying scale. The pictures of Hue in Vietnam during the Tet battles of 1968, of Beirut in 1989 and of the hordes of casualties to both high-explosive and chemical weapons in the Iran–Iraq war testify to the effectiveness of modern non-nuclear weaponry.

Modern conventional warfare on land would differ from that of 1945 in a number of significant ways. Firstly, virtually every weapon is more powerful in nearly every respect than its predecessor,

TABLE 3: VIETNAM WAR[1]

Country	Total Force Mobilized	Military Battle Deaths	Military Wounded
USA	625,866[2]	56,552[3]	153,311
RVN	c.1,000,000	196,863	502,383
Other Free World[4]	72,000	5,225	11,988
North Vietnam and Viet Cong	c.1,000,000	c.900,000	Not known
TOTALS	**2,697,866**	**1,148,354**	**Not known**

Notes:
1. Civilian deaths are impossible to estimate.
2. Maximum in-theatre figure (27 March 1969).
3. Includes 10,326 military non-battle deaths.
4. Australia, South Korea, New Zealand, Philippines, Thailand

[Source: ibid, p 1221]

with longer range, greater accuracy, more rapid firing rate and greater lethality on the target.

Secondly, there are weapons now available which were simply not in existence in the last war, such as anti-tank missiles, while others were just in their infancy, such as fuel-air explosives, anti-aircraft and surface-to-surface missiles.

Thirdly, the power of the air forces in support of the land battle is infinitely greater than before. Aircraft travel at least twice as fast, carry far greater payloads, and the weapons are each more accurate and more powerful than their predecessors, while the means of calling for such support have improved greatly.

Fourthly, the helicopter has brought a whole new dimension to the land battle. Transport helicopters can move men, weapons, equipment and stores around the battlefield at a rate never before considered feasible, and can substantially increase the chances of a wounded man's survival by lifting him quickly and comfortably from near the spot where he was hit direct to a base hospital. In addition to all this, however, the armed helicopter is a truly innovative weapons system, whose potential against enemy troops, tanks and indeed other helicopters, is only just starting to be realized.

Fifthly, the pace of modern warfare is potentially far, far greater than that of the Second World War, or, indeed, of most of the conventional wars since. Every man and every item of impedimenta, from food to ammunition and from spare parts to weapons, in a modern division on the Central Front is mobile in either a tracked or a wheeled vehicle. The scale of radios is such that virtually every minor unit is in communication not only with its superior headquarters but also with its subordinate sections, thus enabling control to be maintained in a fast moving battle.

Next, the very wide scale of issue of effective night vision devices enables units and individuals to move and fight at night in a manner unprecedented in warfare. The hitherto friendly cover of darkness, when food could be brought forward, cables laid, units in the front-line replaced, repairs done and a little sleep snatched is no more. Observation has advanced dramatically as infantry radars and thermal imagers enable front-line troops to see not only through darkness, but through mist and camouflage nets as well.

Means of command and control have also changed out of all recognition. Modern communications systems are divorced from the chain-of-command, are designed to withstand both battle damage

and electronic counter-measures, and provide a capacity and quality undreamed of 45 years ago. Virtually all radio speech is secure (i.e. rendered unintelligible to a hostile listener) by electronic means which are virtually unbreakable. Further, these systems are being used not only to carry voice and telegraph communications more rapidly and efficiently than ever before, but they are also starting to carry data streams linking computers to each other to provide much more effective support to headquarters' staffs.

But (and there is always a 'but') there is another side to all this. For example, the pace is potentially devastating. With the speed resulting from more vehicles, better communications to exercise control and devices to enable operations to continue at night, it might be that men are simply not going to be able to keep up – and, at least on the NATO side, there are precious few reserve units to push into the line to relieve tired units.

Next, there is at least a question mark over the ability of the logistics systems of either NATO or the Warsaw Pact to maintain the supply of ammunition, fuel, spares, rations and replacements required to keep all this going at the pace which is theoretically possible. The finest tanks and aircraft are useless without fuel, guns without ammunition are merely metal tubes, and the fastest mechanical mine-layer with no mines to lay is just a complex machine.

Then, too, there is the electronic warfare (EW) factor. Just as communications have improved, so also have means of interfering with them. Electronic warfare is big business and huge investments have been made in manpower and equipment dedicated to preventing an enemy from obtaining effective use of his electronic systems. There are even cynics who say that there is such a mass of electronic devices on both sides in Europe that jamming will not be necessary as they will simply crowd each other off the air. Whichever is the case, a tank or a company or a surface-to-air missile launching unit without communications is virtually useless.

Inevitably, if war should come it would be a compromise between these two extremes. Armies would come to terms quickly with the new conditions and perhaps some problems that now appear serious would prove to have been illusions, while other new and totally unforeseen problems would appear and answers would have to be found to them also.

This book sets out to paint a picture of what the modern battlefield might look like, what forces would be involved, what equipment they would use and what their

Above: US M113 APCs and M551 Sheridan tank in a rubber plantation in South Vietnam in the late 1960s – a war which has far from disappeared into history.

Left: The armed helicopter is the one truly innovative weapons system in the land battles of the past 20 years.

Right: Despite all the 'new' weapons on the modern battlefield, the infantry remains one of the most vital elements.

problems might be. It makes no moral judgements, makes no predictions of the likelihood of war in any particular area, nor does it seek to suggest who possible opponents might be. In particular, it does not seek to suggest that there would be much glory on a future battlefield, whether conventional or nuclear.

The book also reaches no conclusions on the role of the soldier in the modern state. In the past two centuries military leaders have become more influential in the central affairs of many states, and on numerous occasions they have advocated war as a solution to internal or external

Left: Some of the most dramatic modern battles take place in the invisible arena of the electromagnetic spectrum. This is a Norwegian electronic warfare vehicle.

problems. This was particularly so in 1914, where the generals and admirals in most European capitals pushed the politicians towards war; not, it must be added, that many of the politicians nor, indeed, the public at large, were particularly reluctant. The outbreak of the Second World War saw most general and naval staffs, even in Berlin, advising against war, although in most cases this was because they did not consider their forces ready for war, rather than for any moral reason or reluctance to fight.

In the years immediately following the Second World War there were occasional outbursts as a result of the frustrations of the Cold War. One general even went so far as to advocate a pre-emptive nuclear strike against the USSR 'to bomb the Commies (sic) back into the Stone Age'.

This feeling (although perhaps not so extreme as the last example quoted) persisted until some indeterminate point in the last 20 or so years, where the soldier's role has been perceived to have changed, at least where general war is concerned, from advocating war to actually preventing it. Modern, high-level warfare is so complicated, its tactics so involved and its weapons systems so technologically advanced that few outside the military really understand the potential of the force now available. But many soldiers have themselves realized that a future war would be so destructive – even if it did not involve nuclear weapons – that their true role can only be war-prevention rather than war-fighting.

This has resulted in a cruel paradox for the soldier in Central Europe in that the only apparent way to prevent war is to prepare for it. The soldier thus finds himself preparing for something he does not want to happen; indeed, the more efficient he is, the more unlikely it is that all his training and preparation will be put to the test. However, the soldier, like any other observer of the modern world, knows that capabilities are one thing, intentions are another, and there have been too many instances on the international scene of sudden and unpredictable changes in intention. That, perhaps, is

Below: The dilemma for these Danish soldiers, as in most modern armies, is that the more prepared they are, the less likely they are to have to fight.

the soldier's true role: to prepare and train to fight against a potentially hostile military capability, however friendly it may appear, and thus guard against a change in intention which might otherwise result in that capability being put to use. However, as has been mentioned

already, and as will be made clearer in the pages that follow, there are many, many wars around the world in which there is no (or very little) danger of escalation and so the profession of arms is unlikely to be put out of business for a long time to come!

TANKS

Introduction

The Main Battle Tank (MBT) is the pre-eminent weapons system on today's battlefield. It is characterized by heavy firepower, a high degree of battlefield mobility, good protection and efficient communications. In combination, these enable MBTs to be effective not only as individual vehicles, but also in mass as a striking force at the tactical, operational and even strategic levels. For offensive use, MBTs are seen as the crucial element of the advance, which all other ground-force elements must combine to support. Further, in defence, despite all the other anti-tank systems which are now available on the battlefield, MBTs are regarded as the one element which can defeat the enemy's advancing armour.

Tank Characteristics

The prime characteristics of the MBT are firepower, mobility, protection. It is not possible to optimize all in the same design and thus operational staffs and designers strive to achieve the best balance, based upon operational requirements, national traditions and combat experience. So, the British, following their experiences in the Second World War, have long optimized protection and fire-power, with the result that their tanks have been better armoured and with a heavier gun than most other MBTs – but they have also tended to be heavier, slower and less agile. The Soviets, on the other hand, have developed a greater number of smaller, lighter and less sophisticated tanks, with greater speed. Their previously poor protection has been improved in the late 1980s by adding reactive armour.

Sometimes technology helps to solve problems. For example, in the 1950s if a more powerful MBT engine was needed it inevitably had to be bigger; thus, to make a heavy tank more mobile it needed a larger engine, which meant more space, and an even bigger and heavier tank. Today, however, engines are much more powerful for a given volume than those of 20 years ago. So, although most MBTs are now in the 50–60 ton bracket (compared to 40–45 tons in the 1950s and 1960s) their power-to-weight ratio is much higher, because the engine output power has increased by a much greater amount.

Anti-tank warfare is discussed elsewhere in this book, but the threat which the MBT has to face needs to be examined here. The fact that the MBT is accepted to be the key factor in both attack and defence means that it is also the most important single target on the battlefield; indeed, there is no weapons system on today's battlefield which is the target of so many threats. First, it can be attacked on the front, sides and rear using direct-fire weapons, such as another tank, helicopters, anti-tank guns, remotely-controlled anti-tank mines and ground-launched ATGW; most indirect-

Right: **British Army Chieftain MBT. The British have long optimized protection and firepower in tank design.**

Below right: **US M60A1 gave priority to mobility and firepower, accepting a reduction in protection, but its armour is inadequate against today's weapons.**

Below: No weapons system on the modern battlefield is the target of so many threats as the MBT. As each new threat appears tank designers produce something to overcome it. The one constant has been inexorable growth in size of the MBT.

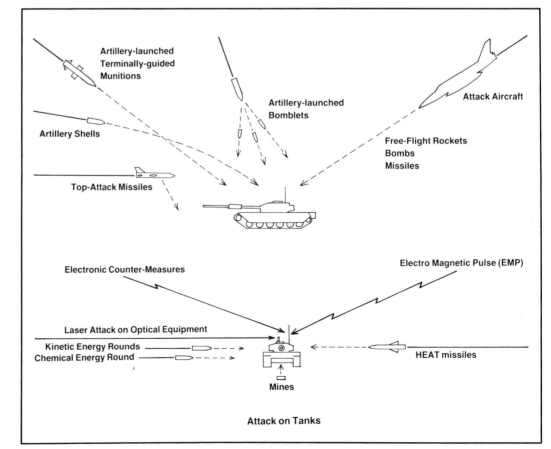

Artillery-launched Terminally-guided Munitions

Artillery-launched Bomblets

Attack Aircraft

Artillery Shells

Free-Flight Rockets
Bombs
Missiles

Top-Attack Missiles

Electronic Counter-Measures

Electro Magnetic Pulse (EMP)

Laser Attack on Optical Equipment

Kinetic Energy Rounds
Chemical Energy Round

HEAT missiles

Mines

Attack on Tanks

Combat Weights of Modern MBTs

Tank	Country	Gun mm	Weight position (see scale below)
Osorio	Brazil	120	✕ ≈45,000 kg
Type 80	China	105	◯ ≈38,000 kg
Leclerc	France	120	✕ ≈54,000 kg
AMX-30	France	105	◯ ≈37,000 kg
Leopard 2	FRG	120	✕ ≈55,000 kg
Leopard 1	FRG	105	◯ ≈40,000 kg
Merkava 2	Israel	105	◯ ≈60,000 kg
C1	Italy	120	✕ ≈43,000 kg
T-80	USSR	125	☐ ≈39,000 kg
T-72	USSR	115	◇ ≈38,000 kg
Challenger	U.K.	120	✕ ≈62,000 kg
Chieftain	U.K.	120	✕ ≈54,000 kg
M1A1	U.S.A.	120	✕ ≈56,000 kg
M60	U.S.A.	105	◯ ≈52,000 kg
Type 64	Japan	105	◯ ≈38,000 kg
Sherman	U.S.A.	76	⌀ ≈32,000 kg

	kg	30,000	40,000	50,000	60,000	64,000
	tons	30	40	50	60	63

Above: **Weights and Armament of Modern MBTs.** Clearly shown here is how British and Israeli MBTs tend to be heavier than their counterparts, Soviet and Chinese designs lighter. Note also the Second World War Sherman, shown for comparison. (Symbols represent gun calibre: ⌀ = 76mm; ◯ = 105mm; ◇ = 115mm; ✕ = 120mm; ☐ = 125mm.)

fire artillery weapons are also capable of a 'last resort' anti-tank role. Secondly, an increasingly important threat comes from above, using indirect-fire weapons (i.e. mortars and artillery), by direct-fire weapons using 'top-attack' munitions and by aircraft. Thirdly, the MBT can be attacked from underneath by anti-tank mines, either lying on the ground or buried.

The ranges of these weapons cover the entire battlefield range spectrum from many miles, such as unseen artillery and mortars up to 30 miles away, to infantry in foxholes at a range of a few yards. The munitions themselves also use different methods of attack, from very high velocity, high density, kinetic energy penetrators e.g. tungsten and depleted uranium armour-piercing, fin-stabilized, discarding sabots (APFSDS) through chemical energy warheads using the 'hollow charge' principle, to the mechanical energy transfer of the high-explosive squashhead (HESH) – in the US, high-explosive, plastic (HEP) round.

The attacks outlined above, if successful, will totally destroy the tank (this is known as a 'kill'). However, the combat effectiveness of a tank can be reduced or even eliminated in other ways as well. For example, one method is to reduce or eliminate the ability of the crew to fight. They can be attacked with neutron, chemical or bacteriological weapons, while an even more recent threat is that of lasers, which can be used to attack the tank's optical and electronic viewing systems, and can also be used to attack the crew's eyes. Nor should the potential value of psychological warfare be overlooked; a reluctant crew will not fight their tank well.

The battle effectiveness of the MBT can also be reduced by attacks on its mobility (an 'M kill'). This can be achieved by destroying or damaging the engine, tracks or suspension gear, or by using, natural or artificial obstacles (rivers, ditches, minefields) to bar its progress. The latter can be used either to prevent MBTs' advance or to canalize

them into a killing zone where other weapons can be used to complete their destruction.

MBTs are of little value unless used in mass, which means that they must be effectively commanded and controlled by radio. This function can be negated using electronic countermeasures (ECM) against their communications systems; for example, jamming. Finally, MBTs use large amounts of fuel and ammunition, and attacks against the logistic supply system to prevent such vital commodities reaching the tanks in the combat area will thus bring the tanks to a halt.

Right: The German-designed Leopard 1, one of the best-balanced 1970s MBT designs.

Below: Despite the PWs, tanks are at their most vulnerable in built-up areas.

Tank Development

It may help to understand the capabilities of modern MBTs if one of today's leading models is compared with its equivalent of 30 years ago; the American M48 makes a useful benchmark, as it was the US Army's principal MBT in 1960. The M48 was the first major post-Second World War MBT and incorporated the lessons of both that war and the recently-ended Korean War. It was rushed into production in the mid-1950s to meet the perceived Soviet threat in Europe and Asia, leading to a number of problems, which had just about been solved by 1960. The hull was constructed of standard armour plate, the main section being cast, but with other sections welded into position. The design was conventional, with the driver at the front, a centrally-mounted, revolving turret containing the armament

and the remainder of the crew, with the engine at the rear. The tank weighed 44,960kg (44.2 tons) and had a road speed of 41.8km/h (26 mph).

The driver sat in the centre of the forward hull, with a manual two-forward/one-reverse gear system. The other three crew members were in the turret: commander and gunner on the right, loader on the left. The main gun was the (then) new 90mm and the tank carried 60 full-calibre, high-explosive and solid-shot rounds (i.e. there were no APDS rounds). A 7.62mm (0.30 in) MG was mounted coaxially with the main gun. A 12.7mm (0.50 in) AAMG was mounted on the turret roof on a flexible mounting, but it could only be fired if the commander exposed his head and shoulders through the cupola.

As with virtually all tanks up to this

time, power was provided by a 12-cylinder Continental petrol engine, with an output of 810hp at 2,500rpm, giving a road range of 113km (70 miles) (somewhat less cross-country). Power-to-weight ratio was 18hp/ton, a reasonable figure for its time. Sensors and vision aids were rudimentary. Crew members were provided with vision blocks and periscopes. Range-taking was achieved using a coincidence range-finder mounted across the turret roof, which was operated by the commander. A very elementary electro-mechanical ballistic computer was fitted, which received inputs via a rotating shaft from the range-finder, but there was no stabilization and the gun could not be fired on the move. The engine compartment contained fire extinguishers but no fire warning system. The communications fit consisted of a

VHF radio, a HF radio and a crew intercom system.

Thus, the 1960 tank was very simple and with few aids to the crew to help fight it and fire the gun. Apart from the periscopes and vision blocks, the crew depended upon the 'Mark One Eyeball' and there was virtually no night-fighting capability. The tank had a petrol engine, with high fuel consumption, a very short range and very combustible fuel. The 90mm gun was adequate for its day, but its chances of a first-round hit were poor and there was no possibility of accurate fire on the move. The only electronics on board were the radios.

Left: One of the best of today's MBTs, the US Army's M1 Abrams is the outcome of a very lengthy development process.

Below: The West German Leopard 2, like the M1A1 version of the Abrams, is armed with a 120mm smoothbore main gun.

M1A1

One of today's leading MBTs is the US Army's M1A1 General Abrams, the result of many years of development and testing. It entered service in the mid-1980s in its original M1 version, and the M1A1 is now also in service.

M1A1 has a crew of four, with the driver forward in the centre of the hull. His controls are, however, quite different from those on M48, with a motor-cycle type handlebar, which actuates a steering lever on the transmission. Speed is controlled by twist-grips on the handlebar, which transmit signals to the electronic engine management system. There is also a 'maintenance monitoring panel', which displays conditions such as fuel levels, battery state, etc. When closed-up, the driver sees using either periscopes or an image-intensifier.

Commander and gunner share an elaborate array of electronic and visual devices. The Gunner's Primary Sight (GPS) has three daytime modes with different magnification: narrow field, ×10 magnification; wide angle, ×3 mag-

nification; and close-in, ×1. Full thermal imaging (TI) optics are provided for night viewing, which are so designed as to give the gunner the same indications as he would get in his day sight. A laser rangefinder gives instantaneous and absolutely precise readouts. All these devices are fully stabilized. There is also an auxiliary sight, with ×8 magnification.

The integrated fire-control system comprises the laser rangefinder, a full solution, solid-state digital computer and the sighting system. All the gunner needs to do is to place his sight graticule on the target and activate the laser to take the range; both these inputs are automatically fed into the computer, which then integrates them with other information (temperature, humidity, wind speed, tank angle, trunnion tilt, barrel wear, ammunition type and characteristics, etc.) to produce a firing solution and apply the necessary offset angles. On seeing the visual indication that all this has been done, the gunner then fires.

The commander has an optical extension of the GPS and six periscopes around

his cupola hatch, giving him 360° vision. If he needs to do so, he can fire the main gun and he can also aim and fire the machine-gun mounted above him on the turret-roof from inside the tank.

Considerable attention is paid to defensive measures. The tank and turret are constructed of an 'advanced armour', similar to that used by the British Challenger and German Leopard 2, which gives protection against most battlefield anti-tank weapons, particularly those using HEAT warheads. The major surfaces, such as the glacis plate, are exceptionally well sloped, and, for the first time on a US tank, skirts are fitted to protect the track and sides of the hull. Ready-use ammunition is held in the turret bustle and separated from the crew by armoured doors. Penetration into this space by a HEAT projectile would result in special panels blowing out to vent the explosion upwards and rearwards. The tank is also fitted with a Halon fire-extinguishing system, which reacts within two milliseconds, and extinguishes virtually all fires within 250 milliseconds.

The gun fitted to the first 3,268 M1s is the M68 105mm, which fires APFSDS, with both tungsten and depleted uranium penetrators, HEAT and training rounds; 55 rounds are carried. The more recent M1A1 mounts the Rheinmetall 120mm smooth-bore gun, firing a similar type of ammunition, but as the rounds are larger only 40 can be carried. A 7.62mm MG is mounted coaxially with the main gun and second 7.62mm is mounted above the loader's position. Above the commander's hatch is a 12.7mm (0.5 in) MG, with electrical power traverse, controlled from within the tank.

The main power unit is an Avco-Lycoming gas-turbine, which normally runs on diesel fuel or kerosene, but which can also use petrol in an emergency. The transmission is fully-automatic, with four forward and two reverse gears. The transmission system also provides power for the brakes, variable hydrostatic steering and pivot steering. The advanced suspension uses rotary shock absorbers, with no less than 361mm (14.2 in) of travel. Combat weight of M1A1 is 57,154kg (56.25 tons). The power output of the Avco-Lycoming engine is 1,500hp, giving a power-to-weight ratio of 26.24hp/tonne (26.66 hp/ton).

Not readily apparent from an external view is the exceptional amount of electronic devices inside the M1. The computer has already been mentioned, but there are also a wind sensor, laser rangefinder, thermal imaging system, tank-attitude sensors, electronic engine management system and a sophisticated array of VHF

radios. There is also a Radiological Warning Device, chemical agent detector and collective NBC protection unit. Devices will also shortly be fitted which give warning that the tank is being targeted by hostile lasers or ground radars.

In overall terms M1 is functionally similar to the M48 of 30 years ago. Both tanks have a similarly shaped hull, with a turret placed above, in which is mounted the main gun, a coaxial MG and with one or more MGs mounted on the roof. The crew is still four strong, and the driver is placed in the front of the tank and the engine at the rear.

However, the differences are great. Perhaps the most obvious is that the gun is much larger (120mm against 90mm), smoothbore instead of rifled and with a much greater range. It also has a much greater rate of fire, uses much more effective ammunition, with a far higher muzzle velocity, is much more accurate, and – using its fire-control system and laser-ranger – has a very much greater probability of a first-round hit. The fully

stabilized gun control system also enables it to fire on the move with a reasonable degree of accuracy.

The armoured protection of the M1 is also of a different order from that of the M48, giving it virtual immunity against shells and missiles with a HEAT warhead. The advances in the electronic field, however, are even more marked and the M1 is a sophisticated, modern fighting machine.

The increase in weight to accommodate all these developments is considerable: the M1A1 weighs 57,154kg (56.25 tons) compared to M48's 44,906kg (44.2 tons), a 27 per cent increase. Ground pressure, too, has increased: M1A1 exerts a ground pressure of 0.96kg/cm^2 (13.66 psi) compared to 0.78kg/cm^2 (11.1 psi) for M48, an increase of 23 per cent. However, the great increase in the power output of the M1A1's engine gives the heavier tank a better power-weight ratio; 26hp/ton compared to 18hp/ton, a 44 per cent increase, which thus makes it a more mobile cross-country performer

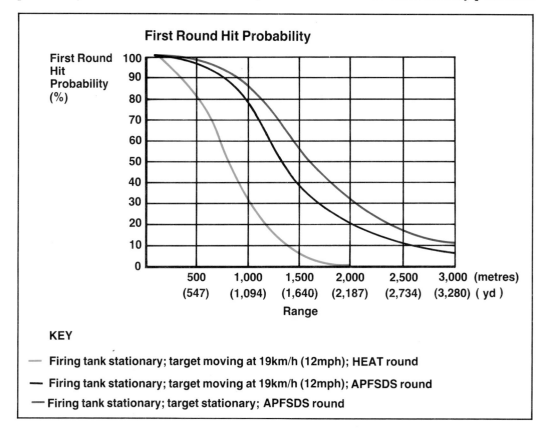

First Round Hit Probability

First Round Hit Probability (%)

Range: 500 (547), 1,000 (1,094), 1,500 (1,640), 2,000 (2,187), 2,500 (2,734), 3,000 (3,280) (metres) (yd)

KEY

— Firing tank stationary; target moving at 19km/h (12mph); HEAT round

— Firing tank stationary; target moving at 19km/h (12mph); APFSDS round

— Firing tank stationary; target stationary; APFSDS round

Above: It is absolutely crucial for a tank to score a hit with its first round, since, with the number of anti-tank weapons on today's battlefield, it is unlikely to get a second chance. This graph shows first-round hit probabilities for a Soviet T-62. It clearly shows the greater probability with a very high velocity round (such as APFSDS), compared to the slower HEAT round; for example, at 1,000m a HEAT round has a 30 per cent chance of a first-round hit, while an APFSDS round has

a 75 per cent chance.

It also shows the fairly self-evident point that the chances are even greater if the target is stationary. The curves extend beyond 2,000m, but in rolling countryside such as that found in Central Europe, and with the smoke and dust inevitably associated with the modern battlefield, it is highly unlikely that targets could be acquired at such ranges.

than its lighter predecessor.

Other Advances

Even the M1A1, however, does not incorporate all the devices available in modern tank technology. A number of nations (e.g. USSR, France) have developed sophisticated automatic loading devices, which enable them to reduce the tank crew to three men. This gives savings in tank height and weight and in crew training time and costs, but has, as yet, not been followed by other major tank nations such as the USA, UK and Germany. For these the four-man crew continues to offer significant advantages for servicing, maintenance, guard duties and repairs (particularly such labour intensive tasks as replacing tracks).

There are other advances too. Explosive reactive armour (ERA), which explodes when hit by an incoming round and thus diverts it sufficiently to render it

harmless, is being fitted as an 'add-on' to numerous older tanks, in order to prolong their useful lives. The recently-revealed Israeli Merkava Mark III takes this process a stage further by being designed from the outset for 'bolt-on' armour, which means that it can take advantage of future developments as they occur. The Israelis also mount the engine forward to add to the frontal protection, particularly for the driver.

A feature introduced by the USSR is that of spall lining, a lead-impregnated plastic foam of uneven thickness, which can absorb the energy of fragments which have penetrated the fighting compartment. It is applied to the inside surface of the hull. In some armies tank crews also wear body armour, in order to give a final protection against flying fragments.

Some nations are also examining the feasibility of overhead gun mounts, in which the very small, slim-line turret

contains the gun and automated loading devices only. This enables the crew to be housed within the hull and also considerably reduces the vehicle's silhouette, particularly when seen from the front. In the USA both the Teledyne Continental Direct Fire Support Vehicle and the Rapid Deployment Force Light Tank use such a design, the former mounting a 105mm gun and the latter a 76mm. Neither has, however, got beyond the prototype stage.

In the 1960s the US Army sought to develop a 152mm gun which would fire both conventional ammunition and an anti-tank guided missile, the Shillelagh, which was mounted in the M551 Sheridan light tank. The combined gun/ missile system failed to work and the Sheridan was relegated to secondary tasks. It came, therefore, as something of a surprise when it was revealed that the Soviet Army has developed an anti-tank

Left: Latest counter to the ever-growing power of anti-tank weapons is **Explosive Reactive Armour (ERA)**. Protruding bolts are welded to vulnerable areas of the hull and used to secure the specially shaped ERA boxes, which contain two metal plates (typically 5mm (0.2in) thick) sandwiching a layer of explosive. When hit by an incoming HEAT round (1) the explosive charge is initiated (2), diverting and absorbing the molten metal jet (3), greatly reducing the effect on the tank's own armour plate (4).

Below: The British Army's Challenger MBT weighs 62,000kg (61 tons) and is armed with the British 120mm gun, which, unlike all other 120mm guns used in NATO armies, is rifled, rather than smoothbored.

missile – AT-8 Songster – which is fired from the 125mm gun fitted to the T-64B and T-80 MBTs. The AT-8 is radio-controlled, using a SACLOS (Semi-Automatic, Command Line-Of-Sight) system in which the gunner simply has to keep the sight on the target to ensure a hit. AT-8, like all ATGW, has a HEAT warhead, which will penetrate up to 600mm (23.6 in) of conventional steel armour, but cannot penetrate the Chobham and reactive armours fitted on most modern Western tanks. AT-8 may also have an anti-helicopter role.

Nobody denies the tactical value of the MBT on the modern battlefield. After nuclear weapons, the huge Soviet tank fleet is seen as the most serious threat to Western Europe, while Soviet generals see Western tanks as the major threat to the success of such an undertaking. The latest MBTs are now very sophisticated weapons systems indeed, and have become very large, very heavy and extremely expensive. However, it seems unlikely that in the two great potential armoured battlegrounds – Central Europe and the Middle East – anything less than the present large, sophisticated machines will be considered in the next few years; the next generation, however, may be quite another story.

Future Tanks

Few countries can afford the enormous expense of the MBTs described above and a number of armies have already elected to use smaller, lighter and cheaper alternatives. Indeed, many have virtually no choice in the matter, since their roads and bridges are simply not capable of taking the loads involved. Thus, once again the question of smaller, lighter and cheaper alternatives is being addressed. Indeed, a number of developments, such as 'light recoil', better armour and more efficient powerpacks are making lighter MBTs a much more effective proposition. Perhaps the most significant of these are the 'light recoil' systems, which enable 105mm guns to be mounted in a chassis of well under 30 tons, an impossible prospect 20 years ago. This will, in time, lead to smaller, lighter MBTs, but it would seem that that time has not yet arrived as far as the major armies are concerned.

One feature now being re-examined is that of liquid propellants, a device which reached trials stage with the British Army in the 1950s. Such a technique has several advantages over the current large cartridge cases and bags of propellant which are awkward shapes to store and to load. Liquid propellants, however, can be stored in containers moulded to fit the

Above: The West German Leopard 2 mounts the Rheinmetall 120mm smoothbore gun, has a crew of four and uses much special armour. It weighs 55,150kg (55 tons).

space available and are safer, since the inert constituents can be stored separately until combined in the breech in a volatile mixture. There are, however, problems, as breech sealing must be extremely tight to prevent leakage, and it is necessary to ensure that the ignition process is carefully controlled and even. Rheinmetall of West Germany is known to be working on a liquid propellant tank gun and there may be others similarly involved. However, no workable weapon has yet been demonstrated.

Another area of development is that of the 'rail gun'*, which actually looks more promising than liquid propellants, and it is possible that demonstrators will appear in the late 1990s, with production weapons in the first decade of the next century. The rail gun first appeared as part of the USA's 'Star Wars' concept, as a method of firing a high velocity projectile in space. It is very attractive for tanks as it appears to offer muzzle velocities of between 4,000m (13,000 ft) and 6,000m (19,700 ft) per second. In a kinetic energy round, where high muzzle velocity is vital, this compares dramatically with today's muzzle velocities of 1,650m (5,400 ft) per second for the West German 120mm APFSDS round.

Such a very high muzzle velocity would mean that time of flight would be negligible and the trajectory at all battle ranges would be essentially flat, and thus engaging a moving target would require little skill. The present complicated sighting graticules needed to enable the gunner to 'aim-off' would just not be necessary.

The rail gun comprises two rigid, parallel conducting rails, between which runs the projectile. A very powerful electrical current (up to several mega-amps) is passed through the rails and the projectile is shot into the gap, fitted with a skirt which makes contact across them and immediately vaporizes into a conducting plasma. As the current flows the projectile is accelerated down the gap

* The 'rail gun' (as distinct from the 'railway gun' – an artillery piece mounted on a railway carriage) is a device in which very high electric voltages are used to accelerate a projectile between two metal bars, or rails.

between the rails, emerging with a very high velocity. SDI demonstration rail guns have accelerated a projectile weighing 300g (10.5 oz) up to a speed of 4,200m (13,728 ft) per second. The theory is sound but there are two present major problems: one is the enormous electrical power needed and the other is the technology of the projectile, which would need to be made of an extremely hard substance to enable it to penetrate an armoured plate at such a velocity without breaking up on impact.

MBTs are currently equipped to counter most threats, but there is one significant weakness. One of the most effective anti-tank weapon systems is the helicopter and more armies are starting to operate rotary-wing 'tank-killers'. At the moment the only weapon on most tanks which might deal with such a target is a 12.7mm (0.5 in) machine-gun, although the Soviet AT-8 Songster ATGM is reported to have a secondary anti-helicopter capability. There appears, therefore to be a strong case to develop a radar for helicopter surveillance and target acquisition, together with a weapon

which could be either a special round for the main gun or a surface-to-air missile.

One major development over the past few years has been the spread of 'retrofit programmes'. Numerous armies, faced by the very high costs of modern MBTs, such as M1A1, Leopard 2, Challenger and Leclerc have decided instead to update their previous generation MBTs. Thus M48s, M60s, Centurions, T-55s and T-62s are being comprehensively reworked and given modern equipment. This can include new powerpacks, new tracks, larger calibre guns with up-to-date fire-control systems, add-on reactive armour, new sensors and the latest communications equipment. The Israeli Army is a past master at this, but others are now almost as skilled in turning an elderly MBT into an acceptable modern fighting vehicle.

Light Tanks

It has already been stated that the current range of MBTs are either too heavy, too big, too sophisticated or too expensive for many armies. Consequently, attention is turning to light tanks, which are specified

as being under 25,400kg (25 tons) in weight. Light tanks have in the past been limited, not only in their size, but also in their firepower, since they were unable to take the recoil stresses of large guns. However, the development of light recoil systems has meant that these lighter tanks can mount substantial weapons; for example, the US FMC Close Combat Vehicle, Light (CCVL) has a combat weight of 19,414kg (19.1 tons) and mounts a 105mm gun, as does the slightly heavier Cadillac Gage Stingray.

Major armies currently consider such light tanks as being suitable only for use in minor theatres and certainly not in a confrontation on the central front or in the Middle East. How long such views will be held remains to be seen, but the proponents of the light tank are convinced that the heavy MBT cannot last more than one generation more.

Below: Soviet MBTs, like these T-62s, are usually much lighter than their Western counterparts, but at least as well armed.

Characteristics of Armoured Units

The primary characteristics of an armoured unit (as opposed to an individual tank) are mobility, armoured protection and firepower. The unit is able to kill tanks and soft targets at long ranges and is relatively invulnerable to enemy artillery and small arms fire. Its built-in communications, training and mobility enable the unit to deploy, redeploy and reorganize with great speed and efficiency.

The limitations of armoured units are that they are vulnerable to anti-tank weapons, other tanks and mines, and they are particularly slow and vulnerable when crossing a water obstacle. The unit also has difficulty in dealing with infantry and anti-tank weapons in close country and in built-up areas.

Tanks in Battle

Individual tank tactics are generally similar in all armies. A tank is vulnerable if it moves, but it must move in order to advance. Therefore, tanks combine in platoons and companies to protect each other in a tactic known as 'fire-and-movement'. Thus, in a platoon of four tanks, for example, the platoon commander will control their moves by radio, ensuring that two tanks are in good fire positions before calling the other two to move from their current fire positions to new ones, which they always do at maximum speed. Once they are established he will move the other two, and so on. In a major attack such combinations will be effected on larger scales. Tanks can also be protected during their moves by the use of covering fire (e.g. from

artillery and mortars) against known enemy positions, and by smoke.

Individual tank positions are adopted to make use of cover for protection. If the commander wishes only to observe he will adopt a 'turret-down' position, in which he can see only from his cupola, but is very unlikely himself to be seen by the enemy. If he wishes to be able to engage targets as well as observe, he needs to move into a 'hull-down' position (see diagram opposite). The tank's visibility at this stage depends upon the size, shape and concealment pattern of the turret, and also upon the radio antennas, which can show up remarkably clearly against certain backgrounds, e.g. sky.

Soviet low-level tank tactics in the attack are somewhat different, being based on the use of overwhelming

Above: The Norwegian Army is one of many to use the West German-designed Leopard 1.

Above right: Light tanks, such as this British Scorpion, are easy to deploy abroad.

strength and deep thrusts into enemy territory. They thus depend upon strength and speed, and are prepared to (and can afford to) accept a much higher casualty rate than any Western army.

However, tanks will seldom be employed on their own. Like all elements on the battlefield they must be used in combination with other combat arms, such as infantry, artillery, army aviation and engineers to achieve their full potential.

Head-on

Side View

"Turret-Down": Observation

Head-on

Side View

"Hull-Down": Observation and Fire

INFANTRY

For no other combat arm have the developments of the past 50 years been as traumatic as for the infantry. At the end of the Second World War the vast masses of infantry serving in all armies were still in their traditional role of foot soldiers. A few units had been given lorries to add to their mobility and some even travelled in tracked, half-tracked or wheeled armoured personnel carriers (APCs) to enable them to keep up with tanks. For all, however, the real fighting, whether in offence or defence was done – as it always had been – on foot.

In the years since the Second World War many armies have been involved in fighting 'minor' campaigns or 'limited' wars. There have been many such campaigns: Malaya, French Indochina, Vietnam, Cyprus, Aden, Algeria, Northern Ireland, Afghanistan, the Falklands, to name but a few. In all of these the infantry have – as always – been the key combat arm, performing their traditional role of fighting on foot. They may have used helicopters, lorries, APCs, parachutes or even ships to reach their operational areas, but once there their role has been the same as it always has: to seek out and destroy the enemy.

Above: The US Army's M1 Bradley Infantry Fighting Vehicle (IFV) is one of the most sophisticated of its type in any army.

Left: Like most IFVs, these West German Marders can ford shallow rivers, but are far too heavy to be amphibious.

Armoured Personnel Carriers

In the few really major conventional conflicts that have occurred (Iran/Iraq war, Korean war, Middle East wars) and in potential conflicts in Central Europe, however, there has been a development in quite a different direction. In these, the infantry has become 'mechanized' or 'motorized', with such units being totally mounted in tracked or wheeled vehicles. At first (broadly speaking from the late 1940s to the early 1970s) such mechanized infantry were mounted in APCs which were, in essence, tracked armoured boxes carrying some 10–12 men. In an attack these APCs delivered their infantry squad/section to a place just

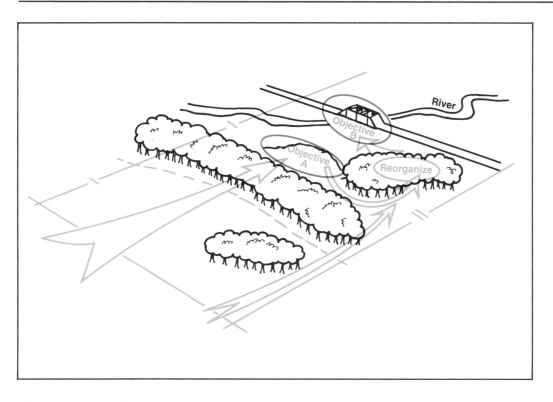

Above: **Flank Attack.** Frontal attacks are sometimes unavoidable, but seldom profitable. Here a force driving for the bridge, Objective B, attacks and clears enemy at Objective A. Some troops remain on A giving covering fire, while others move to the reorganization position, join reinforcements and carry out the second phase of the attack.

short of the objective, from whence they completed the operation on foot. (This type of delivery service gave rise to the APC nickname of 'battle taxi'.) As the APC was a convenient weapons carrier, machine-guns were frequently mounted on the roof of such vehicles. Typical APCs of this era were the US M113, British FV432, French AMX-VCI, Swedish Pbv-302 and Soviet BTR-50P.

There then developed a new theory, led in the main by the West Germans: that the vehicle should be turned into a 'proper' fighting vehicle – well armoured and heavily armed – which could be used to actually 'fight' the infantry it carried onto their objective. This concept had been derived from the German experi-ences fighting the Red Army on the Eastern Front in the Second World War. It led to the German Marder and the Soviet BMP, which were known generically as Mechanized Infantry Combat Vehicles (MICV). Doubts about the validity of the concept were confirmed in the various Middle Eastern wars, where Arab armies using Soviet tactics and Soviet MICVs were badly mauled by the Israelis.

As a result of these experiences a form of compromise has developed, in which the vehicles transport the infantry as far as practicable on the battlefield, but the infantry still 'debus' for the final assault. However, the vehicles (now known as Infantry Fighting Vehicles) are heavily armed, well protected and, in the majority of cases, superbly equipped. Among the best examples of this new breed are the US M2 Bradley, British Warrior, French AMX-10 and Soviet BMP-2.

Once part of an infantry unit has been mounted in such vehicles it is inevitable that the remainder must be similarly mounted to give them the ability to move at the same speed and over the same terrain. As a result most APCs (whether tracked or wheeled) have been used as the basis of a whole series to fulfil specialized functions. Weapons carrier sub-types in-clude mortar carriers, missile launchers and versions with turret-mounted heavy support weapons, such as 90mm cannon. Headquarters are made mobile by the use of command vehicles and communica-tions vehicles, while support functions are carried out by ambulances, repair and recovery vehicles, and logistic load car-riers. Other versions are used by the artillery as command posts, radar carriers and observation vehicles, and by en-gineers as reconnaissance vehicles, mine-layers and bridgelayers.

Within the infantry the widespread use of such vehicles means that greater loads and a wider variety of equipment can be carried than in the days when the soldier fought with what he could carry on his back. Also, such a mass of vehicles needs to be properly controlled and as a result every vehicle has at least one radio, which has led in turn to the issue of radios to the dismounted squad/section.

Twenty-five years ago the infantry battalion was a simple, unsophisticated, 'low-tech', low-cost environment, armed with rifles, machine-guns and mortars. Today, however, the battalion is a very

Left: **NATO is a truly international force; US vehicles cross a West German bridge.**

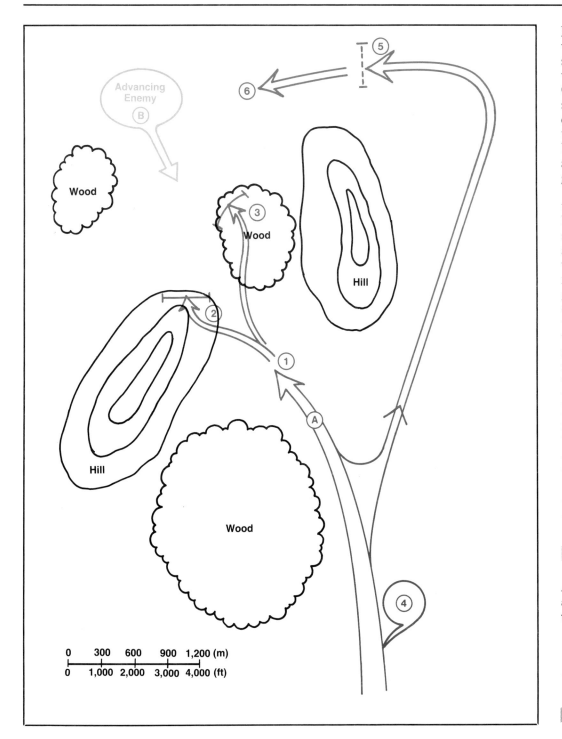

Wood

Advancing
Enemy
Ⓑ

Wood

Wood

Hill

Hill

Wood

⑤

⑥

③

②

①

Ⓐ

④

| 0 | 300 | 600 | 900 | 1,200 (m) |
| 0 | 1,000 | 2,000 | 3,000 | 4,000 (ft) |

heavily-armed unit, using a vast array of very sophisticated vehicles, weapons, sensors and equipment, much of it at the very leading edge of modern technology. Of course, a price has to be paid for such sophistication: the equipment is very expensive, it is much more complicated to operate than in a traditional infantry battalion, many more skilled tradesmen and operators are needed, and much greater logistic support is required.

One further consequence related to the use of IFVs in virtually every army has been that the size of the basic squad/ section has been reduced. About 30 years ago a typical unmechanized squad/section was some 11 strong, comprising a commander and radio operator, a machine-gun team (three men led by the deputy commander) and a manoeuvre (rifle) team of six. In the APC era the vehicles were sufficiently large to accommodate all these men, except that the vehicle itself needed a driver and one other man to stay with it at all times. This reduced the dismounted section to nine men. The IFVs, however, have less room still and many need three men to remain with the vehicle (driver, commander, gunner). As a result the dismounted section comprises even fewer men: eight in the case of the Soviet BMP-2, seven in the US M2 and British Warrior, six in the West German Marder.

Above right: IFVs such as this British Warrior have added a new dimension to the movement and firepower of the infantry.

Below right: One of the most vulnerable moments for IFV-borne infantry is as they 'debus' from the rear of the vehicle.

Above: **Soviet Company in the Advance to Contact.**
Whatever the changes at the strategic level as a result of recent reductions in tension with the West, the Soviet Army still teaches its junior commanders to be aggressive at the tactical level. Here, two forces are advancing towards each other, neither being quite certain of the other's location. The Soviet company (A), moving through the valley between two hills (1), comes under fire from an advancing enemy force (B). Immediately, the Soviet commander throws his forward elements into positions (2) and (3) from which they can pin the enemy down with fire, both direct – from organic weapons – and indirect from mortars and artillery following the forward troops at (4). Concurrently, an attack force is taken from the main body and sent round to a flank, rolling across the start line (5) to undertake an immediate attack (6), supported by fire

from (2) and (3). Such attacks must be mounted with extreme rapidity for maximum effect in order to give the enemy no chance to carry out an attack of their own. With all troops mounted in APC/IFVs and controlled by radio, such attacks are possible.

Tracked Vehicles – the M2 Bradley IFV

One of the finest IFVs currently in service is the US Army's M2 which is the outcome of a development process stretching back over some 20 years. It is constructed of all-welded aluminium, with spaced, laminated armour incorporated into the hull, sides and rear, and an appliquéd steel covering on the lower front and the forward half of the belly to give added protection against mines.

The vehicle weighs 22,590kg (22.23 tons) in combat order and carries ten men. The driver sits at the left front with the power-pack on his right. The turret is

in the centre of the vehicle and offset to the right, with a crew of two: the vehicle commander and the gunner. The seven men of the dismounting squad sit with two tucked-in beside the turret, and the remaining five at the rear of the vehicle. Six of these have access to firing ports within the vehicle.

M2 carries a prodigious array of weapons. Mounted in the 360° traverse, stabilized, electrically-operated turret is a 25mm M242 Chain Gun, with a coaxial 7.62mm machine-gun. The Chain Gun fires APDS or HE rounds (with an APFSDS round under development) at either 200rpm, 100rpm or in single shots. Also on the turret is a twin TOW (Tube-launched Optically-tracked Wire-guided) anti-tank guided missile launcher, which enables the M2 to engage tanks out to a range of 3,750m (12,300 ft), and twin smoke dischargers. There are also six, ball-mounted M231 7.62mm rifles, operated by the members of the dismounting squad. Finally, the squad itself, when dismounted, disposes of a 7.62mm light machine-gun, a Dragon anti-tank launcher and five rifles, three

with grenade launchers.

M2 has been designed specifically to be able to move cross country at the same rate as the M1 Abrams MBT. It is thus highly agile, with a road speed of 66km/h (41 mph) and is amphibious, with a maximum water speed of 7.2km/h (4.5 mph). Road range is 483km (300 miles).

M2 is an excellent IFV giving the infantry squad great mobility, and good protection against small arms fire and all but a direct hit by artillery. It also provides an NBC protected environment.

Wheeled Vehicles – the Soviet BTR-80

Tracked APCs possess a number of significant advantages over wheeled vehicles, the most important of which is a cross-country performance equivalent to that of an MBT. However, they are also very expensive in both original purchase and lifetime maintenance costs. They are also comparatively noisy and are not really suitable for protracted running on roads. Therefore, many nations have developed wheeled APCs, some of which use them in place of and others as

complements to tracked vehicles.

Among the more successful wheeled APCs are the Czech OT-64, French VAB, West German Luchs Transport-panzer 1, South African Ratel, Swiss/Canadian LAV-25 and the Soviet Army's BTR-60/-70/-80 series. The latter are good examples of the type.

The BTR-60P design was started in the mid-1950s, the type being accepted into service in 1960. This is an 8×8 vehicle, with a boat-shaped, open-top body. The driver and commander are seated at the front, with the engine at the rear. The main part of the vehicle is devoted to an open-topped crew compartment for the infantry squad of 16 men. The all-welded hull is constructed of steel plate which will resist small arms fire.

BTR-60P was used as the standard APC of the infantry in motor rifle divisions of the Soviet Army for many years. Many are still in service, especially with Warsaw Pact armies, except for those of Czechoslovakia and Poland, which use the similar Czech OT-64 APC.

BTR-60P has reasonable mobility (but not as good as a tracked vehicle), a good

range, is fully amphibious, and is both sturdy and reliable. However, its main disadvantages are that it lacks overhead cover and, due to the complete lack of doors, exit/entry is over the sides, which is not an ideal arrangement, especially under fire!

Overhead cover was added in the BTR-60PA, which entered service in 1963, together with other, relatively minor improvements. This was followed slightly later by BTR-60PB, which has a turret fitted with a 14.5mm KPV MG and a 7.62mm PKT LMG (the turret is identical to that fitted to the BRDM-2 reconnaissance vehicle and the Czech

Above right: Despite the excellent BMP the Soviets also use the MT-LB APC.

Below left: For its new generation of infantry vehicles the US Marine Corps has opted for the Swiss-designed 8×8 LAV-25.

Below: The highly successful Soviet BTR-60 APC remained in production for many years, despite some tactical drawbacks.

OT-64 APC).

Next came BTR-70 with a fundamentally similar 8×8 layout and the BRDM-2 turret, but with many improvements. Protection is much better for both the vehicle crew and the infantry squad, with particular attention being paid to the frontal arc. The squad has complete overhead protection and is provided with periscopes and firing ports. The eight road wheels have tyres with directional treads and, as on the majority of Soviet wheeled vehicles, the tyre pressure can be

varied by remote-control by the driver. As with BTR-60, there are two engines, that on the right driving axles one and three, and that on the left axles two and four. It is fully amphibious. Rather surprisingly, the engines continue to be petrol fuelled at a time when virtually all other Soviet vehicles had changed to the safer and more fuel-efficient diesel.

The infantry squad, however, has been reduced to nine men. Their arms include normal personal weapons, plus a light anti-tank weapon (e.g. RPG-16), a light

air defence weapon (e.g. SA-7) and two AGS-17 grenade launchers. Entry and exit for the troops continued to be unsatisfactory.

Clearly, the Soviet Army likes this type of vehicle and despite the success of the tracked BMP and MT-LB APC/IFVs the development of the 8×8 wheeled design has continued with the BTR-80. This latest vehicle has much improved entry/exit arrangements, including two side hatches located between the second and third axles. Power is provided by a single diesel engine, which gives improved range and road speed, coupled with greater safety. The turret is similar to the earlier BR-70 but maximum elevation for the 14.5mm MG has been increased from +30° to +70° to give it an anti-helicopter capability. There is a crew of three (commander, driver and gunner) and the infantry squad is now eight (i.e. one less than BTR-70 and eight less than the original BTR-60). Like BTR-70, BTR-80 is fully amphibious and is NBC-proofed.

As with tracked APCs/IFVs, the BTR-60, -70 and -80 chassis have been used as the basis of numerous specialized vehicles. Such versions include: command posts, communications, armoured repair/recovery and forward air controller (FAC). It is clear that the wheeled APC has a firmly-established place in most armies. It will never replace the tracked APC/IFV in some uses, but nevertheless it is a valuable equipment in the right tactical circumstances.

Infantry Weapons

In addition to their APC/IFVs, the infantry's weapons are also undergoing fundamental changes. Automatic self-loading rifles began to replace traditional bolt-action weapons in some armies during the Second World War and by the mid-1960s virtually every army had re-equipped. Typical of such weapons were the widely used Belgian FN FAL and the Soviet AK-47, both 7.62mm calibre weapons. The US M16 (the 'Armalite'), which also entered service in the mid-1960s, used an appreciably smaller 5.56mm round and virtually all weapons now use this calibre, except for the Soviets, who have adopted the slightly smaller 5.45mm.

The consequence of design improve-

Left: A Belgian infantry section takes up defensive positions on debussing from a Spartan APC. The machine-gunner, however, would win no prizes for his fire-position, which affords him no cover at all!

Despite being either fully or semi-automatic, the present generation of rifles are still recognizable descendants of the traditional rifle. It is highly probable, however, that the next generation of rifles may not be. Revolutionary designs, such as the West German Heckler & Koch G11, are now undergoing trials which look like rectangular plastic boxes; many of these have even smaller calibres, such as 4.7mm. Even the ammunition is changing from the traditional bullet fixed in a brass cartridge case to a smaller bullet emplaced in a shaped, caseless lump of explosive. This not only would allow more rounds to be carried both by the individual infantryman and within the supply system, but would also mean that the firing sequence would not have to include extraction and ejection of the spent cartridge case.

Another recent development is the automatic grenade launcher, such as the Soviet Army's AGS-17 Plamya. Resembling a larger machine-gun in size and appearance, this device fires 30mm HE, HEAT and anti-personnel grenades at a rate of 100 rounds per minute out to ranges of about 731m (2,400 ft).

Other infantry weapons seem to have changed less. All squads carry a light machine-gun (LMG). Many armies have devised an LMG which is basically the standard rifle, with an added bipod, but adapted for belt-feed. Thus, for example, the British Army uses the 5.56mm Light Support Weapon, which is virtually identical with the 5.56mm Individual Weapon (rifle) apart from the bipod. The US Army, however, had adopted the M249 5.56mm Squad Automatic Weapon, which is a much more traditional LMG and a quite different weapon from the standard M16A1/A2 rifle.

There are numerous support weapons available within infantry battalions of all armies. All have six to eight mortars, usually of 81mm calibre, which have a very rapid response, a high rate of fire and are today very accurate. They are also highly mobile, being carried by the IFV/APCs; some can be fired from inside the vehicle, others must be dismounted before firing. All battalions also have heavy anti-tank weapons, guns in some armies, but guided missiles, such as the US Dragon, Euromissile Milan and Soviet AT-5, in others.

ments and using smaller rounds is that the weapons themselves are smaller, shorter and lighter, making them easier to control and thus more accurate, as well as easier to carry. Further, since each round is lighter (the old NATO standard 7.62mm round weighs 23.95g (0.85 oz), while the new SS109 5.56mm round weighs 12.50g (0.44 oz)) each soldier can carry either more rounds for the same weight or the same number of rounds at a lighter weight. On the other hand, the marked increase in the rate of fire means that an infantry squad can bring down a much greater volume of fire, which means that not only must fire discipline be far more strictly imposed, but also that the ammunition resupply needs have increased considerably!

Capabilities

It is worth considering the capabilities of the infantry by having a detailed look at a Mechanized Infantry Platoon of the US Army. This force is 38 strong, commanded by a lieutenant and organized into a platoon headquarters and three squads, with four M2 IFVs. They dispose of a remarkable armory of weapons. These may vary slightly depending upon the tactical situation, but typically would comprise:

– Four 25mm Chain Guns, one on each IFV.
– Seven 7.62mm MGs, four coaxially mounted with the Chain Guns and one dismounted with each squad.
– Three Dragon medium anti-tank weapons.
– Four LAW light anti-tank weapons.
– Six grenade launchers.
– Four pistols.
– 28 rifles.
– Three STINGER air defence missile launchers.
– Mines, as issued.

Such a force has a number of capabilities. The speed and mobility of the IFVs, coupled with the built-in radios, give the platoon excellent responses, close control and great mobility. When mounted, the platoon can move as rapidly as the tanks, swim streams and negotiate much soft ground. It can also suppress and kill soft targets, such as dismounted infantry and anti-tank gunners, using the turret-mounted weapons and port-mounted rifles.

When dismounted the platoon can clear woods, buildings, obstacles and dug-in positions, conduct infiltration attacks, dig in and hold ground, provide security, carry out ambushes and lay mines. In such operations the platoon

Below: Today's infantry have unparalleled firepower, including anti-air missile systems such as the US Stinger, which has proved itself in several campaigns.

would normally receive fire support from the weapons on its IFVs, which would be held slightly to the rear. The infantry platoon could also be taken away from its vehicles and used in air assault operations.

There are, naturally, some limitations. Firstly, the IFVs can be attacked by anti-tank weapons or mines, or by direct hits from large calibre artillery weapons or aircraft. Secondly, when dismounted, the infantry are vulnerable to attack by tanks, artillery fire (if not properly dug in), and NBC attack.

Paratroops

A special form of infantry continues to exist in the form of paratroops. Most parachute arms date from the Second World War and their fortunes have varied since. Parachute battalions are basically light infantry battalions, armed with rifles, machine-guns, medium mortars and man-portable anti-armour and air-defence weapons. Despite this lack of sophisticated weaponry (possibly even

because of it!) parachute battalions are expensive to maintain. They require much specialized items of equipment and special-to-role conversions of standard equipment, usually in relatively small quantities, which is inevitably expensive. Also the parachute units, because of their lightweight scales of weapons and equipment, when delivered by air, are unable to sustain protracted operations and must be relieved overland within a matter of days.

Nevertheless, parachute battalions offer some unique attributes. Firstly, they offer a mode of arrival which combines surprise and flexibility, and a parachute assault has often proved to be an essential precursor to a more conventional operation. For example, the French airborne rescue of the hostages at Kolwezi in 1978 could not have been achieved in any other way. Secondly, what might be termed the 'para ethos', which is common to virtually every parachute unit around the world, results in units which are superbly fit, very highly trained and who possess a certain 'elan'. (Their critics might also add that their thrusting tactics almost invite high casualty rates.) But the standards and deeds of units such as the US Army's 82nd Airborne, the British Parachute Regiment, the French 'les paras' and the Soviet Airborne Forces are too well known to need repeating here.

Further, parachute infantry cannot operate alone on the ground. They need their own integral support, particularly with artillery, and extra weapons for anti-tank and air defence tasks. This

Above: The Euromissile Milan has a range bracket of 25–2,000m (27–2,190 yd) and is effective against all known Soviet armoured vehicles, except possibly those fitted with Explosive Reactive Armour.

Below: The US Dragon anti-tank missile has a shorter range than other current systems and is difficult to control.

requires more units, frequently with special equipment and weapons. The Soviet Army has even developed a whole range of weapons for their airborne forces (which few other armies can afford to do), such as the ASU-85 SP gun and the BMD air-droppable APC/light support vehicle.

A parachute operation requires a large force of aircraft such as the US Lockheed C-130 Hercules and C-141 Starlifter, or the Soviet Antonov An-12 Cub and Ilyushin Il-76 Candid. These are large aircraft and their flying at relatively low-level, in close formation and at low speed, as required for a conventional parachute 'drop', invites retaliation. Whether such an operation could be carried out in a general war in Central Europe is debatable, but its capabilities in other operational settings is undeniable.

Air Mobile Operations

The rapid development of the helicopter has introduced a new element to the battlefield and to the mobility and roles of the infantry. Although, as with any aspect of military operations, troops specially trained in a particular role provide the ideal solution, it is nevertheless true that almost any infantry unit can serve in the helicopter-borne air-mobile role. Further, low-flying helicopters taking full advantage of every scrap of cover and taking with them their own offensive/defensive attack helicopters, appear to have a better chance of survival than a large formation of multi-engined, low-flying, fixed-wing transports.

This has to a certain extent undermined the role of parachute units in general war. Thus, as described in the chapter on helicopter operations, following the US experiences in Indochina there has been a marked upsurge in the formation of air mobile units, such as the British 24th Infantry Brigade.

Conventional Infantry

Modern infantry cannot, however, concentrate on their mounted role alone, as the more traditional 'foot-slogging' role remains as important as ever. The infan-try must still carry out dismounted roles in environments like Central Europe where their IFVs are vulnerable, for example, in close country, in very mountainous terrain and in built-up areas. The latter (cities, towns and villages) occupy an increasingly large proportion of the countryside, and fighting in them will require increasingly specialized techniques. Outside Central Europe the infantry retain their traditional role in operations such as those conducted by the British in the Falklands and the US Army in Grenada.

The Future

In the case of general war in Central Europe and other 'hi-tech' environments the role of the infantry is inextricably involved with that of the armoured force, and the two will almost always operate together in combined arms battle groups. In this type of warfare the infantry will have to use ever more sophisticated fighting vehicles, fire a greater variety of weapons and operate an ever-increasing number of sensors. Furthermore, as the pace of battle quickens, the infantry will, of necessity, become more adaptable and flexible. Thus, the days when the infan-try was a 'non-technical' fighting arm,

Above: The 'hi-tech' mounted role has become central to modern infantry training, often to the detriment of more traditional 'foot-slogging' tasks.

Above right: French infantry exhibiting the ultimate in land mobility!

Below right: 'Battle-taxis' like the British FV432 seem to have had their day.

whose most complicated weapon was a machine-gun are long since over. In fact, the modern infantryman has to be unprecedentedly flexible, capable of switching from 'hi-tech' to 'low-tech', from IFV-borne to foot-slogging to heliborne, all at days notice. In addition, he must be capable of handling the most ancient of weapons such as a knife or bayonet, or undertaking hand-to-hand combat, while at the same time being capable of operating the most modern equipment, such as a turret-mounted chain-gun or an air-defence missile.

BATTLEFIELD ARTILLERY

Descriptions of experiences of soldiers in both world wars and in post-1945 conflicts all indicate that the soldiers' greatest single fear was of artillery. Other weapons are somehow more bearable, perhaps because the average soldier feels that he can do something about them, either to take cover when their imminent arrival is detected or to fire back. But artillery fire generally arrives unheard, can be devastating in its effect and somehow seems quite arbitrary in its results. Most infantry memoirs, from the First World War to the Falklands, are laced with comments on the efficiency and effectiveness of the opposing artillery; statistically it is one of the most efficient means of killing and wounding on the battlefield. In the Korean War, for example, of the casualties on the United Nations' side, 35 per cent of those killed and 75 per cent (a very high proportion) of those wounded were victims of artillery fire.

In the past 40 years artillery has undergone a quiet revolution. The mobility of the weapons has increased dramatically, rates of fire have increased by a factor of at least three in the case of larger weapons and by a factor of ten with the smaller types. But perhaps the most significant development is not immediately apparent as it lies in the area of computer support, electronics and communications, which are used to acquire targets and to control and coordinate the use of the weapons at a particular commander's disposal. The consequence of all these is that artillery is now able to bring heavier fire to bear, more quickly, far more accurately and with much greater effect than ever before.

Modern land artillery can be subdivided into a number of areas:
– Field artillery, firing guns, howitzers and, in some cases, heavy mortars, the great majority mounted on tracked or wheeled self-propelled (SP) chassis. Some weapons, particularly those for use in less-developed areas, are still towed.
– Missile artillery, firing rockets from tracked or wheeled self-propelled launchers.
– Air defence artillery, firing both guns and missiles against aircraft and helicopters in the battlefield area.

Field Artillery

During the Second World War most field artillery was of 105mm calibre or less, although some 155mm and 175mm guns and howitzers were in use. The vast majority of these weapons were mounted on wheels and towed by trucks, which also carried the gun crew and first-line ammunition, although some horse-drawn artillery was in use right through to 1945! The Americans, British and Germans introduced tracked SPs during the course of the war, but their use was by no means widespread. The fire of the guns tended to be coordinated at a relatively high level, although actual control was at a low level, thus ensuring efficient use of the resources available and rapid responses.

After the war the trend towards increased mechanization continued and field artillery pieces were more frequently mounted on tracked SP chassis. The Second World War SPs were mostly constructed by taking a towed artillery piece and placing it in an open mount, with good elevation but very limited traverse, on a converted tank chassis. Post-war, however, it was realized that such designs had several limitations, including the need to move the entire SP to make a substantial change in traverse and a lack of protection for the crew. Even the relatively late US Army M110 203mm (8 in) SP howitzer, which was fielded in the 1970s, has a traversing limit of 30° left and 30° right. There was thus a move towards turret-mounted artillery pieces, which made for a heavier, more complicated – and more expensive – vehicle, but which also solved the traverse problem and gave protection against NBC and small-arms fire to the crew.

The vast majority of field artillery pieces in NATO armies in the 1950s and 1960s were of 105mm calibre, with smaller numbers of 155mm weapons in 'medium' and 175mm in 'heavy' artillery units. However, the 1970s and 1980s have seen a general move towards 155mm calibre, abandoning 105mm on the Central Front except for four regiments of Abbot with BAOR. The Soviet Army has long used somewhat larger calibres than the West, their standard towed field artillery being 122mm and 130mm at the time that NATO was standardized on 105mm, with 152mm in heavier units. Today 152mm is the Soviet standard although using 122mm 2S1 SPs, remain in service.

The two current leading weapons in this class are the Soviet 152mm 2S3 and the US M109. The Soviet weapon fires a 43.6kg (96.1 lb) projectile to a maximum range of 24km (14 miles), while M109A1 fires its 42.91kg (94.6 lb) shell to a range of 14.6km (9 miles).

In all calibre-by-calibre comparisons Soviet weapons fire heavier shells to a greater range, an advantage with an important tactical benefit, since they can be used in counter-battery fire (i.e. to attack enemy artillery) against NATO weapons at ranges which the latter cannot match.

Several methods of increasing the range are under examination. The most

common is to use a small rocket motor at the rear end (base) of the shell. Such rocket assisted projectiles (RAP) possess the greater range required, but tend to be

Above: At the 'higher' end of the spectrum of indirect fire weapons are gun/howitzers, such as this French Army GIAT Canon de 155mm Tracte.

Right: The Soviet 122mm D-30 entered service in 1963. The breech, seen clearly here, is of the vertical, sliding wedge type and in semi-automatic operation. Towed by the muzzle, when deployed the wheels are lifted off the ground.

less accurate. In 'base-bleed', a combustible compound is burnt at the base of the projectile during flight, emitting a gas at subsonic velocity, which creates a positive over-pressure in the immediate vicinity and reduces base-drag by as much as 80 per cent. Because of its low velocity the gas does not operate as a propellant and thus does not affect the accuracy.

Other methods under examination include such sophisticated propulsion as ramjets which are essentially tube-launched missiles. However, there would appear to be considerable problems in designing a missile with components which can survive the acceleration stresses in the barrel.

An artillery projectile is simply a carrying vehicle for transporting a (normally lethal) payload rapidly and accurately to the target. For many years such payloads have comprised explosives, chemical or bacteriological agents, nuclear weapons or smoke. However, several armies are now developing 'sub-munitions', small anti-personnel and anti-tank mines which are scattered in predetermined areas in remotely-laid minefields. For example, in one typical system, a six-gun 155mm battery can lay an anti-armour minefield 300m (984 ft) deep by 250m (820 ft) wide with two salvoes.

Among the more esoteric roles is that of delivering expendable communications jammers, which are designed to penetrate the soil at the target, deploy an antenna and then jam enemy transmissions at particular frequencies for a predetermined period. Heat generators can also be fired to confuse the enemy's infra-red detection systems.

Great efforts are being made to increase the rate of fire, since the effects of artillery are reduced if men, particularly in the open, have time to take cover. Many modern artillery weapons are being designed to have a 'burst' capability, usually of three rounds in ten seconds, although this could not be sustained for long; even six rounds per minute would be a very high rate. The sustained rate is much more likely to be of the order of two rounds per minute.

In the USA trials are being held with a 'trajectory-shaping' technique in which a gun fires four rounds on different trajectories designed to enable all four to arrive simultaneously on the same target. However, it must be restated that increases in the rate of fire place yet further loads on the resupply system as ever more ammunition is demanded by the artillery arm.

British 155mm Artillery System 90 (AS-90): Following the failure of the very ambitious Anglo-German 155mm SP-70

programme in 1986, the British Royal Artillery has accepted for service the VSEL AS-90, which will replace all of the elderly, small calibre 105mm Abbot SP guns currently remaining in service in the British Army of the Rhine (BAOR), together with at least some of the ageing 155mm M109s.

Unlike many modern SPs, AS-90 is not based on a converted MBT chassis, but utilizes a totally new, purpose-built chassis, optimized for the artillery role. Thus it has the largest possible turret ring to give maximum space for the crew – actual diameter is a very large 2.7m (8.86 ft) – and hydropneumatic suspension to keep the floor clear of torsion-bars. The driver sits at the front on the left, with the Cummins V-8 diesel engine on his right.

The design of AS-90 has the turret mounted at the rear of the vehicle. Again, this is a major consideration, since a tank has its turret centrally mounted, and SPs based on converted tank chassis (such as

the French 155mm GCT and the Israeli Soltam M72) have less than ideal layouts as a result and lack the crew space of a design such as AS-90. Some consideration was given to constructing AS-90 of aluminium, but it was decided to use welded steel construction instead, mainly because it is easier to 'work'; it has a maximum thickness of 17mm. Elevation and traverse are electrically-powered, with manual back-up. The 155mm/39-calibre ordnance, a British Royal Ordnance design, can be elevated between −5° and +70° and is fitted with a double-baffle muzzle brake and a fume extractor. Forty-eight rounds are carried on the gun, 32 of which are in the turret bustle. There is a four-man crew: commander, driver and two ammunition handlers.

Particular attention has been paid to getting the gun into action quickly. An inertial navigation system and an on-board computer enable survey parties to be dispensed with and the gun position is

Above: The French GCT SP gun/howitzer uses a modified AMX-30 chassis as a mount for a 155mm ordnance in a new turret with 360° traverse. It is in service with French, Iraqi and Saudi Arabian armies.

Opposite: The VSEL AS-90 can fire a burst of three rounds in ten seconds, with a sustained rate of fire of two rounds a minute. Using standard ammunition and charges the 39-calibre barrel achieves a range of 24,700m (81,036 ft).

known with great accuracy, virtually as soon as it comes to a standstill. Coupled with the burst-fire capability this means that the gun can move into position, be in action within less than two minutes, engage a target with great accuracy using only predicted fire and then disengage and move on before enemy counter-battery fire can be brought to bear.

Czechoslovak 152mm Self-Propelled DANA: Effective as tracked SPs are, they are also expensive in initial and operating costs, hard to maintain and not suitable for long journeys, especially by road. As a result a small number of armies have developed SP weapons on wheeled chassis. Of these, the most effective is the Czech 152mm DANA, which is highly rated by both Warsaw Pact and NATO experts.

The DANA weapons system consists of the Soviet M-1973 (2S3) 152mm howitzer, installed in a totally new turret which is mounted on a considerably modified Czech Tatra 815 8×8 chassis. The barrel lies in an open slot in the gun housing, and, as there is thus no prospect of gasses entering the crew compartment, there is no need for a bore-evacuator. The driver sits at the front of the vehicle, while the turret crew consists of two men, who share what must be a somewhat cramped compartment with an automatic loader. A hydraulic crane on the turret roof assists in ammunition supply. Maximum range is some 20,000m (65,616 ft), although this could be increased with rocket-assistance. Full NBC protection is provided. Three stabilizing legs are fitted, which are lowered prior to firing.

This is a neat and practical weapon. The Czechs believe that in Central Europe, where there is a huge network of roads and tracks, there is less of a requirement for the much more complex and expensive tracked SPs. Thus, they believe that their wheeled DANA will give all the mobility that is needed and they could well be correct.

Artillery Rockets

Artillery rockets have been used since Napoleonic times, but the first effective systems were introduced in the Second World War with weapons such as the Soviet Katyusha quickly establishing an awesome reputation. Even these were relatively inaccurate area bombardment systems, but there has been a steady improvement over the past 40 years. Rocket systems today are cheap and easy to produce, although the rockets themselves are more expensive, round for round, than standard artillery high-explosive shells, and reload time is longer.

Rockets are ideal surprise weapons and this, coupled with the noise of a rocket attack, gives them a marked morale effect. They are also very effective counter-battery weapons; i.e. attacking enemy artillery positions. They are particularly effective at delivering smoke and chemical-agents, being able to create high concentrations much more rapidly than howitzers.

Above: The highly successful American M109 155mm SP howitzer is in service with many armies. Maximum range of 14,600m (48,000 ft) is short and efforts are being made to extend it.

Below: The US-developed Multiple-Launch Rocket System (MLRS) is a highly effective 227mm (8.93 in) artillery rocket system, which is now entering service with a number of NATO armies.

Rockets have always been less accurate than tube-launched shells. Rockets are today more accurate than earlier systems, the Soviet 240mm BM-24, for example, having a circular error probable (cep) of 93m (300 ft) at 7.25km (4.5 miles), and a cep of 118m (387 ft) at its maximum range of 11km (6.9 miles). Nevertheless, they are not in any way suitable for precision attacks against pinpoint targets.

The most modern Soviet system is BM-22, a 220mm calibre rocket, weighing 300kg (660 lb) and with a maximum range of 40km (24.9 miles). Payloads include high-explosive, chemical and minelets. Sixteen launch tubes are mounted on an 8×8 ZIL-135 truck chassis, fitted with stabilizing jacks. The rate of fire is such that each firing vehicle is accompanied by a resupply vehicle carrying a complete reload of 16 rockets. The Soviet Army has numerous other rocket systems, one of the most interesting of which is the RPU-14. This comprises 16 launch tubes mounted on two-wheeled trailer chassis, the whole device weighing 1,835kg (1.8 tons). It is used by Soviet airborne forces, with a battalion of 18 in the artillery regiment of each Soviet Airborne Assault Division.

The Czechoslovak Army is frequently independent in armament matters, and has produced some thoroughly practical and well-engineered weapons. A case in point is their M-70 system, in which they have mounted a Soviet BM-21 launcher on a Czech Tatra 813 (8×8) truck. There is sufficient space for a full 40-round reload pack on the platform, which reduces reload time from some 20 minutes in the Soviet version to just 2–3 minutes.

The US Army 227mm Multiple Launch Rocket System: Most NATO armies disposed of their Second World War rocket systems in the late 1940s and did not replace them. The West German Army 110mm Light Artillery Rocket System (LARS) entered service in 1969, but it was virtually the only Western system until the US Army formulated a requirement for a General Support Rocket System in 1976. This has since been redesignated the Multiple-Launch Rocket System (MLRS) and is now in service with the US Army and is destined for service with the French, British and West German armies as well.

The rocket is 3.937m (12.92 ft) long, has a diameter of 227mm (8.93 in) and weighs 272kg (600 lb); it has a maximum range of 30km (18.6 miles). There are three warheads: M77 anti-personnel, AT2 anti-tank mines and a chemical round. The M77 shaped-charge sub-munition (bomblet) weighs 0.23kg (0.5lb); 644 are carried in one rocket.

Range is 32km (19.9 miles) and a time-fuse deploys the sub-munitions over the target, each bomblet being stabilized during its descent by a ribbon streamer. A salvo of six rockets would scatter 3,864 M77s over an area the size of four US football fields, a very dense concentration which would make enemy movement extremely difficult.

The second type is the West German-developed anti-tank warhead, a 236mm (9.3 in) diameter rocket, weighing 107kg (235 lb), which carries seven four-mine dispensers. Each of the 28 AT2 anti-tank mines weighs 2.2kg (4.8 lb) and consists of a 103.5mm (4 in) diameter shaped-charge warhead, which can pierce 140mm (5.5 in) of armoured plate. The rocket overflies the target at a height of some 1,200m (4,000 ft) and an explosive charge opens the dispensers, scattering the parachute-retarded bomblets. A single MLRS vehicle can launch 12 rockets in one minute, which will scatter 336 mines over an area of 1,000 × 400m (3,280 × 1,312 ft). As with M77, this is a quickly-laid, remote minefield, with a density which will cause the enemy considerable problems.

The Phase III warhead is a terminally-guided sub-munition (TGSM) weapon with a unique capability. Each rocket will carry six TGSMs, which will be deployed at a predetermined point on the flight-path by a time fuse. Each TGSM will then glide for a brief period while on-board sensors determine its height, at which point it will pull up into horizontal flight. An on-board 96 GHz active radar will then search a ground area, some 2,000 × 1,000m (6,561 × 3,589 ft) in size. Return signals will be fed into the warhead's computer until a valid AFV target is acquired, at which point the TGSM will pitch over into a dive and attack the AFV's highly vulnerable upper side, using its contact-fused, shaped-charge to achieve a K-kill.

An even more capable weapon is under development in the USA – the Tactical Missile System (TACMS). This rocket is 3.962m (13 ft) long and 0.61m (24 in) in diameter; i.e. marginally longer, but some three times greater in diameter than a standard MLRS rocket. Four missiles will be mounted on an MLRS launcher. They will have a range greater than that of the current Lance and will introduce an off-axis launch technique (i.e. the rocket will change course after launch), which will prevent enemy radars from tracking along the rocket's trajectory to the launch vehicle and then undertaking a counter-battery fire mission. Numerous warheads are planned, including 1,000 M77 bomblets; a new type of precision-

Below: The Soviet BM-22 is one of the latest in a long series of very effective, truck-mounted artillery rocket systems, which are widely used by the Soviet and other Eastern European armies.

guided, anti-armour submissile; a runway-attack system; a bunker-buster for use against buried HQs and bridges; minelets and ECM jammers.

This exceptionally versatile MLRS system has the same battlefield mobility as armoured formations, being mounted on a tracked vehicle, derived from the M2 IFV, carrying a trainable and elevating, 12-round launcher. The rockets are launched from self-contained, six-round pods, with a ten-year shelf-life, with two pods on each launcher. MLRS promises to be a very effective weapon, but this capability is gained at the cost of a markedly more complex and expensive weapons system than the Soviet types such as the BM-22.

Heavy Mortars

A mortar is a simple, tube device, firing a large 'bomb' at a relatively large angle (normally 60°+). Because the stresses are small the barrel is of light construction and the mortar is particularly popular for use within infantry battalions, using calibres up to 81mm. Mortars of greater calibre are normally accepted to be artillery weapons and for many years after the Second World War 120mm mortars were the largest to be produced, and those in relatively small numbers.

Soviet 240mm Self-Propelled Mortar, 2S4: As in so many fields, the Soviets use some very heavy mortars and have recently introduced the 240mm Self-Propelled Mortar M-1975 (2S4). Again, as is so often the case with the Soviet Army, they have taken two well-proven systems – the 240mm M-240 breech-loading mortar and the GMZ tracked minelayer chassis – and put them together to produce a new and highly effective system. The mortar and its baseplate are mounted on top of the vehicle and are hydraulically lowered to the ground for firing, the baseplate pivoting on an axle on the rear of the vehicle. Maximum range is some 12,700m (41,666 ft) and minimum range 800m (2,624 ft).

The F-864 HE bomb for this massive mortar weighs 130kg (286.6 lb) of which 34kg (74.96 lb) is payload. As a comparison, the heaviest US HE shell currently in use is the 203mm M106, which weighs 92.53kg (204 lb), with a payload of 17.59kg (38.7 lb) of Comp B explosive.

The Soviet SP mortar fires HE, chemical and concrete-buster rounds, as well as a nuclear round, but unlike lighter mortars the rate of fire is low, about one round per minute. Loading involves swinging the barrel away from the breech into the horizontal position; five men then lift the round and push it into the open end of the barrel, which is swung back to mate with the breech again.

How Will it All Work?

Artillery Tactics: The great majority of armies organize their artillery along generally similar lines. The artillery is formed into units, usually called battalions (regiments in the British Army), comprising a number of batteries, each with six or eight guns. Such a battalion would be allocated to support an infantry or armoured brigade with each battery sub-allocated to an infantry or armoured battalion.

The artillery batteries move according to a plan made by the artillery battalion so that there are always guns in position ready to fire, while others are moving to a new position. Such moves are essential, first to keep pace with the battle, but also because each side will devote considerable resources to trying to locate and then eliminate enemy artillery. Thus, to stay too long in one spot will be very hazardous, to say the least; current US Army planning, for example, is based on each fire unit moving about 22 times per day, although how long such a pace can be kept up is open to some question!

The artillery is deployed in support of the infantry and armoured forces and thus close coordination is essential. This is achieved by the artillery commanders travelling with the commanders of the units they are supporting, leaving their deputies in command of the guns. Thus, in an infantry brigade, for example, the artillery battalion commander will travel with the brigade commander and the artillery battery commanders will travel with the battle group commanders. In addition, many armies send artillery

observation officers to move with the forward troops, who have radio contact with the guns and who can control the fire by direct observation.

Further artillery resources are held at divisional, corps and army group level. These consist of heavy artillery battalions (typically 175mm or 203mm guns and, in the Soviet case, 240mm mortars). These are allocated as the relevant commander deems necessary for a particular operation. Thus, a brigade attack might be allocated, in addition to its own artillery battalion, a battery of 203mm guns and a battery of heavy mortars. It would then be up to the commanders of those artillery units to position the guns and mortars where they could best support the attack and to send officers to the brigade headquarters to obtain the requirements and to translate them into orders for the guns.

All this presupposes an intricate network of communications dedicated to use by the artillery; indeed, the artillery are among the most prolific users of communications, particularly radio. This has an additional benefit in that the radio can be used to coordinate fire between different artillery units. Thus, for example, an artillery battalion supporting one brigade can be used to give fire support to another brigade when its own parent brigade does not require its services.

Field Artillery Fire Control: A further consequence has been the ever-increasing sophistication of artillery command-and-control and peripheral systems. To opti-

Above: Soviet artillery observation post. An example of the traditional OP at work; the latest systems are highly automated to give better, quicker responses.

Top: A superb picture of the mysterious Soviet 2S4 Self-Propelled 240mm Mortar (here in service with the Czech army) clearly shows the huge barrel and baseplate.

Right: The VSEL Ultra-lightweight Field Howitzer (UFH), weighing just 3,628kg (3.57 tons), can be carried by the UH-60 Blackhawk helicopter.

mize the utilization of the firepower now available, computer-controlled systems are necessary, which can control and coordinate artillery fire support on a divisional and corps basis. Further, target acquisition methods have had to be improved in order to give the guns timely and accurate information on enemy locations, and to take advantage of the weapons' range capabilities.

No army will ever admit to having sufficient artillery and all have concluded that the key to making more effective use of the field artillery they already have on the modern battlefield is to automate the control function, as far as is practicable. Some computerized systems have already been fielded, such as the British FACE and American Tacfire, and similar systems exist in Warsaw Pact artillery arms. The purpose of all such systems is to enable the artillery commander to put the right type (nature) and quantity of rounds on the correct target and the time required in the fire plan. Such a requirement is by no means new – the old manual systems did this, too – but the new systems not only enable hours of work to be done in seconds, but can also handle the complexities of planning, coordinating and integrating the fire of field artillery, artillery rockets and other fire support agencies, such as infantry mortars, close support aircraft and naval gunfire. Built-in interoperability with allies' systems further ensures that all this can also be done on an international scale.

The next US Army system will be the Advanced Field Artillery Tactical Data System (AFATDS), which is due to replace the current Tacfire in the early 1990s. The first function of AFATDS will be to prepare, distribute and modify fire plans at the pace demanded by modern warfare. However, it will do much more than this. It will also present multiple options to the fire control staff, draw attention to changing priorities, and even indicate when a unit has spent more time than is wise in one location and needs to move on to avoid counterbattery fire. It will record (and display graphically) the location of all guns, their ammunition state, their fuel state and other information as required by the commander. AFATDS will use off-the-shelf microcomputers, with no major space or power requirements, and a distributed data base, which will place considerable processing power at every station on the system.

Air Defence

The Threat: One of the most serious conventional threats to ground troops

---

TACTICAL SYMBOLS

All armies use systems of symbols to mark maps to show the disposition of units. The most widely used is the NATO system, based on that developed by the US Army. In this system a tactical unit is depicted by a rectangle ☐ , with the size of the unit above it, e.g. ☐ (a company); the type of unit indicated by a symbol inside the rectangle: ⊠ (an infantry company) and the unit designation to the right: ⊠ A (Company A).

Size is indicated by:

• Squad	ı Company	× Brigade	×××× Army
••• Platoon	ıı Battalion	×× Division	××××× Army Group
	ııı Regiment	××× Corps	

A bridge across the size symbol indicates an all-arms team:

Team/Combat Team   Task Force/Battle Group

The type of unit is indicated by a symbol, illustrative of the role:

⊠ Infantry	◿ Anti-tank	▽ Parachute unit
⊠ Mechanized infantry	Air defence	⊞ Medical
⊟ Armour	⊠ Communications	• Artillery, towed
Cavalry/Scout	Chemical	◈ Artillery, SP
⊶ Helicopter/Aviation	✳ Transportation	
⊓ Engineer		

A rectangular symbol on its own indicates a unit in the area it is placed. A line from the symbol indicates that the HQ of that unit is at the end of the line. In the NATO system friendly units are indicated in blue/black and hostile units in red. Thus, for example:

Task Force based on Mechanized Infantry battalion   ••• Air defence platoon

Armoured Company Team   ⊠ 1/12 1st Battalion, 12 Infantry Regiment

Mechanized Infantry brigade HQ   Engineer company

3rd Armoured Division   ◈ Company, SP artillery

An area occupied by a unit is indicated by a line demarking the area and one of the size symbols described above. Thus,

Area occupied by a company

Area occupied by a battalion, with companies as shown

Weapons can be shown, with bars being added to indicate 'medium' and 'heavy'. Thus:

⊏—< Light anti-tank (e.g. US LAW, Soviet Sagger)	←—○ Medium mortar (82–199mm)
⊏—< Medium anti-tank (e.g. US DRAGON)	←—○ Heavy mortar (200mm +)
⊏—< Heavy anti-tank (e.g. US TOW)	⊏—◁ Light air defence (e.g. US REDEYE)
←○ Mortar, 81mm or less	⊏—◁ Medium air defence (e.g. US VULCAN)

Vehicles can also be shown:

⪢ Light tank	⊞ Medium tank	⊟ Heavy tank
◇ Light, tracked APC	◈ Medium, tracked APC	◇ Heavy, tracked APC

Further symbols include:

Nuclear explosion   Direction of advance   Minefield

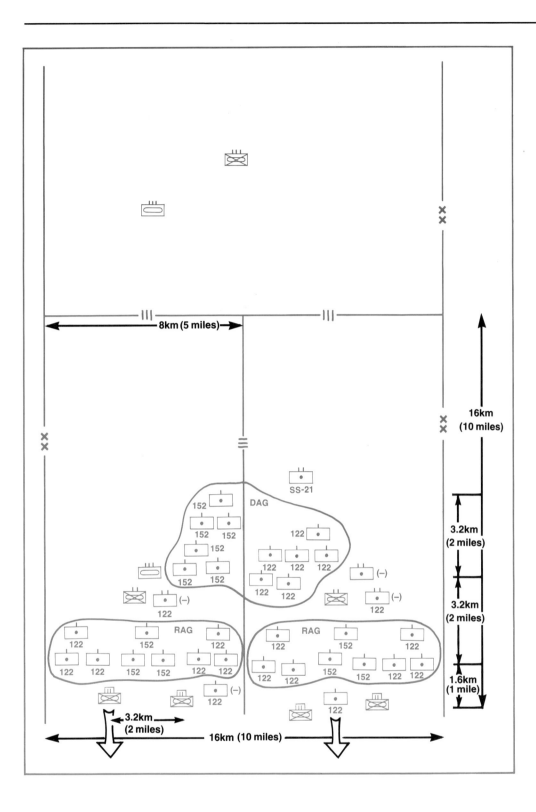

The diagram shows the possible disposition of artillery assets available to a **Motor Rifle Division** in an attack.

KEY

122mm battery

152mm battery

SS-21 (FROG) battalion

(−)   Unit less than strength due to detachments

DAG   Divisional Artillery Group

RAG   Regimental Artillery Group

Alternatively, aircraft targets can be acquired by ground-based radars, such as the AN/MPQ-53, associated with the Patriot weapon system. This one set is capable of searching for targets, detecting and tracking them, identifying them using an Identification-Friend-or-Foe (IFF) system, and then tracking and guiding the missile. It is also fitted with ECCM. The system's human interface is at the Engagement Control Station, where judgement on 'go/no-go' can be exercised. However, the system is capable of totally automatic operation, which may be necessary in a future conflict. (Although not a land system, in the Falklands War in 1982 the Royal Navy used the Seawolf system against low-flying targets, especially missiles; sometimes the first a ship's crew knew of an approaching target was when the Seawolf missile was launched by its automatic system!)

As in other areas the air defence scene is increasingly dominated by electronic battles. Aircraft use increasing numbers of devices to frustrate attack by ground-based weapons, while the men on the ground are always coming up with new devices to break through this invisible shield and shoot the aircraft out of the sky. An additional problem exists for the ground defences in that they clearly must not shoot down their own aircraft. This is overcome in part by the use of IFF, while procedural methods, such as the use of flight lanes for 'own aircraft', can also be used. However, all aircrew are apprehensive when they overfly their own troops who have just been hit by enemy aircraft; despite all the precautions the chances are that someone will just blaze away.

Like other weapons areas, battlefield air defence systems range from small, individual hand-held devices, such as the

comes from the air, in the form of fixed-wing aircraft, helicopters, remotely-piloted vehicles (RPVs) and drones. Most manned aircraft attacks will be delivered at very low level, by aircraft flying between 400 and 600 knots. Such aircraft are extremely difficult to detect, let alone with sufficient time to be able to actually respond by firing a weapon at them.

Without a doubt the most effective means of acquiring such a target is with an airborne early warning aircraft, such as the US Boeing E-3 Airborne Warning and Control System (AWACS) or the Soviet SUAWACS, which have exceptionally powerful radars, capable of 'seeing' far across into the enemy's airspace. The fighter directors on the AWACS can then either vector one of their own fighters to deal with the hostile attack or they can pass the details of the target to a ground station, which is done fully automatically. The ground station can then pass the information to a suitably placed ground defence weapon site.

shoulder-launched British Blowpipe and US Stinger, to the massive systems with large launchers giving area coverage, such as the US Army Patriot and Soviet SA-12. There are two main weapons types in use – guns and missiles – each with its own advantages and disadvantages.

Soviet SA-8 'Gecko' Low-Level SAM: The Soviets have produced a long series of air defence SAM systems, starting with the widely-used SA-1, which was used with some success in the defence of North Vietnam. They have constantly sought to maintain a layered protection over their ground forces, with a combination of guns and SAMs covering the lowest level, and then all-missile systems for medium- and high-level. Currently the most widely used of their low-level SAMs is the system known in NATO as SA-8 'Gecko', but whose Soviet designation is ZRK-SD Strela 3.

SA-8 is a very neat design, with the missiles, together with their radars, mounted on a purpose-built six-wheeled vehicle; crew is three. The missile launcher is mounted on the top of the vehicle; in the SA-8a there are four unboxed missiles, but in the latest SA-8b there are six missiles in boxes.

In all three systems a complete reload is carried on the launch vehicle, while each battery of six launchers (four in peace) is directly supported by two TZM missile resupply vehicles, with further reloads available from the regimental resupply company.

SA-8a is a high acceleration, single-stage, solid propellant missile, with a maximum speed of about Mach 2. It is 3.1m (10.17 ft) long and 0.21m (8.27 in) in diameter, and is fitted with small indexed tail and canard control surfaces. Minimum altitude is 10m (33 ft) and ceiling is 13,000m (42,650 ft). The latest SA-8b missile appears to be the same length as SA-8a but of less diameter; it has a higher speed and improved guidance, and has a maximum height of 15,000m (49,212 ft).

The radar installation is exceptionally neat, and highly effective in practice. The main radar scanner is mounted above the missile launcher; it operates in the H-band and has a maximum range of some 30km (18.6 miles). The scanner folds back on top of the missiles for air transportation and high-speed road travel. In front of the launcher is a J-band target-tracking radar with a 25km (15.5 mile) range, flanked by two I-band missile-guidance radar antennas. These latter operate on different frequencies, each controlling one missile, which enables the system to attack an aircraft target with

two missiles on different frequencies and thus overwhelm its ECM defences. Mounted on top of each missile-guidance scanner is a Low-Light TV system, which is used for target-tracking in poor visibility and an adverse ECM environment.

The vehicle is the Transporter 5937, a 6×6, diesel-engined design. Like many Soviet Army vehicles it is fully amphibious.

Soviet 2S6 4 × 30mm SP Air Defence Gun System: Despite the widespread use of missile systems for air defence, guns have remained in service. However, in order to cope with modern battlefield

Right: Key to the operation of the US Army's Patriot SAM system is the multi-function AN/MPQ-53 phased-array radar.

Far right: The British Field Artillery Computer Equipment (FACE).

Below right: Towed howitzers are no longer suitable for the European theatre.

Below: The latest Soviet 2S6 SPAD has four 30mm cannon, eight SA-9 SAMs and radar, all on a self-propelled chassis!

conditions they have had to become much more sophisticated, mounted on self-propelled chassis and, in the majority of cases, with on-board target acquisition and fire-control radars. For many years one of the most effective of these systems has been the Soviet ZSU-23-4, which has inspired a very healthy respect among any aircrew flying against it.

ZSU-23-4 is based on a PT-76 tracked reconnaissance vehicle chassis, with a turret in which is mounted a quadruple 23mm automatic cannon. An antenna is mounted on the turret for the multi-purpose 'Gun Dish' radar, which performs search, detection, automatic tracking, and ranging functions. Maximum effective range in the air defence role of the 23mm cannon is 2,500m (8,202 ft) and one, two or all four cannon can be used in an engagement. Cyclic rate of fire is 1,000 rpm per cannon in bursts of 3–5, 5–10 or a maximum of 30 rounds. The cannon are water-cooled.

Having seen this Soviet weapon in service the US Army developed the M247 Sgt. York DIVAD, which, like the ZSU-23-4, sought to integrate existing guns, chassis and radar into a new air defence system. However, the problems associated with this eventually proved insuperable (at least in the eyes of the US Congress) and it was cancelled.

Meanwhile, the Soviet Army has developed a new gun system – the 2S6, which marries four 30mm cannon and no less than eight SA-19 missiles to a T72 MBT chassis. Maximum effective range in the air defence role is 3,800m (12,467 ft). The search radar antenna is mounted at the rear of the vehicle roof and the tracking radar antenna at the front of the vehicle, the whole turret design and arrangement bearing a striking resemblance to that of the West German Gepard air defence gun.

Nuclear Artillery

One highly specialized area is that of nuclear artillery. In the early 1950s a huge cannon – the US Army's 280mm (11 in) 'Atomic Cannon' – fired the W19, a 15kT fission warhead, but had no ability (nor, indeed, at that calibre, any requirement!) to fire conventional artillery shells. The reason for such a large calibre was that that was the smallest shell that could accommodate an atomic warhead at that time; since then technological

Right: Soviet 152mm 2S3 SP howitzers rumble through Red Square. These excellent weapons are nuclear-capable.

advances have enabled nuclear shells to be designed which can be fired from normal howitzers. Current dual-capable howitzers include the US Army's 155mm M109 and 203mm M110, Soviet 152mm M-1973 (2S3) and 203mm M-1975 (2S7) and British 155mm AS-90.

The M109A2, for example, is a tracked 155mm self-propelled howitzer, which can fire a full range of conventional shells. The standard HE shell has a range of 18.1km (11.2 miles), which is extended to 24km (14.9 miles) in the Rocket Assisted Projectile (RAP). The current nuclear shell is the W48, which weighs 54.2kg (119.5 lb), has a yield estimated to be in the region of 0.1kT and a range of 1.6km (1 mile) to 14 km (8.7 miles). The Soviet nuclear shell for the 2S3 has an estimated yield of 0.2kT; range is of the order of 18km (11.2 miles).

While field commanders set considerable store by their own organic nuclear artillery there has been considerable debate about the utility of these weapons. The problem is that their range is quite short and they would thus have to be positioned as near to the FLOT (Forward

Line of Own Troops) as possible. Thus, realistically, weapons such as M109A2 with a 14km (8.7 miles) range would need to be located at about 7,315 to 9,144m (24,000–30,000 ft) from the FLOT to fire their nuclear shells. This, however, makes them vulnerable to detection and destruction, especially as their dual-capability, coupled with the need for every single gun to be used in the conventional role means that they cannot be held back to wait for a nuclear mission.

Left: British Javelin shoulder-launched SAM, developed from the Blowpipe, which was used in the Falklands War.

Above right: ADATS is the latest in the US Army's search for an air defence system.

Below right: The US Army Patriot SAM system is now being fielded in Europe.

Below: British Royal Artillery gun crew with the widely used American M110A2 203mm (8 in) self-propelled howitzer.

BATTLEFIELD HELICOPTERS

A very few helicopters were used in the final months of the Second World War in the casualty evacuation role, but it was not until several years later that the true potential of this revolutionary type of aircraft began to be appreciated. In the 1950s helicopters were used to deliver troops to landing zones in remote areas in the numerous counter-insurgency wars, such as those in Malaya, French Indochina and Algeria. The Suez operation of 1956 saw helicopters used for the first time to land marines from naval ships standing off the coast, but it was the Vietnam war which led to the most startling developments.

In Vietnam the helicopter appeared to offer an answer to many of the problems being encountered by the US forces. Transport helicopters could move men and equipment very rapidly from one part of the battlefield to another; indeed, complete units could be lifted into jungle sites which would have been virtually inaccessible on the ground, unless a disproportionate amount of time and effort had been expended. Further, fast-flying, well-armed attack helicopters were introduced to protect the slower and much more vulnerable transport machines. Lifting capacity rose dramatically, although speeds increased by a less marked amount, but reliability and sophistication were of a new order – the helicopter had come of age as a weapons system.

There was, however, another dimension, in that the new capabilities of the helicopter and awareness of its further potential began to generate new tactical concepts. Massed landings by forces of battalion size in areas held by the enemy

Above right: **The crews of two Polish Mil Mi-6 transport helicopters are briefed for their next mission. The wings span 15.3m (50 ft) and are removable.**

Right: **Mil Mi-24 (Hind-D) undergoes pre-flight maintenance checks. These excellent, combat-proven aircraft are in widespread use around the world.**

Below: The helicopter's first great campaign was in the Second Vietnam War, where this archetypal 1967 shot of a machine-gunner firing twin 0.5 in Brownings from the door of a UH-01 'Huey' was taken. The installation is archaic by today's sophisticated standards.

Above: Polish Mil Mi-2 (Hoplite), with special attachments on its exhaust systems, generates smoke to screen off a 2S1 122mm SP battery position.

required careful planning, good control during the approach and effective command if a firefight developed. This led to additional roles, with special equipment fits for armed reconnaissance, airborne command posts, airborne radio-relays and the like.

This was also the time when it began to be realized that helicopters were not just a new toy, but a major (and very expensive) component of the new armies. Special aviation units were formed and in

not a few nations intensive fights took place between the army and air force for control of these new machines.

The US Army was the first to see the need for a totally new type, not a transport helicopter with weapons added, but a battlefield attack helicopter. This gave rise to the Lockheed AH-56 Cheyenne, an extremely sophisticated and very expensive machine, whose main problem was to be twenty years ahead of its time. As a result of the AH-56's cancellation in 1966 an interim type, the AH-1 Hueycobra, provided the US Army with an attack capability until the AH-64 Apache entered service in 1985.

Meanwhile, the Soviet Army, which had also been a keen proponent of battlefield helicopters, introduced the Mil Mi-24 'Hind', an attack aircraft of exceptional capabilities. Well armed and heavily armoured the Hind has served in numerous campaigns, but principally in Afghanistan and Nicaragua. As with the US in Vietnam, the Soviet Army has learnt that helicopters are very effective if handled properly, but that they are very vulnerable to well-directed ground fire. In Vietnam US helicopter losses were very heavy and even in Afghanistan the small number of air defence weapons used by the Mujahideen forced the Soviet helicopters to fly very high and use

Above: Hind-E with rocket pods and AT-6 'Spiral' missiles mounted below the stub wings. Under-nose cannon is the GSh-23L.

Opposite: Agusta A-129 Mangusta (Mongoose) is an Italian-designed aircraft for attack and anti-armour missions.

Below: The Bell UH-1 'Huey' did more than any other machine to establish the helicopter as a mature system.

numerous defensive devices.

Since the early 1970s two new roles for battlefield helicopters have appeared. The first of these is as anti-tank weapons platforms. The helicopter has a number of advantages in this role. First, it is exceptionally flexible, its inherent mobility enabling it to move rapidly from one threatened area to another. Secondly, it can carry a very useful payload, especially of anti-tank guided weapons, such as the US TOW, Soviet AT-6 or the French HOT, as well as free-flight rockets and heavy cannon. Thirdly, it is capable of 'nap-of-the-earth' – NOE (see page 66) – flying and of hovering behind cover, which enables it to remain concealed in a quite remarkable manner. As a result, not only are transport helicopters being fitted with missiles, but more armies are now developing specialized anti-tank helicopters, such as the Italian Agusta Mangusta and Soviet Mil Mi-28 'Havoc'.

The second of these new developments is occurring in the 1980s and 1990s as it has been realized that the threat from helicopters is now such, especially to tanks, that countering them has become a major requirement. An increasing number of ground weapons are being given an anti-helicopter capability, but this is not enough. As a result increasing thought is being given to helicopter 'fighters' which will be optimized for destroying enemy helicopters. The whole sequence is, in fact, a remarkable echo of the early years of the aeroplane, which developed in its first ten years from a rickety and hazardous device into a reasonably reliable and effective machine capable of militarily useful tasks such as reconnaissance and artillery spotting. In these latter roles it became such a threat in the first year of the First World War that defensive measures became necessary and armed 'fighters' were developed to shoot down enemy aircraft.

The Attack Helicopter – US McDonnell Douglas AH-64 Apache

The McDonnell Douglas (originally Hughes) AH-64 Apache is one of the most sophisticated aircraft in service today and almost certainly the most expensive helicopter in production, costing a reported $13 million each in 1989. It is designed to be an all-weather, day/night attack aircraft capable of destroying enemy armour, particularly main battle tanks. Maximum take-off weight is 8,006kg (17,650 lb) and there is a crew of two, with the pilot sitting above and behind the copilot/gunner in the nose. Power is provided by two 1,696shp General Electric turboshaft engines, giving a maximum forward speed of 302 km/h (188 mph) (one of the highest among current service helicopters) and mission endurance of 1.83 hours.

There is a large range of armament. The principal weapon is the 30mm Hughes M230 'Chain Gun', a single-barrel cannon, powered and timed from an external source. It has a cyclic rate of fire of 625rpm (+/−25rpm) and in the AH-64 1,200 rounds are carried. A great variety of missiles can be carried on the two stub wings. There are four stations for underwing pylons, each of which can carry a variety of payloads, including a quadruple Hellfire missile launcher (maximum 16), a quadruple TOW missile launcher (maximum 16), or a 19-tube 2.75 in rocket launcher (maximum 76). Alternatively, an 871 litre (192 gal) external fuel tank (maximum four) can be carried.

Development is under way to mount an AIM-9L Sidewinder on a launch rail on each wingtip, to give the AH-64 an air-to-air capability against other helicopters or aircraft. These weapons give the Apache a very effective capability against enemy tanks.

The heart of the Apache lies in its avionics and electronics, the main system being the Target Acquisition/Designation Sight and Pilot's Night Vision Sensor (TADS/PNVS). TADS and PNVS are,

in fact, separate systems, but are interlinked and work in parallel. TADS consists of a direct-view optical system, a TV camera, a laser spot tracker, and a laser rangefinder/designator, all mounted in a turret under the nose, which can rotate +/−120° and elevate +30°/−60°. The PNVS is a Forward-Looking Infra-Red (FLIR) system, mounted above the nose in a small turret, which can rotate +/−90° and elevate +20°/−45°. The information from these sensors is fed to the pilot's and copilot's Integrated Helmet

and Display Sighting System (IHADSS), and these also show such flight information as airspeed, altitude and heading. A number of other systems also assist in the flying of the aircraft; for example, a simplified inertial system stores exact target locations, and this is backed up by a Doppler navigation system. Such sophisticated systems are essential to enable the two crewmen to fly the aircraft at high speed and low altitude, avoid obstacles, observe for hostile aircraft and ground weapons, and fire the weapons.

The aircraft also carries a host of

electronic devices. There is a suite of radios to communicate (mostly in secure mode) with various ground stations (parent unit, support unit, friendly aircraft, etc.). A Radar Warning Receiver (RWR) indicates that the aircraft is being 'painted' by a hostile radar (the usual prelude to launching a missile or firing a gun), while an Identification Friend-or-Foe (IFF) is used to challenge other airborne targets. The ECM suite includes a radar jammer, an infra-red jammer, chaff dispensers and a radio-band jammer. Passive countermeasures include

Left: The West German MBB Bö-105 (PAH-1) is one of several first-generation anti-tank helicopters and is basically a reconnaissance machine adapted to take a variety of weapons and sensors. Note the six launch tubes for HOT ATGW.

Below: The quite unmistakable profile of the Soviet Mil Mi-28 'Havoc' attack helicopter, which, despite its newness, is now regularly shown to Western experts.

main variations are in size and complexity. However, some armies have endeavoured to produce an attack helicopter by arming a transport type. This has been done by the West Germans with the PAH-1 version of the MBB Bö-105 and the British with the armed version of the Westland Lynx, but these can never be more than compromises.

Mil Mi-28 Havoc

The Soviet Army is second only to the United States in helicopter-operating experience and in the size of its helicopter force. However, the Soviets have produced some remarkable aircraft, which rival anything the US has produced, including the huge Mil Mi-6 Hook and Mi-26 Halo transport machines and the very successful Mil Mi-24 Hind attack helicopter. Latest from the Mil stable is the Mil Mi-28 Havoc, an attack helicopter which is clearly in the same class as the AH-64 Apache; but, despite a similar layout the Soviet machine is by no means a copy of the American.

The Mi-28 first flew in 1982 and development has been slow, mainly due to changes in the Soviet Army's statement of requirements to incorporate lessons from the war in Afghanistan. Like the AH-64, the Mi-28 is a single rotor machine, with twin turboshaft engines, a heavily armoured fuselage and a two man crew mounted in tandem. There are two shoulder-mounted stub wings, a fixed undercarriage and a large cannon mounted under the nose. One fascinating difference is that the Mi-28 has a small cabin in the rear of the fuselage with a door on the port side, which is designed

to be used to rescue one or two men from downed aircraft or in other emergencies.

Primary weapon is the AT-6 Spiral, a beam-riding anti-tank missile: 16 are carried in four quadruple launchers on the wing-tip pylons and the prominent thimble radome on the nose is part of their control system. Other armament can include two rocket pods, each housing 20 57mm free-flight rockets and SA-14 missiles modified for the air-to-air role. There is a chin-mounted 30mm cannon (apparently derived from that used on the BMP-2 IFV) with a double-feed system which enables it to fire either armour-piercing or high explosive shells.

Survivability is given a high priority – not surprising after the experiences in Afghanistan. There is internal composite armour to protect the crew and the somewhat small cockpit windows are all of armoured glass. The seats and undercarriage are stressed to absorb crash landings of up to 15m/sec (50 ft/sec). Even the transmission is capable of running for between 20 and 30 minutes with no oil.

It appears, however, that the avionics are nowhere near as sophisticated as those on the AH-64. The pilot's head-up display is fixed, unlike that on the American machine, which follows the pilot's head movements. Also, on the Mi-28 the gunner's sight is a plain direct-vision

Below: The mighty AH-64 Apache. Armament is (from left to right) Sidewinder AAM, eight Hellfire ATGW, Stinger AAM and a Hughes 30mm chaingun in the chin position.

'black-hole' IR suppressors, fitted over the engine exhausts, in order to avoid presenting a target to enemy IR-homing missiles.

The US Army has ordered no less than 975 AH-64s, which will serve in 34 aviation battalions, as well as training units.

The majority of other current generation attack helicopters are essentially similar in overall design to the AH-64, with a two-man crew in a slim cockpit, undernose cannon and sensors, and stub wings for weapon mounts/launchers. The

device with a built-in laser for range-taking only. The Soviet machine also has night-vision devices, but, again, much less capable than those on the AH-64. However, the Soviets are traditionally good at producing rugged, simple and reliable aircraft and, as in many other cases, it may be that the simpler aircraft stays serviceable for longer than the much more complicated type.

The Soviets will, without a doubt, use the Mi-28 in much the same way as the US. Its primary task will be anti-armour, hunting in pairs to attack with its heavy battery of AT-6 missiles. It will also be used against other softer targets, such as IFVs and command post vehicles, using its rockets and 30mm cannon. It is an altogether formidable machine.

The Transport Helicopter – Boeing-Vertol CH-47 Chinook

There are numerous military transport helicopters in service with many armies. These range in size and capability from the 10–12 man (i.e. squad/section) lifter such as the Westland Lynx and the Sikorsky UH-60A Blackhawk, to the giant Soviet Mil Mi-26, which can carry up to 100 troops. One of the most successful – and enduring – designs is the Boeing-Vertol CH-47 Chinook, which

first flew in 1962 and is still in production in 1990 on three lines in the USA, Italy and Japan.

The CH-47D is a twin rotor helicopter, powered by two Avco Lycoming turboshafts, each of 4,500shp. The fuselage is 15.54m (51 ft) long, but the usable-space in the cabin is 9.17m (30.17 ft) long, 2.51m (8.25 ft) wide and 1.98m (6.5 ft) high. Access to the cabin is by two side doors at the front and by a full width, electrically-operated ramp at the rear. This gives sufficient internal space for 44 fully-equipped troops on seats, 24 stretchers and two attendants, or for a variety of vehicles, such as field cars, and light guns. (Such figures are very dependent upon a variety of factors, including the fuel load, mission range, current weather conditions, etc. During the Falklands War in 1982 one RAF Chinook flew a tactically critical mission with some 86 soldiers aboard; it was a case of 'standing room only' as in a bus or train in the 'rush-hour'!)

Many loads are simply too bulky for the internal cargo hold and have to be carried externally. There are two cargo hooks on most Chinooks, three on the RAF version. In the latter the front and rear hooks are rated at 9,072kg (20,000 lb) each and the centre hook at 12,700kg

(28,000 lb). There is also a hydraulic winch for cargo handling and rescue work. A typical mission for the CH-47D is to carry a payload of 10,446kg (23,030 lb) over 56km (35 mile) range; such a capability (23,030 lb = 10.28 tons) could easily include an M198 howitzer *and* its first-line ammunition *and* its crew.

The toughness of the CH-47 is legendary. US Army versions in Vietnam absorbed considerable battle-damage and still flew to complete their missions. In the Falklands War only one Chinook survived the sinking of the *Atlantic Conveyor*, but it flew until the end of the campaign despite a lack of maintenance and a total lack of spares. At one stage on a low-level mission over the sea the windscreen wipers were inoperable and in a sudden rainstorm the pilot became slightly disoriented and actually hit the water – the aircraft ('Bravo November') simply bounced back into the air again and flew on.

The Chinook is not permanently armed, but machine-guns can be mounted in fixed mounts firing forwards or on flexible mounts in the cabin doorways. The aircraft has a ferry range on internal tanks of some 2,058km (1,279 miles), and certain versions can also be fitted with a long probe for air-to-air refuelling.

The ability of helicopters such as the Chinook to move men, weapons, ammunition or equipment is too easy to under-estimate. The normal payload is in the region of 10,160kg (10 tons) and on a typical battlefield resupply mission of 48km (20 miles), transit time would be ten minutes. Offloading a slung load is very quick, so total time for each journey would be in the region of 25 minutes. If three aircraft are available, then one load will be uplifted about every 10 minutes,

Left: Special handling arrangements are needed on the ground to utilize the exceptional capability of large helicopters such as these CH-47 Chinooks.

Above right: French Army SA.341 Gazelle, armed with fixed GIAT M621 20mm cannon.

Right: RAF Chinook HC.1 with underslung engineer vehicle; three hooks are mounted on the underside of the helicopter.

Far right: The helicopter enables anti-tank teams (such as this French Army Milan team) to be redeployed around the battlefield with exceptional rapidity.

which means that the ground organization will have to generate one ten ton load every ten minutes or 60 tons an hour, and at the far end a similar weight/volume will have to be received and dispersed! The huge effort that is involved in assembling such large loads at such a rapid rate is extremely difficult to visualize; in fact, the 'productivity' of such helicopters is so great that special ground organizations have to be set up, otherwise aircraft must sit idle while the next load is prepared.

Helicopter Tactics

In general terms, the method of flying on or near the battlefields depends upon the terrain, the weather and the threat. The nearer the ground a helicopter flies the more concealed he is likely to be from enemy observation and fire. However, at low level there are large numbers of obstacles, ranging from the natural, such as hills, valleys, and trees, to man-made, such as towers, masts, pylons, wires and buildings. These can, of course, give cover, but they can also be extremely hazardous to the aircraft.

Weather, too, is a factor. Poor visibility can enhance the helicopter's survival from enemy action, but it can also make flying even more hazardous, especially at very low levels, where obstacles will be even more difficult to see.

The pilot must balance all these against each other in planning his mission. The most efficient and fastest – 193 to 225 km/h (120 to 140 mph) – route will be at an altitude just sufficient to remain clear of all obstacles, but this will place the helicopter in a position in space where it is relatively easy for the enemy to observe, using radar, infra-red or the 'Mark 1 Eyeball'. If this makes the aircraft too vulnerable then the pilot must 'contour fly', which means that he comes down somewhat lower and flies at a more or less constant height over the ground, gaining or reducing height according to the profile of the terrain below. He will fly over most obstacles, but may have to fly around some. This contour-flying is necessarily slower, typically 113 to 129km/h (70 to 80 mph).

Finally, there is 'nap-of-the-earth'

Right: Flying low and very fast a Hughes AH-64A Apache is the most sophisticated attack helicopter in service today.

Far right: In a very low hover an AH-64A waits to spring an attack on an 'aggressor' during a training exercise.

Above: Using 'nap-of-the-earth' flying AH-64s would be difficult to see and also remarkably difficult to hear; even more so from inside a closed-down tank.

Right: A lean and extremely mean fighting machine the AH-64 is designed to fight and to survive at very low level at the Forward Edge of the Battlefield (FEBA).

(NOE) flying, which is practised in areas of maximum threat. Here, the pilot comes right down to about 6 to 12m (20 to 40 ft) and flies around and behind obstacles. Again slower, typically 80 to 113km/h (50 to 70 mph), the pilot must devote virtually his entire attention to the actual flying of the aircraft at this height and speed.

These three examples have dealt with the flight profile in terms of height above the ground. The pilot must also, however, plan his flight to make maximum use of the cover between his aircraft and the threat. Thus, he would fly behind a wood, around (rather than over) buildings and other obstructions, and avoid skylines or placing himself in front of contrasting scenery. Where tactics dictate that he must fly in the open, he will do so for the minimum time, flying at maximum speed from one piece of cover to the next. Close-to, helicopters seem very large, very noisy and easy to detect; however, a skilful pilot can render his aircraft very difficult, if not virtually impossible, to detect and follow. Thus, a scout or anti-tank helicopter with a masthead sight can hover behind cover, with its spinning rotor just beneath the top of the cover, and remain undetected while it observes.

The survivability of an individual helicopter is increased by operating in twos or threes, using the age-old technique of 'fire/observe-and-movement'. Operating against an armoured column, for example, three attack helicopters would select ambush positions using woods or buildings as cover, hovering so that they could just see the killing ground. Such positions should also have good, covered entry and exit routes for concealed arrival and departure. Once enemy tanks enter the killing ground the helicopters break cover long enough to fire their ATGW and then return to cover to track the missile onto the target. It is thus similar in many ways to a ground ambush, but with the addition of the third dimension.

Air Assault Tactics

An air assault operation has similar characteristics, whatever the army. The characteristics of such a formation are that it is capable of attacking from any direction, it can move rapidly into otherwise inaccessible areas with most of its combat support (including artillery) and it can concentrate, disperse or redeploy very quickly. It can also maintain a high tempo of operations and can carry out attack, defensive or surveillance missions, as required.

The other side of the coin is that the helicopters in an air assault force require

landing zones and they are vulnerable to attack by enemy aircraft, air defence artillery or other helicopters. Also, they cannot fly in really poor weather conditions, or, in some cases, at night.

Any air assault operation must be planned with great care since it involves large numbers of helicopters, men and weapons, and a normally fairly complicated movement, especially if there is to be more than one pick-up from the same landing zone. The best way to undertake this planning process is to work backwards in sequence from the final event in the operation, the landing of the troops at their destination, since the air operation is simply a means of transportation to fulfil a ground mission.

Thus, the first essential is for the ground force commander to decide upon his tactical plan for the ground operation at the destination; i.e. what is the ground troops' mission, which units need to be positioned where by the helicopter to

Above: British infantry run to board an RAF Puma helicopter. The British formed an air-mobile brigade in the 1980s for deployment on the Central Front in war.

achieve that mission, and what fire support is required?

Next comes the landing plan, which gives details of how the troops, artillery and supplies will be landed. This will include the landing zones, timings, sequence of arrival and other details necessary to ensure that the requirements of the tactical plan are met.

From these two plans the plan for the air movement operation can be developed. This decides on the grouping of aircraft, the routes they are to follow, speeds, altitudes, formations, action on aircraft becoming unserviceable, possible changes of plan due to bad weather or

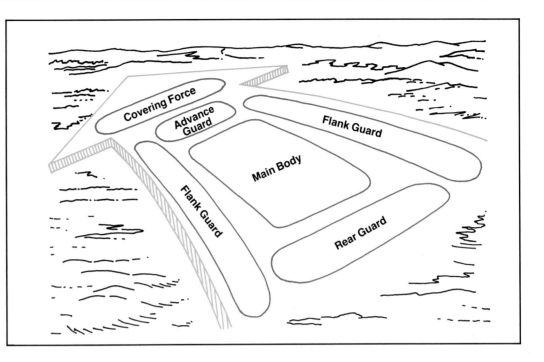

Above: **Advance to Contact.** A large force, such as that shown here, will make extensive use of helicopters. Leading is the covering force with scout helicopters well forward. The Advance Guard covers the Main Body and deals with light resistance. Flank and Rear Guards also protect the Main Body.

enemy action, and so on. Flight routes are planned so that they make best use of terrain to provide cover against observation and fire from the enemy.

Still working backwards, the next element is the loading plan, which is designed to ensure that the right troops and equipment are loaded into the right aircraft. Finally, the staging plan ensures that the right troops and equipment move to the correct pick-up points to meet their aircraft.

There is, of course, a need for yet one more plan, which is the operation to suppress enemy aircraft defences which are in a position to detect and attack the helicopters during their flight to their objectives. This will involve artillery support, attack helicopters and air force fixed-wing aircraft in a combined and coordinated operation.

Major operations of this type will involve many elements. Reconnaissance of landing zones and routes will be an

Above: **OH-58D in a low hover fires 69.8mm (2.75 in) rockets, using its prominent mast-mounted sight, which is fitted with TV and FLIR.**

essential prerequisite, which will be carried out by scout helicopters, drones, or fixed-wing photo-recce aircraft. Attack helicopters will be required to clear the routes immediately prior to the operation. Finally, helicopters will be required to lift the troops, artillery and supplies.

Heliborne assaults can be conducted by virtually any infantry unit, with only a little training and preparation and very little specialist equipment, unlike parachute assaults which require specially trained troops, using special-to-role equipment. Heliborne assaults are vulnerable during the air move, although less so than parachute assaults, since helicopters are able to fly lower and are more agile than the lumbering fixed-wing transports. Finally, both types of assault are at their most vulnerable in the period on the ground immediately following landing; however, heliborne assaults will have the immediate support of attack helicopters and will almost invariably be within range of friendly artillery support.

BATTLEFIELD SUPPORT BY FIXED-WING AIRCRAFT

The air activity over the land battlefield in any future war will be intense. Air forces of both sides will seek to support the ground forces in the land battle, but they will inevitably be forced to start any campaign with a struggle against each other in order to gain air superiority. This battle will involve not only air-to-air fights against opposing aircraft, but also strikes against enemy airfields and air command-and-control systems. There will also be a major effort devoted to destroying or neutralizing enemy air defences, with which will be associated a massive electronic warfare (EW) battle, since all air activities now involve a huge amount of electronic systems and devices. Then, concurrent with all this, the air forces will carry out their tasks in support of the land battle itself: reconnaissance (both photographic and electronic); airborne surveillance and control; attacks on tank, vehicle and troop concentrations and positions; moving men, vehicles and equipment; and, all the time, remaining poised to take part in the nuclear battle should the conflict escalate.

It is important to appreciate that this air battle will not be a separate activity. In future the land and air battles will be totally integrated and will be coordinated with each other in every way and at every level. In both NATO and the Warsaw Pact the command structures are such as to ensure joint control.

There is a plethora of fixed-wing aircraft dedicated to supporting the armies in the land battle; indeed, on the crucial Central Front that would be their primary task. On the NATO side, for example, battlefield support could range from

large Boeing B-52 bombers of the US Strategic Air Command tasked with battlefield interdiction operations against highly critical targets, through operations against highly critical targets, through operations by American FB-111, and British, West German and Italian Tornado swing-wing aircraft, down to small aircraft in the ground-attack role, such as the Alpha Jet. In addition, many light aircraft, including propeller-driven types, continue to serve in tasks such as

Right: The joint French-West German produced Alpha Jet is an attack aircraft with air-to-air and anti-shipping capability using laser-guided bombs and missiles.

Opposite: USAF-15E fires a Hughes TV-guided Maverick air-to-ground missile.

Below: West German Tornado dispensing MBB anti-tank bomblets; such weapons would be vital in any anti-armour battle.

radar surveillance, jamming and general reconnaissance. A similar variety of aircraft and types exists in the Warsaw Pact.

The very serious threat posed by such aircraft has given rise to a huge array of ground defences. There are numerous radars to provide early warning of aircraft threats and to track the targets once they have been acquired. These are backed-up by a vast range of air defence weapons, ranging from sophisticated missile systems, through gun systems mounted on tracked chassis down to individual soldiers using rifles or machine guns. So effective are these modern defences that they have, in their turn, caused the air forces to design a whole new range of techniques to overcome them, known as Suppression of Enemy Air Defences (SEAD).

The air battle during the United States' campaign in Vietnam illustrated the potential of modern air forces. Although some of the roles and achievements of aircraft in that war were controversial, there can be no doubt that there were cases where tactical air support turned the tide in particular land engagements. A particular example was at the Battle of Khe Sanh, just south of the Demilitarized Zone (DMZ), where attempts by the North Vietnamese Army to overrun an isolated garrison of the US Marine Corps (as they had done with the French at Dien Bien Phu in 1954) were prevented by the tactical airpower of the US Navy and USAF.

Unfortunately for the United States, the North Vietnamese also showed just how effective properly controlled and sited air defence systems could be. Even though the overall 'air-defence system' was relatively unsophisticated and did not use the most modern weapons and sensors available, the losses suffered by US aircraft and aircrews *at all heights* were far greater than had ever been anticipated. Many aircraft were lost over North Vietnam, but, taking just three types of (then) modern aircraft no less than 17 B-52s bombers, and 83 F-8 Crusader and over 300 F-4 Phantoms fighters were lost to air defences in North Vietnam.

To understand the potential of modern air power on the battlefield, it is first necessary to look at a few aircraft, which are representative of those available.

Right: A flight of three B-52 bombers drop 1,000 and 750 lb bombs on a target 25 miles from Bien Hoa Air Base, Vietnam, December 1966.

Below: The North Vietnamese air defence was more than a match for the firepower of the F-4 Phantom.

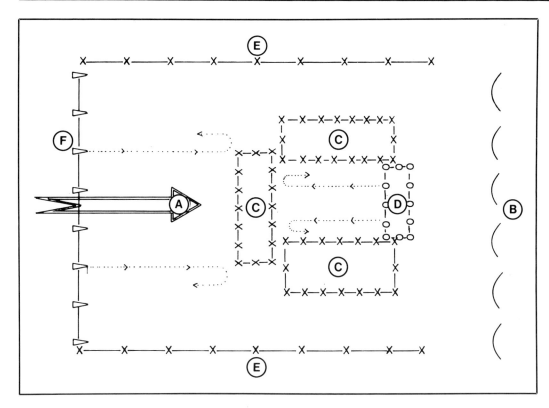

Left: **Artillery/Air Cooperation.** US forces evolved some deadly techniques in Vietnam to combine artillery and air power. This example, taken from the Battle of Khe Sanh (1968), shows enemy advancing in column (A) towards US positions (B). American 155mm batteries fire concentrations (C) on three sides of a box with the open end towards their own positions. Another battery fires a rolling barrage (D), moving up and down. Infantry (B) deal with any survivors driven towards them and 175mm guns fire fixed linear concentrations (E). Meanwhile radar-controlled A-6 attack aircraft drop a rolling barrage of bombs (F) to catch the reserves.

Below: **The Kinh No rail yard and storage facility after a B-52 strike in December 1972. Situated seven miles north of Hanoi, the complex was a major distribution point for supplies coming into North Vietnam.**

Above: Latest RAF version of the unique V/STOL Harrier is the GR5, seen here with underwing pylons and long-range tanks.

Ground-Attack Aircraft

The McDonnell Douglas/British Aerospace AV-8B Harrier II is in production for the US Marine Corps as the AV-8B and as the GR Mk 5 for the British RAF; the two types are virtually identical, differing only in the avionics fit. The AV-8B is unique among fixed-wing aircraft, because it is not only designed to undertake battlefield support missions, but it is also designed to spend its entire combat life within the battlefield environment. This is because its Vertical/Short Take-Off and Landing (V/STOL) capability enables it to operate away from highly vulnerable fixed airbases and to be based in concealed extempore airfields virtually anywhere. The original Harrier conclusively demonstrated this during the Falklands War in 1982, when, within days of the successful landing in San

Carlos Bay, RAF aircraft were operating ashore from a 'strip' consisting of about 60m (200 ft) of steel matting. No other fixed-wing aircraft in the world could have done that.

The AV-8B is a relatively small aircraft with a length of 14.12m (46.33 ft), with the pilot sitting well forward under a large canopy with exceptional visibility. The small wing is mounted in the shoulder position and is swept at a modest angle with a span of 9.25m (30.33 ft). The undercarriage has two main legs in tandem under the fuselage and two small, steadying legs located at about half-span on the wings.

Key to the AV-8B's unique capability is the Pratt & Whitney F402 engine, a licence-built version of the Rolls-Royce Pegasus 11-21E. This aircraft has four rotating nozzles, which enable it to lift or lower the aircraft vertically or propel it horizontally in forward flight. The engine has a thrust of 9,979kg (22,000 lb), which enables the aircraft to lift a very significant warload, particularly in the Short Take-Off mode.

Maximum speed is Mach 0.93 1,083km/h (673 mph) and this means that when operating from a forward field base only a few miles behind the FLOT, the AV-8B is over the target very quickly indeed. The actual payload on any one mission depends upon the weight of fuel to be carried to achieve the desired range and the intended take-off mode, since more fuel is needed for a vertical take-off (VTO) than for one requiring a short forward roll (STO). Thus, the maximum all-up weight in the VTO mode is 8,867kg (19,550 lb), while in the STO mode it is 13,494kg (29,750 lb).

A very wide range of weapons can be carried. The AV-8B has a number of underwing points, on which can be carried HE bombs, cluster bombs, laser-guided (smart) bombs, anti-radar missiles or fuel tanks. In addition, there are two 25mm cannon mounted under the fuselage and the aircraft can also carry two AIM-9L Sidewinder AAMs for self defence against other aircraft.

It is astonishing that the AV-8B Harrier II (and its predecessor, the AV-8A

76

Right: USAF A-10 is a purpose-built attack aircraft, specializing in low-level attacks against ground targets.

Harrier I) remain the only battlefield V/STOL aircraft. This aircraft provides a unique capability, being designed for ground attack and operating within the area of the ground forces being supported. More than this, however, the modern large fixed airfields are such obvious, high-value targets that they are bound to be attacked very early in any conflict. Thus, aircraft based on such airfields will be either prevented from operating or will be concentrating on their own survival. But the AV-8B is able to operate away from all this, away from virtually any field, with an adjacent wood for cover for the ground facilities sufficing for this excellent aircraft.

A completely different approach was taken by the USAF in developing its specialized ground attack aircraft, the Fairchild Republic A-10. Whereas the

AV-8 has V/STOL capability to give it survivability and to enable it to operate from near its area of operations, the A-10 is a conventional take-off and landing aircraft (CTOL), but its powerful engines and specially-designed undercarriage enable it to operate from 'austere' forward strips. The AV-8B is small, fast and unarmoured, but the A-10 is large, relatively slow and heavily armoured; both are designed to fly very low in the forward combat area. The AV-8B concept was proven (in its RAF/Royal Navy Harrier (AV-8A) form) in the Falklands War but the A-10 has yet to operate in a live conflict. Which would prove the better in a 'high-tech/high threat' environment such as the Central European front must (and hopefully will) remain an open question.

The A-10 was the outcome of a 1960s competition designated 'AX' (attack-experimental)', to produce a highly survivable aircraft, powered by turboprops or turbofans, with a high first-round lethality against armoured targets, to fulfil the USAF's ground-attack mission. Two finalists reached the 'fly-off' stage, the

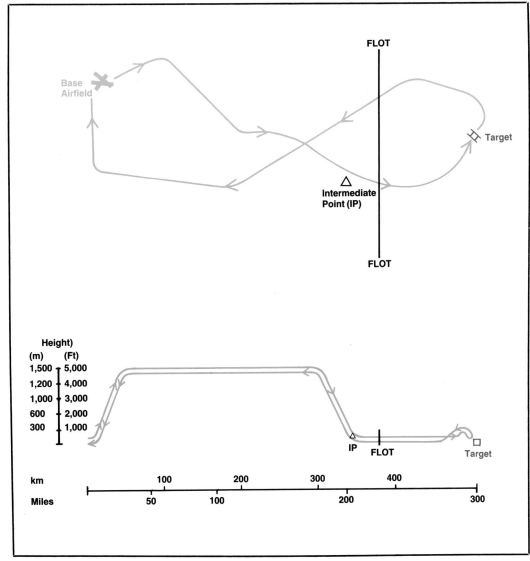

Left: **Ground-Attack Mission.** When ground troops identify a target for attack the aircraft will normally transit at about 1,500m (5,000 ft), descending to very low level to cross the FLOT. An easily identifiable Intermediate Point (IP) will be used to guide him to the target. (The top diagram is the plan view while the lower shows the side elevation.)

A-10 and the Northrop A-9; the A-10 won and the A-9 disappeared, although the Soviet Union's Sukhoi Su-25 'Frogfoot' ground-attack aircraft bears a marked resemblance to it!

The A-10 is large: it has a wing-span of 17.52m (57.5 ft) and a length of 16.25m (53.33 ft), and a maximum all-up weight of 22,680kg (50,000 lb). It is thus the same size as, and about twice the weight of a loaded 30-seat turboprop airliner! The A-10 has straight wings and two 4,112kg (9,065 lb) General Electric TF-34 turbofans, which give it a maximum speed of 681km/h (432 mph) and a fully-laden take-off run to 15.2m (50 ft) of 1,220m (4,000 ft).

Because the A10 must inevitably operate in a high-threat environment it has great built-in survivability. The pilot sits in a titanium 'tub', which is proof against 23mm rounds (clearly, the requirements staff had the Soviet ZSU-23-4 in mind), with a canopy made of armoured glass. The fuselage is heavily constructed and all controls and fuel lines are routed for maximum protection, as well as being duplicated and widely separated. The twin engines are mounted high on the rear fuselage, both for survivability and

to minimize the infra-red (IR) signature, and the aircraft can return home with one engine completely shot away. The twin-fin tailplane also possesses 50 per cent redundancy.

However, the task of the A-10 is not so much to survive as to deliver ordnance against enemy targets and to destroy them. Perhaps the most dramatic element of the A-10's weapons is the built-in GAU-8/A Avenger, seven-barrel 30mm Gatling cannon, with a magazine of 1,174 rounds. This huge weapon is 6.4m (21 ft) long, fires 30mm heavy armour-defeating depleted-uranium rounds and its recoil forces are so powerful that the aircraft visibly slows down as it fires. The effect of this weapon on even a heavily armoured MBT is devastating.

The A-10 also has 11 stores pylons: four under each wing and three under the fuselage. A great variety of stores can be carried, from Paveway laser-guided 'smart' bombs, cluster bombs, Hellfire anti-tank missiles, free-flight rockets, Snakeeye retarded bombs and HOBOS (homing bombing system) to electronic warfare pods and fuel containers.

The USAF, the only user of the type, has 565 A-10s (107 of them operated by

the Air Force Reserve), the great majority of which would be committed to NATO's Central European Front in war. Considerable efforts have been made by the USAF to evaluate the A-10's capability and survivability in war, and it appears, albeit in the absence of actual combat experience, that it will be highly effective.

Deep Attack

The AV-8B and A-10 are designed to undertake ground-attack missions in the forward areas of the battlefield; i.e. up about the enemy's divisional rear boundary. Many aircraft are designed for deeper attack missions; i.e. to about army rear boundaries.

Such types include the US Vought Corsair II and General Dynamics F-16 Fighting Falcon, British BAe Buccaneer, British/German/Italian Panavia Tornado and the Soviet MiG-23. Perhaps one of

Below: **A USAF F-16B Fighting Falcon. This is one of the most important aircraft in NATO, in service with the US, Belgian, Danish, Dutch and Norwegian air forces.**

Above: The Sukhoi Su-25 'Frogfoot' is the Soviet ground-attack aircraft; it makes interesting comparison with the USAF A-10 (see page 77) but is a generation newer.

Right: An RAF Jaguar comes in at very low level past Schloss Hohenzollern in southern Germany. Note the large 'recce pod' on the centreline position.

the most important and capable in this class is the Soviet Sukhoi Su-27, known also by the NATO reporting name of 'Flanker'.

This large, two-seat aircraft has twin engines and swing-wings, and is specifically designed for low-level penetration of enemy airspace. It has a maximum speed at low level of some 1,400km/h (870 mph), but when carrying external weapons and fuel tanks (which would almost always be the case in the battlefield area, at least on the outward leg of a mission) maximum speed is about

1,000km/h (620 mph). Combat radius on a typical tactical mission, flying low all the way ('lo-lo-lo' in air force jargon) with a 8,000kg (17,640 lb) underwing load is some 322km (200 miles).

The avionics fit is very sophisticated and is designed to enable the aircraft to penetrate deep through enemy air

Left: US Army pilot shows off one of the cameras fitted in his Grumman OV-1 Mohawk. Having entered service in 1961 the Mohawk will remain in the US Army's inventory well into the 21st Century.

Below: The interior of the US Army's Sikorsky EH-60A Blackhawk electronic countermeasures (ECM) aircraft, showing the two operators at their consoles.

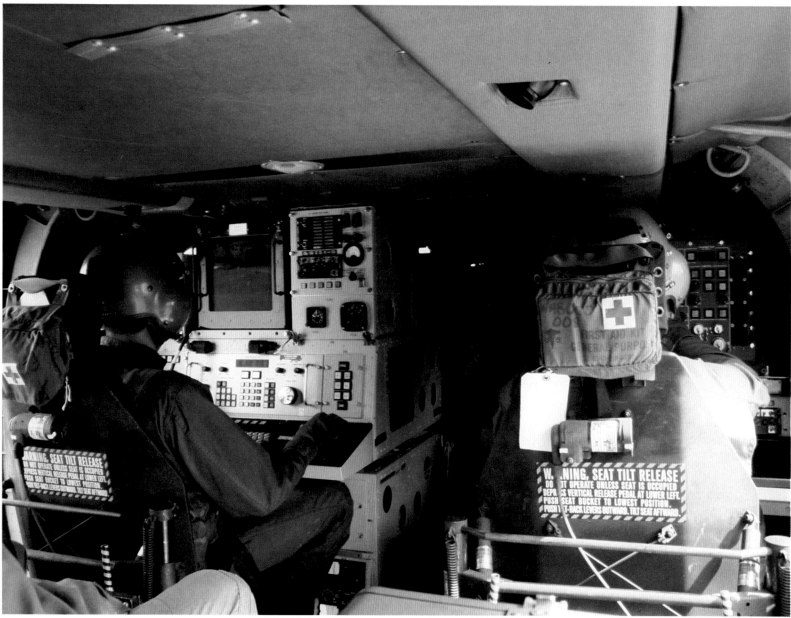

defences and then deliver its weapons with extreme accuracy. Such is the range of equipment fitted, including radar warning receivers (RWR), EW jammers, and ECM systems such as chaff dispensers, that a second crew member is necessary to operate them all.

Electronic Warfare Aircraft

As described in the section on communications (see page 116) a huge effort is now devoted to electronic warfare (EW) and many of the EW resources of direct relevance to the land battle are mounted in aircraft. There would, in fact, be a host of EW aircraft in or near the forward areas operating both in direct support of the land battle and of strike aircraft carrying out attacks against enemy targets.

The US Army has operated for many years the Grumman DV-1 Mohawk, a small, two seat, twin-engined aircraft. One of the two current versions is the OV-1D, equipped with sideways-looking airborne radar (SLAR) and photographic and infra-red (IR) sensors capable of monitoring enemy operations in daylight, night and bad weather. Its primary task is thus gaining information on enemy movements in the forward areas.

The other version of the Mohawk is the RV-1D, known as the 'Quick Look' system, which is an airborne, computer-controlled electronic intelligence system. Its primary mission is to provide forward commanders (i.e. at division and corps level) with information on the location and type of enemy radars and other 'non-communications' emitters. As with the OV-1D, the RV-1D can operate in any weather and by day or night.

The third US Army type is the Guardrail system, using a twin-engined light utility transport aircraft, based on the very successful civil Beechcraft King Air and Super King Air. The RU-21H Guardrail V, the current system, is designed to intercept and locate enemy communications transmitters, particularly microwave systems, which are difficult to intercept from the ground because of their line-of-sight characteristics. The Guardrail V aircraft is festooned with antennas and packed with equipment. A newer version, the RC-21K Improved Guardrail V, is fitted, in addition, with a satellite communications system, thus freeing it from dependence upon communications with ground-based radio stations.

Finally, the US Army has an EW

Above: **USAF TR-1 reconnaissance aircraft emerges from its hangar for a high-level flight. Sensors in the nose and pods enable the TR-1 to operate successfully at heights in excess of 26,000m (85,000 ft). Designed for strategic missions, the TR-1 is now also used tactically.**

helicopter in the shape of the Sikorsky EH-60A 'Quick Fix', which is organic to divisions and armoured cavalry regiments. This is a special version of the Blackhawk and is fitted with equipment to enable it to intercept, locate by direction-finding (DF) and, if required, jam enemy radio transmitters and systems. The EH-60A has a crew of five and can remain on station for up to two hours. (A less capable aircraft, an EW version of the earlier Bell UH-1 'Huey', the EH-1H, is also in service.)

USAF EW aircraft would be based and would tend to operate a little further to the rear, in support of corps and army group operations. The first of these would be Lockheed TR-1As (the most recent version of the Lockheed U-2 'spy-plane'). These aircraft are fitted with

Above: USAF and German Air Force operators work side-by-side in a NATO E-3A AWACS aircraft on a patrol over Western Europe.

the Advanced Synthetic-Aperture Radar System (ASARS), which gives an extremely high definition radar picture in all weathers, by day or night, out to 55km (35 miles) to one side of the flight-path. Some TR-1As also carry the Precision Emitter Location Strike System (PLSS), which, when used by three TR-1As flying well-separated race-track orbits and cooperating with each other, can pinpoint the location of any emitter within range with an accuracy of +/− 1m (3 ft). Also operating in the same area would be Lockheed EC-130H 'Compass

Call' aircraft fitted with high-power jammers, linked with similar systems on the ground to give a comprehensive capability against enemy command and control communications systems.

Yet further to the rear, but still within the battle zone, would be Boeing E-3A Sentry Airborne Warning and Control System (AWACS) aircraft, of which NATO owns and operates 18. These remarkable aircraft have a huge radar scanner mounted back-to-back with an IFF (Identification Friend-or-Foe) system in a rotating dome ('rotodome') mounted on a pylon above the rear fuselage. Operating in 'race-track' orbits these aircraft can scan vast areas of airspace, and identify enemy targets out to great distances. They can also vector friendly aircraft against enemy targets.

The E-3A force is vital to the conduct of the modern land–air battle.

On the Soviet side there is a similar array of aircraft devoted to the support of the land battle on the Central Front. A special EW version of the venerable Mil Mi-4, the 'Hound-C' has five sets of the Yagi antenna arrays protruding from its fuselage, and this appears to be intended to jam NATO communications in the VHF and SHF bands; i.e. tactical radio nets and possibly some of the microwave trunk systems, which are difficult to jam from the ground. There are also specialized EW versions of the Soviet equivalent of the Lockheed C-130, the Antonov An-12 'Cub'. For example, Cub-B, an ELINT platform, is fitted with numerous receivers, signal analysers and air-to-ground communications links for real-time passage of information to ground stations, while Cub-C and D are ECM aircraft designed to jam ground communications.

There are also two Soviet AWACS platforms. The first, the now somewhat elderly Tupolev Tu-126 'Moss', is a turboprop aircraft with, like the US E-3A, a very large rotodome mounted on a pylon above the rear fuselage. This was an interim type with a limited performance, but nevertheless one of these aircraft lent to India (together with its crew) during the 1971 war with Pakistan was reported to have provided a very valuable service. A few remain in service, but more important today is the definitive Soviet AWACS, the Ilyushin Il-76 'Main-

stay'. Like the E-3A, this is also a conversion of a four turbofan-powered, transport airframe and, again, has a large rotodome on a pylon above the rear fuselage. The Il-76 can be assumed to offer a similar performance to the Boeing E-3A.

Tactical Transport Aircraft

Also playing a critical role in the land battle and very active in the battlefield area will be air force operated fixed-wing transport aircraft. These will be involved in a multitude of missions, including flying in reinforcements and supplies to forward airstrips, air-dropping urgently needed supplies, moving troops and equipment from one part of the battle

area to another, and possibly in paratroop drops. Their use, of course, depends upon the tactical air situation and they would be unlikely to be used where the enemy had total air superiority. However, even in the Central Front they have an important role, while in other theatres their support would be crucial to success.

Below: Tactical transport aircraft have a vital role and come in many sizes. Typical of the smaller end of the range is the Spanish CASA C-212 Aviocar, seen here at Farnborough in 1988, in military camouflage and fitted with winglets.

Features of virtually all of these military tactical transports are a short take-off and landing capability; a large, unobstructed cargo hold; a tail ramp for loading vehicles and equipment; at least one exit door for paratroops; and a high wing, mounting two or four turboprops except for the Soviet Il-76, which has four turbojets. All are capable of deliver-

Above: The intercontinental range of the Lockheed C-141 Starlifter enables it to fly non-stop from the USA and drop paratroops direct onto a European battlefield.

Left: The Transall C-160 was jointly built by France and West Germany as a medium military tactical transport.

ing their loads to a forward airstrip, and most are also capable of air-dropping men and equipment by parachute.

At the smaller end of the scale are twin-engined aircraft, such as the Spanish CASA C-212 Aviocar. This has a capacity of 24 troops, or 23 paratroops and a jumpmaster, or 2,770kg (6,107 lb) of freight. It can also carry some light vehicles, such as a Land Rover, although its capacity in this respect is somewhat limited. (Many military transport aircraft frequently reach the limits of the volume of their holds before they reach their payload limits.) The slightly larger Shorts 330 is very similar to the Aviocar in concept and capability.

In the medium-size area there is a large number of types. The Transall C-160 is a twin turboprop aircraft with a carrying capacity of 93 troops or 16,000kg (35,725

lb) of cargo. The Transall is a good aircraft, but far more successful is the similarly sized, but four-engined Lockheed C-130 Hercules. Carrying 92 passengers, 64 paratroops or five standard pallets, the Hercules has been in production since 1951, is used by at least 44 different nations and exists in some 30 different versions. The ruggedness, flexibility, reliability and adaptability of the Hercules are legendary and it is employed in roles as diverse as strategic transport, EW platform, special operations gunship and short-range, short-field tactical lifter. The Hercules was also used to pioneer the now widely used, low-level extraction system, in which pallets or vehicles on special platforms are pulled out of the rear door by a drogue parachute, while the aircraft flies at a height of some 5m (15 ft) above a landing strip.

The USSR produces a generally similar four turboprop transport, the Antonov An-12 'Cub', but this is being replaced by the four turbojet Ilyushin Il-76 'Candid'. The Il-76 can seat 140 troops and take 40,000kg (88,185 lb) of freight, although, as with all transport aircraft, heavier loads can be carried over shorter distances. One record held by the Il-76 is the dropping of a stick of paratroops from a height of 15,386m (50,479 ft), which speaks very highly not only for the altitude performance of the aircraft, but also for the courage of the men jumping from such an immense height, although the military application of such an undertaking is difficult to envisage!

Finally come the super-heavy aircraft, which, despite their size, still have some tactical capability due to their short-field performance. The USAF Lockheed C-5 Galaxy has been in service for 20 years and for some time was the largest, heaviest and most powerful military

Above: **Paratroops are given a final briefing before a free-fall jump. The role of paratroops on the modern battlefield is the subject of debate.**

Above right: **Groundcrew in full NBC outfits making final adjustments to a BL755 cluster bomb on an RAF Jaguar.**

Right: **Soviet Antonov An-124 Condor at the 1988 Farnborough Air Display.**

transport aircraft in the world. It can carry almost anything in the US Army inventory, including two M1 tanks, five M113 APCs, 36 standard cargo pallets, 16 three-quarter-ton trucks or 345 troops. It can fly intercontinental ranges and then land on a forward, semi-prepared strip.

The first Soviet transport in this category was the four turboprop Antonov An-22 'Antei', with a maximum payload

of 80,000kg (176,350 lb). It can carry virtually any item of equipment in the Soviet inventory. Even bigger, however, is the Antonov An-400 'Condor', a four turbofan aircraft with an empty weight of 180,080kg (397,000 lb or 177 tons) and a payload estimated to be well in excess of 119,750kg (264,700 lb).

Aircraft Weapons

Combat aircraft are only the means of transporting weapons, which must then be delivered against ground targets, and there is now a vast range of such weapons available. At the 'low-tech' end is the traditional, free-fall 'iron bomb', which can still be used to great effect. Modern aircraft can carry a large number and even ground-attack fighters can carry large bombs of up to 907kg (2,000 lb) in weight. The explosive content of these bombs is considerable and their effect is enhanced by the use of modern subst-

ances, such as air-fuel explosives. The Soviet Air Force, for example, has a series of HE bombs, ranging in size from 100kg (220 lb), through 250kg (551 lb), 500kg (1,102 lb), and 750kg (1,653 lb) to 1,000kg (2,200 lb). Many air forces use retarding devices on such bombs, in order to permit the aircraft to be clear of the danger zone before the bomb hits the ground.

A relatively simple and cheap means of increasing the accuracy (and thus the effect) of iron bombs is to fit a laser-guidance head and rudimentary control surfaces. In combination with a laser target marker (LTM) (either air- or ground-based) these enable the bombs to be delivered with great precision. During the Falklands War one such bomb, delivered by an RAF Harrier, was guided by a ground-based LTM literally through the door of a tent being used as an Argentine artillery command-post.

Above: RAF Jaguar with Paveway II laser-guided bombs on inboard pylons. Chaff/flare pod is on the starboard outer pylon.

Above right: Jointly-designed by Italy and Brazil, an AMX attack aircraft drops retarded bombs at low level.

Right: Latest night/all-weather attack version of the AV-8B, armed with bombs, missiles and machine-guns.

Because modern air defences are such a threat, it is operationally necessary for ground-attack aircraft operating in support of ground forces to deliver such bombs at very low-level. One device which seeks to overcome the weapon-aiming problem this entails is the cluster bomb, such as, for example, the British Improved BL 755, in which a bomb-

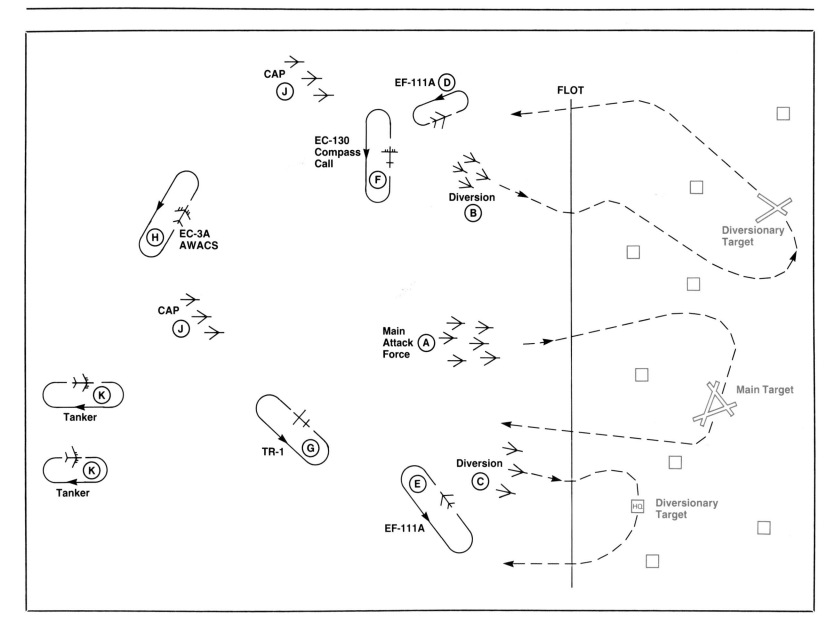

shaped container is used to transport 147 bomblets. When the bomb is released by the aircraft it falls until a preset time delay activates the primary cartridge which blows off two sections of body-skin, following which the main cartridge ejects the bomblets in a predetermined manner to ensure even coverage of the target area. The bomblets deploy a small drogue, arm themselves after a short period of flight and, on impact, use a shaped charge to penetrate at least 250mm (9 in) of armour.

A particular type of target is the enemy airfield runway, which is attacked as part of the counter-air battle to prevent aircraft taking-off or landing. This is, in many ways, a particularly difficult target and special weapons have been developed to overcome this. The USAF Direct Airfield Attack Combined Munition (DAACM) is one of the most advanced of these and consists of two types of munition packaged in a standard Tactical Munitions Dispenser (TMD). The fore-

A Major Air Attack. The diagram represents schematically (not to scale) the major elements which might take part in an attack. The Main Attack Force (A) comprises attack aircraft armed with runway attack weapons, fighter escorts and an electronic countermeasure (ECM) aircraft. Two diversionary attack forces (B) and (C) are similarly made up. Each attack group is routed to avoid known radar and air defences.

EF-111As (D) and (E) use their ECM against enemy air defence surveillance and target acquisition radars. A Lockheed EC-130 flies an ECM mission (F), and a Lockheed TR-1 (G) surveys enemy air space with its synthetic aperture radar. Following a racetrack pattern high over the rear area, an E-3A AWACS (H) provides surveillance of the air situation on both sides of the FLOT and is ready to vector CAP aircraft (J) in support of the raids. Finally, tankers are airborne (K) to replenish aircraft running short of fuel.

part of the TMD contains eight Kinetic Energy Penetrators (KEP). On being dropped from the aircraft the TMD after a preset delay dispenses the KEPs, which look like small rockets. Each KEP then deploys tail fins and a drogue which pulls out the main parachute to slow down the missile until it is pointing downwards at an angle of 65°. At that point the missile's rocket motor fires, the parachute is jettisoned and the KEP is driven into and through the runway, exploding when it is deep enough to create a fair-sized crater. The other element of the DAACM are 24 British-designed Hunting area denial sub-munitions, small HE devices which scatter over the cratered area to prevent movement and delay repairs to the runway.

A weapon first used in the Second World War is still widely used in the ground-attack role: the unguided aircraft rocket. Such rockets are housed in streamlined pods and are fired singly or in a ripple, as decided by the pilot, and are aimed by pointing the aircraft at the target. These rockets are of various calibres, ranging from 37mm (1.45 in), through the widely used 57mm (2.25 in) and 70mm (2.75 in) and 81 mm (3.2 in) to as large as the Soviet 240mm (9.4 in). A typical rocket is the Swiss Oerlikon SNORA 81mm rocket, which has three different warheads; anti-tank, fragmentation and practice. The fragmentation rocket is 1,783mm (70 in) long, weighs 19.7kg (43 lb) and has a range of some 10km (6.2 miles). On impact the explosive (2.8kg (6.2 lb) of trityl) scatters 2,133 tiny metal fragments at high velocity around the target area. The effect on troops being hit by a strike of 24 such rockets simultaneously is devastating unless they are exceptionally well protected. There is also an anti-tank warhead, using the hollow-charge principle.

Also still highly effective against ground targets is the aircraft cannon. Most powerful of all currently in service is the General Electric GAU-8/A, de-scribed above in the section dealing with the A-10. Another weapon from the same company is the five-barrel GAU-12/U; this marries the same multiple rotating barrel principles as the GAU-8/A to the outstanding 25mm round, which has a muzzle velocity of 1,097m/sec (3,600 ft/sec). There are tracer, high explosive and APDS rounds. When combined with a rate of fire of 4,200 rounds per minute this produces a weapon which fully merits its name of 'Equalizer'! The standard cannon in Soviet aircraft is the single-barrel GSh-23, a 23mm weapon, but a newer multi-barrel weapon, believed to be 30mm calibre is being introduced. Both would be devastating against soft targets such as trucks and APC/ IFVs, but would not be totally effective against MBTs.

Aircraft-launched guided-missiles are used for a variety of roles in attacking ground targets. One of the most important roles is that of attacking hostile radars. The US Shrike anti-radar missile is still in use by the USAF on Wild Weasel aircraft and by Israel; it was also used by the British in the Falklands War. Its successor, now entering service, is the High-speed Anti-Radar Missile (HARM), which has three operating modes. The first is *self-protect*, in which the carrying aircraft's radar warning receiver is used to detect threatening radar transmissions; the launch-control computer analyses and prioritizes the emissions and tells the pilot when to launch. Second is the *target of opportunity* mode, in which the missile seeker head detects certain predetermined radar parameters and homes onto them. The third, *pre-briefed*, involves launching HARM into an area known to contain radars and if one of these should emit HARM, it will immediately attack it.

Below: Panavia Tornado of the West German Navy *(Bundesmarine)* armed with HARM missiles.

Missions

Attacking aircraft will have to fly low and fast when in enemy airspace, especially if they are overflying the land battle area, which will be covered with sensors and with layered defensive weapons systems. There will also, of course, be defensive aircraft, waiting to deal with hostile targets.

Among the major consequences are that most flights over hostile territory will be made at very low level, i.e. below 76.2m (250 ft) and relatively high speed, 724–966km/h (450–600 mph), and that, to avoid detection, aircraft will seek to use only passive sensors. However, in order to fly so low and so fast, human control will not be adequate, nor will passive sensors suffice for the very precise and rapid requirements to avoid obstacles, and thus active terrain-following radar (TFR) will be essential.

Ideally, one aircraft would contain all the necessary weapons and sensors for an operation, but this is very unlikely to be feasible. Thus, aircraft will operate in at the very least pairs, but far more likely is a multi-aircraft operation; some major attacks might involve up to 60–70 aircraft in one way or another. Preliminary analy-

Above: To reach their targets in any future war, strike/attack aircraft such as the Tornado would have to fly very fast and very low.

sis of the proposed routes to the target would give a (hopefully) accurate indication of the enemy's sensors and weapons within attacking range of the proposed route. A plan would then be made to take out these sensors and defences in a progressive manner during the course of the operation; in effect, the raiders fighting their way through. This is known as 'suppression of enemy air defences' (SEAD).

Thus, taking the USAF as an example, to fight a small attacking force through to their targets deep in enemy territory could involve:

– Preliminary reconnaissance of sensors, using specialized EW aircraft, such as the USAF's Lockheed TR-1, and other EW intelligence (for example, by ground-based direction-finding (DF) techniques).

–Preliminary reconnaissance of aircraft and ground-based air defence weapons systems, using low-flying 'recce' and satellite photography.

– One or more AWACS aircraft flying at considerable height, but standing well back from the FLOT, controlling the operation and giving advance warning of enemy aircraft movements.

– Three or more stand-off jammers, operating against enemy ground-defence radars, and against the airborne-intercept (AI) radars on airborne interceptors. On the NATO side these would be USAF EF-111A Raven or Luftwaffe Panavia Tornados with special anti-radar fits.

– A special operation against enemy SUAWACS to either destroy it (or them), or at least to reduce or negate its capability during the actual attack mission.

– A stand-off jammer aircraft operating against enemy air defence command and control systems. The USAF EC-130H 'Compass Call' version of the Hercules transport aircraft is specially fitted for this role, and the Soviet Antonov AN-12 'Cub-C' is thought to have a similar role.

– Airborne tankers to refuel the main attack force before entering hostile airspace.

– Attack aircraft grouped according to their targets. One or more of these groups

might be accompanied by EF-111A Ravens or McDonnell Douglas F-48 Advanced Wild Weasel aircraft, which are specially equipped for the radar suppression mission.

– Fighters to deal with enemy fighters.

The grand total of aircraft involved in such an operation could come to as many as 50 aircraft, and would be a major operation of war. Nevertheless, this is the price which modern ground defence sensors and weapons, together with air defence fighters compel an attack force to pay.

Below: The USAF EF-111A Raven is a sophisticated modern aircraft whose electronic warfare capabilities were used to full effect in the US raid on Libya.

Tactical Nuclear Operations

One of the major results of the Intermediate-Range Nuclear Forces (INF) Treaty has been to increase the importance of air forces in delivering nuclear weapons. This is because the treaty has done away with nuclear-capable missiles such as SS-20 and Pershing, and it appears that shorter range missiles may be discontinued as well. In such a case the air forces would be the only delivery means left.

Implications for the Ground Battle

The effect of air power on the ground battle is enormous. The hostile air threat is an element of the equation which every ground commander must take into account at all times, except in the unlikely event that one side achieves complete domination in the air battle. This has only happened in the past in the case of the Western Allies in the final stages of the Second World War, where the German air effort was entirely defeated. It seems unlikely that such a situation could happen again.

Thus, ground commanders must en-

sure that their forces do not concentrate sufficiently to offer attractive targets to the enemy's air forces, and that at all times cover is taken from air observation/ attack. This means using camouflage and deceptive methods against visual, optical, thermal and infra-red observation. It also means that large-scale movement must be confined to the hours of darkness, and even then it may not achieve as effective concealment from enemy observation as was the case in the past, since modern methods, such as radar and thermal-imaging, can 'see' just as effectively at night as they can in daylight.

The air threat also means that large resources must be devoted to air defences, and in most armies today this means a great deal of manpower and equipment. It also requires a large and sophisticated command-and-control organization for the air defences, to ensure that they are properly positioned, that they are ready to meet the anticipated threats and that they are supplied with missiles and ammunition. So demanding is this requirement that some armies are today developing communications

Above: The Lockheed TR-1 is a high altitude reconnaissance and research aircraft equipped with the most up-to-date electronic warfare equipment. It has an operational ceiling of 27,430m (90,000 ft) and a maximum range of 4,830km (3,000 miles).

systems solely for the air defence use.

The other side of the coin is that a side's own air forces can be used to strike at the enemy and to observe his movement. This, too, requires close coordination, especially as most air forces, particularly in the Western nations, have a separate command chain from the army, which necessitates special joint operations centres and the deployment of air liaison officers, usually down to brigade level.

Most land force commanders, when asked what the top priority for the air force should be, will say that it is to keep the enemy air forces from interfering with their ground operations. Whether in modern conditions this is possible is difficult to say.

INTELLIGENCE AND SURVEILLANCE

No effective military operations can take place without proper intelligence. First, it is essential that the commander knows everything it is possible to know about the enemy – his strength, locations, dispositions, tactics, doctrine, equipment, and present and possible future intentions. Secondly, the commander must have a thorough knowledge of the terrain over which he is fighting, in order to identify avenues of approach open to his own and the enemy forces, to know where fighting and movement is possible and where it is not, and to be aware of what natural obstacles there are and their possible effects on friendly and enemy operations. Thirdly, the commander must know the current and future weather over his area of the battlefield and what effect it is having or will have on possible operations. Finally, the commander must know the current and future dispositions of his own and other friendly forces in the area of his concern, which is not as simple a task as it sounds in today's fast-moving battle.

All this might appear to be a blinding glimpse of the obvious. But, as will be shown, the provision of up-to-date and accurate intelligence is one of the most complicated, time-consuming and difficult tasks on the modern battlefield.

Establishing Intentions

The intelligence function starts in peacetime, as national intelligence staffs seek to identify possible hostile threats to their country or to an alliance of which it is a member. They then seek to build up a picture of the armed forces involved, their composition, dispositions, strengths, weaknesses and their possible capabilities. There is, however, a significant difference between such capabilities and the actual intention to use them, a problem that is exacerbated by the fact that while capabilities are long-term, intentions can change almost overnight.

Thus, for example, throughout the 1970s and into the early 1980s the Argentine armed forces had a *capability* to invade the Falkland Islands, a fact that was tacitly acknowledged by the British who stationed a small military force on the islands. However, the British clearly judged the actual Argentine *intention* to invade as very remote, as witnessed by the fact that the force actually stationed there was some 40 Royal Marine Commandos, a tiny force compared to the size of the islands and the capability of the Argentine armed forces. However, at some time in late 1981 or early 1982 the Argentine intention changed – a fact that seems not to have been appreciated in the United Kingdom until it was too late to take preventive action.

It should be added that there was an equally serious failure in Argentina, where the intelligence staffs appear to have completely underestimated (perhaps even ignored) the possibility that the British not only had the capability to retake the Falklands, but would actually undertake to do so.

Even countries facing well-established threats from neighbours and who possess a demonstrable capability to attack can be taken by surprise, due to an intelligence failure to see the change in intentions. For example, the Israelis have been

Below: An Israeli Centurion in a ruined Lebanese town. The Middle East is an intelligence jungle: capabilities and inventories are known down to the last item; the problem is judging intentions.

under almost continuous threat from their Arab neighbours since the state was founded in 1949. They fought several wars in defence of their existence and even outside the periods of overt conflict found themselves under regular attack. In their very successful 1967 war they gained considerable territory, taking the tactically vital Golan Heights in the North, while, in the South, they captured and held the eastern bank of the Suez Canal. It was obvious that an Arab attempt to retake both at some future date was inevitable. However, in the early 1970s, despite very noticeable rearmament in all the countries concerned, the Israelis were clearly unconvinced of any actual intention on the part of the Arabs to go to war again, at least so soon after their defeats in 1967.

By 1973 there were distinct signs of an Arab build-up, the great majority of which were seen and reported by the very efficient Israeli intelligence services. In late September the annual Egyptian mobilization exercise took place, with a scheduled end-date of 8 October. The Israelis had been expecting the exercise and appear to have taken only the most routine of precautions, indicating that no attack was seriously expected, especially as it was the month of Ramadan, the Muslim fasting period. Even when the families of Soviet civil and military advisers in Arab countries were observed to be leaving the area and Soviet ships were starting to leave Egyptian and Syrian ports in some numbers, the significance seems either to have passed unnoticed or to have been misinterpreted.

By 3 October junior Israeli intelligence officers were predicting war, only to be told that they were being 'alarmist'. By 5 October, the Israeli Southern Command had become so concerned by the concentration of forces on the western bank of the Suez Canal, still under the guise of the 'exercise', that they requested authority to implement the prepared reinforcement plans. The response was to be told that this would be 'provocative'. Then, in the early hours of 6 October the Israelis received a copy (albeit a somewhat dated one) of the Egyptian operation order, which gave details of the plan, including timings, with H-hour (the time of the

crossing of the Suez Canal) being given as 18.00 hours that night. The Israeli cabinet ordered partial mobilization at 10.00 hours, but when the Egyptians crossed the canal at 14.05 hours precisely (H-hour had been brought forward some weeks previously) the Israelis were far less prepared for war than they could have been if they had read the signs earlier.

It is worth mentioning that not only was there a failure at the strategic level, but there was also a further intelligence failure at the tactical level concerning the method of crossing the canal. The Israelis had built a massive wall of sand on the bank of the canal in order to prevent the early movement of vehicles, particularly tanks, during any possible Egyptian attack. The wall was some 12m (40 ft) high and with a very wide base and was a very formidable obstacle, and it clearly gave the Israelis a feeling of confidence. However, the answer to such apparently intractable tactical problems is frequently not only brilliantly simple but also is only revealed to very junior officers and so it proved in this case. A junior Egyptian engineer officer (regrettably his name is not known) saw that all that was required

were some powerful water monitors, as used, for example, in open-cast mines, and there was certainly no shortage of water. So, having established a foothold on the far bank, the Egyptians simply washed away a breach in the wall, a possibility not apparently foreseen by the defenders.

Peacetime Intelligence Gathering

All nations' defence ministries seek to gather as much information as they can during times of peace about possible hostile powers. The main problem is not that the information is difficult to obtain; indeed, the major problem is more one of trying to process the enormous volume that is available. The 'open' press is read avidly by all intelligence staffs since it is full of potentially useful military information. The open press, however, goes far beyond newspapers, popular magazines, television and the radio. There is available today a vast range of professional journals in most countries, both military and civil, which describe military equipment and discuss strategic and tactical matters.

To the surprise of many people in the

Right: The SR-71 is an invaluable element in the Western intelligence-gathering organization. Cruising at the outer limits of the atmosphere it is equipped with numerous electronic, photographic and infra-red sensors.

West the range of such journals in Eastern Europe is also very extensive, although not as great as in the West, and has been so since well before the advent of *glasnost* and *perestroika*. However, the journals there tend to be more about doctrinal than equipment matters. In fact, Soviet Army journals have always been particularly open on tactical matters and in the early 1970s Westerners followed with fascination a discussion in the correspondence columns of one such journal on the role and use of the BMP IFV. The correspondence involved captains, colonels and generals, and the Western readers learned a considerable amount from it. Technical matters are treated more circumspectly, although even the efficient Soviet security machine has its lapses. One occurred, for example, when a university professor produced a very dry, technical text-book on radar propagation techniques, which included details of antenna technology unheard of in the West and which applied to the very

latest equipment then just being fielded in the Soviet Army.

Also in peacetime, there is very considerable activity in monitoring radio and other communications, and the Soviet Union is particularly active in this sphere. They launch intelligence-gathering satellites regularly, and also have a large fleet of ships involved in monitoring Western activities. These ships may appear at first sight to be primarily involved in naval matters – for example, watching the launch of the latest US Navy submarine-launched missile – but they are, in fact, equally involved in monitoring land-based activities.

Finally, there is the covert gathering of information, at which, again, the Soviets are especially adept. From time to time evidence of such activities becomes public knowledge, as, for example, when a spy is arrested and tried, or when a KGB-planted electronic device is discovered in a Moscow embassy. Such incidents,

Above: For some 40 years the Soviets have deployed many hundreds of intelligence gathering ships (AGAIs) at critical points around the world. Many, such as that shown here, are converted trawlers, but some are large, purpose-built ships.

however, only represent the 'tip of the iceberg' in a never-ending process.

Tactical Intelligence

On the land battlefield intelligence staffs are concerned with tactical, rather than strategic, matters. The first requirement in any battlefield intelligence process is to evaluate the threat to the unit or formation involved. This involves conducting a detailed study of the enemy forces, their organization, composition, weapons and equipment, and their tactical doctrine. The aim of this process is to identify enemy capabilities and to determine their

normal methods of operation. This last point is especially important. For example, the Soviet tactical doctrine is somewhat different from that in the West, since, as is described in more detail elsewhere in this book, the Soviets employ 'tactical echelons', and it thus becomes particularly important to NATO intelligence staffs to identify the Soviet 'second echelon' in an attack.

A knowledge of enemy doctrine, both tactical and organizational, is essential but must not, however, be allowed to assume that the enemy will become stereotyped. For example, if a NATO divisional intelligence staff were to become aware that they are faced by a Soviet motor rifle division, it would be folly to assume that the division must necessarily be organized and equipped exactly according to the manual. All organizations can be altered in detail; thus, a motor rifle division could have more or fewer tank battalions than in the standard table, because the army commander has redistributed his assets to meet the tactical situation. Similarly, the equipment may not match the perceived

'norm' and the division might be equipped with T-72 tanks instead of the expected T-80, or may be the first to receive some previously unknown item of equipment, a totally new mortar, say.

Next comes the evaluation of what are known to operations and intelligence staffs as 'areas of influence' and 'areas of interest'. An area of influence is the tactical area in which the commander requires to be able to acquire and attack targets. The extent of this area depends upon the unit concerned, its means of

Above: The Soviet T-72 Main Battle Tank is seen here fitted with fabric skirts and smoke mortars on either side of the turret front.

surveillance and target acquisition, and upon the tactical situation. Typically, such areas of influence might be as shown in Table 1.

TABLE 1: Tactical Group	Distance Beyond Forward Line of own Troops (FLOT)	Information Lead Time	Maximum Processing Time
Task Force/Battle Group	5km (3 miles)	0–3 hours	Less than 10 minutes
Brigade	15km (9 miles)	3–12 hours	Less than 30 minutes
Division	70km (43 miles)	12–24 hours	Less than 60 minutes
Corps	150km (93 miles)	24–72 hours	Less than 2 hours

The significance of these figures is that they tell commanders what distance into hostile territory they need to be able to keep under surveillance and (in the right-hand column) how long they can permit for such information to be processed into intelligence. Thus, a task force needs to be able to acquire targets out to ranges of 5km (3 miles) with its own surveillance devices and weapons, processing the information in less than ten minutes and then engaging them with its own organic weapons. It is also directly interested and affected by what the enemy is going to do in the next three hours. A corps headquarters, however, is interested in a much deeper area, takes a longer-term view, can allow slightly longer for the information to be processed, and plans the battle one to three days ahead.

The area of interest is that which is occupied by enemy forces which are capable of affecting commanders' future operations. This is inevitably larger than the area of influence and typically might be as shown in Table 2.

From these figures it can be deduced that at divisional level, for example, surveillance systems are required which can carry out reconnaissance up to 150km (93 miles) into enemy territory and produce information which can be processed and in the hands of the staff within two hours. How is this to be done?

Surveillance

The oldest and still highly effective methods of short-range combat surveillance are the eyes and ears of the forward troops. With suitable training a large amount of information can be picked up and even the seemingly old-fashioned reconnaissance patrols have a vital place in the intelligence-gathering plan. For example, dead ground within a mile or so of the FLOT can only be examined by an aerial platform or a man.

However, there are now a large number of surveillance systems available to forward units. For example, lightweight, infantry radars can detect moving men or vehicles. The US Army's AN/PPS-15B weighs 15kg (33 lb) and can be mounted on a vehicle, held in the hand or mounted on a tripod. It has a detection range of some 3,000m (9,862 ft) and can be used to cover a 350m (1,148 ft) segment, subdivided into seven 50m (164 ft) gates. Sector scan is also variable between 22° and 180°. The range and bearing of moving targets are displayed on a solid-state LED display, and both audio and visual alarms are fitted. Such a device is ideal for guarding the edge of a defended area and for giving early-warning of the approach of men, vehicles, or, on a river or lake, boats.

An equipment evolved during the Vietnam War was the remote sensor and the latest such device – the Remotely Monitored Battlefield Sensor System (REMBASS) – is now in service with the US Army. This uses sensors which respond to seismic disturbance, heat, acoustic, infra-red, or magnetic field changes as men or vehicles pass by. The remote sensors are positioned on likely approaches (tracks, track junctions, bridges, and the like) by hand, artillery shell or aircraft. The information is sent back by FM radio, which is only switched on when there is a signal to transmit and repeaters are available to extend the range.

TABLE 2: Tactical Group	Distance Beyond Forward Line of own Troops (FLOT)	Information Lead Time	Maximum Processing Time
Task Force/Battle Group	15km (9 miles)	0–12 hours	30 minutes
Brigade	70km (43 miles)	12–24 hours	60 minutes
Division	150km (93 miles)	24–72 hours	2 hours
Corps	300km (186 miles)	72–96 hours	4 hours

Left: On the battlefield, electronics now help the human senses in the intelligence battle; this is the Remotely Monitored Battlefield Sensor System (REMBASS).

Above: Two very well camouflaged infantrymen using night observation devices; one free-standing, the other combined with the rifle sighting system.

Also available to the infantry are electro-optical devices for observation in poor visibility or at night. Early equipments used infra-red, but this is an active technique and easily detectable by the enemy. These were succeeded by image-intensifiers, which use electronic processes to enhance the observed images, but these are tending to be replaced by thermal imagers, which are more robust and give rather better discrimination. Thermal imaging is used in hand-held observation devices suitable for an infantry patrol, in heavier, tripod-mounted equipment for artillery observers, and as an integral part of a weapon sight to give it a night-firing capability. Ranges for

such devices cannot be given since they depend upon the differences in temperature between a target and its surroundings, which is clearly a very variable factor.

An important requirement on the modern battlefield is to locate enemy weapons and here, too, radars are frequently used. The British Claribel mortar locating radar, which is typical of a number of different models in service with various armies, detects a mortar bomb in flight, plots two points on its trajectory and then, having measured the slant range and bearing of these two positions, feeds them into its computer which backtracks to the mortar baseplate position. All this is done within 30 seconds and thus the firing mortar's actual position can frequently be known before the bomb has reached its target.

Locating artillery gun and rocket positions is a little more difficult. Sound-ranging, a technique developed during the First World War, is still used in some

armies. This depends upon a series of highly-directional microphones being positioned in a long and virtually straight line, and connected to a central control point by cable or radio. A particular gun is detected by its firing sound by a number of the microphones and the difference between the time that sound takes to reach each of them is recorded. It is then a matter of geometry to work out the position of the gun, which can then be engaged with counter-battery fire.

Radars are, however, quicker, simpler and require less manpower to do the same job. The US AN/TPQ-37 can locate enemy guns and rocket launchers at their normal ranges and is being fielded on a

Right: US 'Firefinder' radar can spot incoming enemy shells, mortar bombs or missiles and backplot their trajectories to determine the position of the weapon.

Above: The Fuchs Armoured Personnel Carrier equipped with Battlefield Surveillance Radar.

Left: British Cymbeline mortar-locating radar can pinpoint a mortar's position before the bomb has hit the ground.

scale of two per division. This equipment uses a combination of radar tracking and computer-driven signal processing to detect, verify and track projectiles, and then compute their start point. It can track several projectiles at the same time and can be programmed to ignore projectiles originating from a gun or rocket position already identified.

Radars are also being used for more general ground surveillance and the Israeli EL/M-2121 can be used for surveillance of moving targets deep into hostile territory. This equipment, mounted in a transportable shelter is claimed to be able to detect large vehicles out to a range of 120km (75 miles), small vehicles out to 40km (25 miles) and a walking man or woman at ranges of up to 20km (12 miles). Such ranges can, of course, only be obtained if the radar is well sited and there is a line-of-sight between the antenna and the target.

There are a large number of radars on the battlefield fulfilling tasks such as air surveillance, air control, weapon target acquisition, and weapon tracking and guidance, as well as the ground tasks described above. All such radars are, by definition, active emitters and thus can be identified and located with great precision by hostile forces, and then attacked either by artillery or by anti-radar missiles which home in on the radar transmissions. Counter-measures can be taken, such as transmitting in short bursts, frequency hopping, frequent physical moves and so on, but it should not be thought that radar is an impregnable system.

Visual and photographic tactical reconnaissance deep into enemy territory was traditionally the task of fast, low-flying aircraft. This is still done, but the cost of such missions in the face of modern air defences is potentially very high. As a result, attention has moved to alternatives, one of the more widely-used being remotely-piloted vehicles (RPVs), which are controlled from a distant command post using radio links between the two, or by drones which follow a flight profile programmed into the vehicle before take-off. Both types of vehicle can be equipped to record information and take it

back to base, or can be fitted with communications to enable the information to be transmitted to a ground station in real time.

One of the most successful drones is the Canadair AN/USD-501, which is in service with the British, French, Italian and West German armies. It is a small airframe fitted with small cruciform wings and canards, and is launched from a medium truck, using a rocket booster. It flies at an altitude of between 300 and 1,200m (980–3,900 ft) at a speed of 740km/h (400 knots) and as it is only 260cm (8.5 ft) long and 33cm (13 in) in diameter it is extremely difficult to see let alone engage. Prior to take-off, the flight profile is programmed into the control system (height, track, turns, etc.) and one of two sensor packs fitted; one

contains a Zeiss camera, the other an infra-red line-scan. The drone returns to a beacon at the launch site, where the motor stops and it descends under a parachute.

At the next level come manned aircraft, standing back from the FLOT and observing the enemy using sideways-looking infra-red, sideways-looking airborne radar and electronic devices. These are described in the previous section (see page 94).

Other Sources Of Information

There are, of course, many other sources of information. Prisoners-of-War are particularly valuable, both for short-term, 'hot' information obtained rapidly by questioning in the forward areas, and for long-term information resulting from

slower, in-depth questioning further to the rear.

A major source of information is the electronic warfare (EW) organization, which monitors enemy communications (i.e. radio, microwave, etc.) and non-communications (i.e. radar) transmissions. These can be used for direction-finding (DF) to locate the transmitters,

Above: Heron-26/Mizar unmanned air vehicle (UAV). UAVs are increasingly used for battlefield reconnaissance.

Right: Boeing E-3A Sentry of the NATO Early-Warning Force based in West Germany.

Right: Ever greater resources are being devoted to electronic warfare equipment, such as this US Army AN/MSQ-103A.

Below: Satellites are also essential to intelligence gathering efforts. Images from this French SPOT were used to monitor the long-running Iran–Iraq war.

Above: Armies have detected a gap in their intelligence-gathering capability, which must be filled by a fixed-wing aircraft such as this Defender/Castor.

or to listen in and analyse the traffic, or to give jammers target frequencies, although the latter precludes obtaining any further information. As a guideline, ground-based intercept stations working against ground-based targets should be able to intercept at ranges up to very approximately those shown in Table 3.

TABLE 3:	
Ground radars	25km (15 miles)
VHF radio	40km (25 miles)
HF ground wave	80km (50 miles)
HF skywave	Unlimited

Other information will come from the rear, normally in the form of processed intelligence. This will have been obtained by aircraft reconnaissance, electronic warfare, satellite reconnaissance, and, perhaps, covert means.

Thus, in front of every unit on either side there is a network of information gathering systems spreading far and wide into enemy territory. By use of these systems commanders hope to find out more about the enemy – and more quickly – than the enemy does about him. However, all these sensor systems and the information they produce are of little value unless it can all be put to effective and timely use.

Processing Intelligence

Sensors and reconnaissance produce raw information, which has to be verified, collated and analysed before it becomes intelligence. One of today's major problems on the battlefield is that there are so many means of obtaining information, and it is disseminated so widely and rapidly that intelligence staffs are being simply overwhelmed by its sheer volume.

Computer systems are being gradually introduced to cope with this problem, although the process is taking longer than originally anticipated due to the unfore-

seen difficulties in integrating the systems and in writing the software. The US Army, for example, is in the process of developing the All Source Analysis System (ASAS). This is a computer-driven battlefield intelligence support system which receives, stores and fuses information in real-time and, since each station is connected to the Army Tactical Command and Control System (ATCCS), passes it on to all other stations on the system. Further, connections to the similar Air Force system ensures that not only do they all update each other as the battle progresses, but also all commanders, whether army or air force, are looking at the same picture of the battlefield.

Such systems are not, however, intended to automate the entire process and to drive the human intellect from the loop. Far from this being the case, commanders will, in fact, have greater management over the information-gathering process and will be able to make much better use of sensors and other agencies as they will be able to identify and prioritize requirements at a much earlier stage.

ENGINEERS

On today's battlefields the engineers would be one of the busiest of the combat arms, since their tasks are numerous and their resources always insufficient. Engineers' basic missions are to facilitate the movement of their own troops about the battlefield and to hamper the movements of the enemy. This includes such tasks as building bridges for their own troops to cross, destroying bridges so that the enemy cannot use them, laying minefields to impede the enemy's movements, and clearing enemy minefields to enable their own troops to move. It also means making and improving roads, clearing obstacles and digging major defence-works, and, on the other hand, creating obstacles to delay the enemy and destroying his defence works. Engineers also create and lay explosive charges and booby traps, and conversely, clear them. In many armies engineers also pick up a number of miscellaneous, but nevertheless vitally important tasks, such as camouflage and water supply.

Every army has a corps of engineers, which is organized into companies and battalions, and distributed throughout the tactical formations to provide direct support to the combat troops. There are also usually engineer units in the rear echelons for major undertakings and for providing greater engineer support to tactical formations when required for a specific operation.

Mine Warfare

Mine warfare seemed to be overlooked for some years in the 1950s and 1960s with little development taking place, and a continuing reliance being placed on Second World War stock and techniques. There was then a resurgence of interest, however, possibly due to the success of mines and booby-traps used by the North Vietnamese Army and the Viet Cong during the Vietnam War.

Above right: A vital engineer's task is the destruction of bridges, efficiently carried out in this case by Pakistani sappers in the war against India in 1971.

Right: British Royal Engineer examines an Argentine anti-tank mine laid in the peaty soil of the Falkland Islands.

Mines can be used in both offence and defence. In offence they can be used when temporarily assuming the defensive (e.g. to defeat a counter-attack) and for flank protection. In the defence, minefields are used to create obstacles, either to stop the enemy altogether or to canalize his advance into channels selected by the defence. In both cases it is essential that the minefields are covered by fire, otherwise they will be breached by engineer mine-clearing teams. Minefields have become particularly important to NATO armies in Central Europe, where one of the methods of dealing with the threat of a sudden, multi-pronged, Soviet armoured advance is rapidly laid minefields covering the major areas of advance.

Many countries manufacture mines and a typical anti-personnel mine is the Austrian ARGES Bounding Mine, Model SpM75. This is quite a large cylindrical device, weighing 6kg (13 lb), mounted on a base-plate and fitted with three tripwires, which are stretched radially from the mine. A man knocking one of the tripwires causes a firing-pin to release a tensioned spring which throws the mine straight up into the air. A thin wire, some 1.5m (4.9 ft) long connects both base-

plate and the mine, and when this is stretched taut it pulls out a firing-pin which detonates the charge, which fires 4,600 spherical fragments outwards at high velocity at about the height of an average man's chest. Like many anti-personnel mines, the SpM75 is designed to maim and not to kill, on the grounds that a wounded man is more of a liability than a dead one to the opposing army.

As part of the overall anti-tank battle much attention is being devoted to the development of anti-tank mines. Rapid laying is described later, but the actual mines themselves are of considerable interest. The USA produces a great range of mines, among them the M19 plastic anti-tank mine. This device is 332mm (13 in) square by 94mm (3.7 in) deep; it weighs 12.6kg (27.7 lb) of which the explosive accounts for 9.53kg (21 lb). It is activated by a pressure fuse mounted under the top pressure plate; i.e. a tank has to drive right over it to set it off. The entire device is constructed of plastic and it has two anti-lift fuses. It is also waterproof to enable it to be used on river beds.

Traditionally mines, both anti-tank and anti-personnel, were dug in by engineers, a time-consuming and labour

Above: British bar-mine laying plough towed by an FV432 APC. Mine laying is always a battle against time and automated methods have had to be adopted.

intensive task. Modern warfare allows insufficient time for this and engineers have turned to mechanical devices to speed up the process and to improve the productivity of the minelaying sappers. Mines are no longer buried as deep as before, and are either laid in shallow trenches or simply scattered on the surface.

The US Army uses a system known as the Ground-Emplaced Mine-Scattering System (GEMSS), in which the mines are laid by a large trailer, which can be towed by any suitable prime-mover, such as an M113 APC or a 5-ton truck. The trailer-mounted mine dispenser holds up to 800 mines, each weighing 1.8kg (4 lb) and laid at intervals of 30 or 60m (98 or 196 ft), the interval being determined by the rate that mines are fed into the launch chute and the speed of the laying vehicle. By this means a 2,500m (8,202 ft) surface minefield can be laid in less than six hours, its purpose being to canalize enemy armoured forces into constricted areas where they will form rewarding targets for defensive anti-tank forces. The mines have a magnetic-influence triggering device and do not need to be actually run over by the tracks of a tank.

Soviet minelaying techniques are similar in principle, using both tracked and trailer-mounted minelayers. Typically, on suitable ground three tracked mine-layers moving parallel to each other some 20–30m (65–98 ft) apart and dispensing anti-tank mines at intervals of about 5m (16 ft) can lay 1,000m (3,280 ft) in 30 minutes. Three PMR-3 minelaying trailers lay about 500m (1,640 ft) in the same time. The PMR-3 is towed by modified BTR-152 trucks, each carrying 120 anti-tank mines in racks; as one truck is emptied it disconnects and moves off to collect more mines while a loaded vehicle connects to the plough and carries on. Both the tracked minelayer and PMR-3 minelaying trailer have plough blades which open up a continuous furrow into which the mines are laid and a trailing back-fill plate which pulls the soil back over the mines.

Soviet anti-personnel mines can be laid by various means, one being from chutes fitted to any convenient truck, which trail along the ground. Mines are placed on the chutes at set intervals and they slide down to the ground where they are armed and camouflaged by men following on foot. One squad/section can lay 200 mines in 20 minutes.

It should be noted that while mine-laying, using the techniques just described, is a traditional engineer operation, a recent development is the laying of mine-fields using artillery or aircraft. These are very small mines (usually called 'mine-lets'), which can only lie on the surface, but their great advantage is that they can be used to lay remote minefields at short notice. Obviously, it is a headquarters task to coordinate such mine-laying activities between engineers and artillery.

One of this new generation is the US Army's Area Denial Artillery Munition (ADAM), which is a mine device fired from 155m M109-series howitzers, with a maximum range of 17.7km (11 miles). There are two types of projectile, both carrying 36 M74 minelets, the only difference being that those in the M692 have a self-destruct time greater than one day, while those in the M731 have a life of less than a day, both being pre-set at the time of manufacture. The projectile contains a fuse which functions at a predetermined time during flight, following which the wedge-shaped M74s are projected from the rear of the shell, the spin of the shell imparting a lateral dispersion, while its

forward flight gives linear dispersion. The M74s, having landed, deploy seven trip-wires and arm themselves. When detonated a fragmentation unit containing 21.25g (0.9 oz) of explosive is propelled upwards and explodes at a height of about 1.5m (5 ft).

The converse task is mine-clearing. This is a task to which the Soviet Army has paid considerable attention, since its tactics (at least until very recently) have

Above: **The British mine plough, here attached to an AVRE, is designed to push mines to one side and thus maintain the momentum in an armoured attack.**

been based on rapid advances and thus defensive minefields must be brushed aside quickly. First measures are the KMT-4 mine plough (usually fitted to one-third of the tanks in the leading echelons) or the KMT-5 mine-roller/plough combination. These armour- or infantry-operated equipments clear lanes one vehicle wide, but engineers then widen the lanes, normally with the use of explosives. One relatively recent device is an explosive hose, which is projected across the minefield and then detonated, creating a lane some 6–8m (20–26 ft) wide and 180m (590 ft) long.

Traditionally, the Soviet Army also places great reliance on manual mine-clearing. The IMP transistorized mine detector weighs some 7kg (15.4 lb), and can detect metallic mines at a depth of 45cm (18 in), although few modern mines contain any metallic components. Clearance is then by men using prodders, who carefully clear the earth from around the mine and then, having disarmed any anti-lift devices, clear it away. However, the

Above: US Marine trainees learn how to search for mines using their bayonets, a method still necessary although it is slow and can be very hazardous!

great difficulties the British Army experienced in clearing Argentine minefields in the Falklands Islands following the 1982 war has shown that such modern mines are exceptionally difficult to clear. (In fact, in the Falklands the cost in lost limbs became so great that many minefields in uninhabited areas have been simply marked and abandoned.)

Bridging

Any withdrawing force always seeks to make its enemy's advance as difficult as possible. One of the means of achieving this is to destroy bridges, especially those over natural obstacles, particularly rivers. It therefore is necessary for the advancing force to have means of crossing such obstacles.

One of the first means is to make as many vehicles as possible amphibious and this the Soviets, in particular, have done on a fairly large scale. Secondly, tracked vehicles can be waterproofed and given snorkel tubes to enable them to ford rivers. However, neither of these is as good an answer as it first appears, since amphibious vehicles' waterproofing must

Left: Mine hunting with hand-held detectors. Modern mines contain few metal components and are difficult to detect.

be checked very carefully before committing them to a crossing, while fording requires very careful reconnaissance and choice of crossings, and is especially unpopular with crews. Thus, although swimming or fording may be necessary for the very first elements, in all other respects bridging is a more reliable and efficient answer.

All major armies use single-span and multi-span bridges, pontoon bridges and ferries. Most rapid to lay of all assault bridges are the armoured bridgelayers – usually known by the US Army abbreviated designation of AVLB (armoured vehicle-launched bridge). The majority of these consist of a scissors bridge mounted folded and lying horizontally on top of modified MBT chassis. The bridge is launched by raising it, still folded, to the vertical, upon which the forward leg starts to open, and as the rear leg is lowered the forward leg straightens until the bridge is laid flat over the gap. The laying vehicle then disengages and moves away to allow traffic to start crossing the bridge, which can, of course, be recovered later and reused.

Thus, the Soviet AVLB is the MT-55, which consists of a scissors bridge capable of spanning a gap 16m (52.5 ft) wide and taking a 50,800kg (50 ton) load. It is mounted on an T-55 chassis and takes 2–3 minutes to lay. The US Army's current standard AVLB is based on the M60 tank chassis and can take a variety of bridges. Largest of these is 28.3m (92.83 ft) long and can span a 27m (88 ft) gap, taking a 60 ton load. It takes three minutes to lay.

The West German Army considers scissors bridges to suffer from a tactical disadvantage, in that when they reach the vertical during laying they are so high that they are very easy to observe from a

Above: Bridge-laying tanks are essential to maintain the momentum of an advance.

Right: West German M2 amphibious bridge and Biber armoured engineer vehicle.

distance. So they have developed a bridge, based on the Leopard 1 MBT chassis, known as the Biber (Beaver), which launches its bridge horizontally to span gaps of up to 20m (65.6 ft).

Next come amphibious ferries, which are based on wheeled or tracked chassis. These drive into the river at the selected site and rotate a platform which is then married up with another similar vehicle to form the ferry. The Soviet GSP ferry, for example, is a tracked vehicle which can carry loads of up to 52,000kg (51.18 tons), which covers all known vehicles in the Warsaw Pact armies. The US Army uses the Mobile Assault Bridge/Ferry (MAB).

Further up the scale comes the floating bridge, in which the Soviet Army, once again, is the leading exponent. The PMP, for example, consists of a series of pontoons carried on 8-ton trucks, which also act as the launchers. BMK-130 bridging boats are then used to manoeuvre the pontoons into position. This bridge can take any Soviet MBT.

Other bridges are built from one bank of a gap to the other and numerous varieties exist. One of the most widely used is the British Medium-Girder Bridge (the successor to the Second World War Bailey Bridge), which can be assembled in a variety of ways to suit the width of the gap and the load to be carried. It can also be used with pontoons to build ferries.

Above: The British Army's combat engineer tractor (CET) is a very versatile, fully amphibious vehicle.

Engineer Vehicles

Engineers in every army use a whole variety of civil engineering plant, such as bulldozers, tractors, graders, dump trucks, and so on. Since these are designed for extremely tough construction jobs the only step in their 'militarization' is to give them a coat of green paint. However, there are some jobs, particularly in the forward areas where a specialized, usually armoured engineer vehicle is needed. Many of these are based upon a suitable MBT chassis. Thus, the Soviet IMR (Combat Engineer Vehicle) is a T-54 chassis, with the turret removed and a dozer blade and multi-purpose crane fitted. Similarly, the West German Armoured Engineer vehicle is based on the Leopard 1 chassis and is fitted with a dozer blade with special teeth for ripping up roadways and a large earth-auger.

The British, however, have developed a Combat Engineer Tractor (CET), a 17,272kg (17 ton) tracked vehicle, which is designed to undertake a number of tasks. At the rear of the vehicle is a large, light alloy bucket which can be used for digging or bull-dozing and can also be used as an earth anchor. There is also a powerful winch which can be used for

Above: NATO cooperation at work as a column of Canadian Army M113 APCs cross a floating bridge laid by West German engineer troops. There are many such wide rivers in central Europe.

pulling loads or even for self-recovery of the CET itself. A second earth anchor is mounted on the roof, but this is rocket-propelled with a range of 91.4m (300 ft) and is used to help the CET climb steep river banks. The CET is fully amphibious and has a crew of two.

The US Army looked at the CET, but did not buy it, developing the Counter-Obstacle Vehicle instead. The COV is based on the chassis of the M88 armoured recovery vehicle, but is fitted with an impressive array of engineer devices. At the front is a V-shaped, combined dozer-blade/full-width mine-plough. On each side of the hull are two telescopic arms, normally fitted with detachable digging buckets. However, these can be replaced by grapples, lifting hooks, augers or hammers. A rear-mounted towing hook can be used to tow a number of engineer trailers, while side-mounted hydraulic outlets can be used to power hand-held power tools.

Runway Repair

Air forces are increasingly targetting each other's airfields and, in particular, the runways. As a result rapid runway repair is an increasingly important task for engineers. This requires a great deal of conventional engineering equipment such as bulldozers, graders and rollers, but, in addition, special matting has been developed to lay over the top of repairs.

When an airfield has been hit the first task is to carry out reconnaissances to establish what damage has occurred and where. This information is transferred to a runway plan and a minimum operating strip plotted, normally a minimum of 1,500m (4,921 ft) long by 15m (49 ft) wide. The area round each crater is then cleared of debris and after preparation the crater is either filled with pre-stocked aggregate, or, if none is available, the debris is simply pushed back into the crater. Once the crater has been filled and compacted the damaged area is levelled and covered with a repair mat.

Various types of matting are in use. The USAF uses AM-2 matting, which consists of various sizes of aluminium planks which have ingenious interlocking devices to enable them to be connected to each other. The top surface of each plank has an anti-skid coating. The various sizes of plank are laid in a brick-pattern, which gives the eventual runway a high degree of lateral stability, but allows longitudinal flexibility. Matting of this type was used by the British to rehabilitate and extend the runway at Port Stanley following the Falklands War and it gave excellent service until the new purpose-built runway at Mount Pleasant was opened.

The British use a repair mat of portable roadway, which is stored ready for use and transported to the site on a special trolley towed by a medium tractor. It is then spread manually, anchored by expanding bolts and fairing panels fitted. A crater formed by a 350kg (770 lb) bomb requires a 22 × 16m (72 × 52 ft) mat.

COMMAND, CONTROL AND COMMUNICATIONS (C³)

The organization and structure of the forces involved in the land/air battle is now so complex, the amount of information to be handled so vast and the speed of reaction required so great that the demands made of the C³ system are increasing exponentially. Just to take one area as an example – information – the amount of data flowing around the system is extremely high. Sensors increase every year in both number and capability, and the raw data they produce is sent rearwards in ever-increasing volume, which in itself require communication systems which can not only handle more data, but also do so more expeditiously. At some point all this information data has to be sorted and analysed and turned into intelligence, which then has to be disseminated to all those who need to know it.

To try to meet this challenge the communications systems are in an almost constant process of expansion, while within headquarters automation continues apace. First and second generation automated data processing (ADP) systems are now in widespread use, but very exciting third generation systems are soon to be introduced, which will not only have larger capacities and greater operating speeds, but will also introduce such new concepts as expert systems and aids to military decision making.

Command and control are inseparable, but not identical. Command is the authority exercised by an individual, which has been given to him by his superiors to enable him to direct, control and coordinate the military forces placed at his disposal. Command inevitably involves the exercise of 'leadership', a quality which is difficult to define, but which involves encouraging others to do what is needed to fulfil the mission, sometimes in conditions of great, perhaps even mortal, danger. Different people exercise leadership in different ways as, for example, with some of the best known Second World War generals. Patton, Montgomery, Rommel and Zhukov were all very successful field commanders in their own way and yet utterly different as individuals, both in their personalities and in their national characteristics, and in the manner in which they led their troops.

Control, on the other hand, is the management of military force and the

Left: **A West German tank commander surveys the ground. Everything he sees will have to be communicated either to his crew or to his troop leader by radio.**

technicalities of its execution. This involves the carrying-out of a plan in line with the directions of the commander. Thus, at a divisional headquarters, for example, it is the divisional commander (a major-general) who exercises *command*, and it is the divisional staff that executes the *control*.

In modern warfare the forces involved are so large and the distances between headquarters so great that the exercise of both command and control cannot be achieved on a face-to-face basis, as it was in the days of Wellington, Napoleon and (more recently) of Stonewall Jackson. So, both commanders and controllers require

Right: Section briefing for soldiers of the British 1st Battalion, The Parachute Regiment. Britain's many small wars have bred highly skilled junior leaders.

Below: US Army platoon commander receiving orders by radio, his essential link to the higher echelons of command.

Above: Infantry battalion HQ; in war the vehicles would be inside the barns.

the inseparable third element of the triad: *communications*.

Headquarters

All commanders exercise command and control from a headquarters (HQ), whether it is the lieutenant and his two-man group in a platoon HQ or the four-star general and his many hundreds of staff officers and assistants in an army group HQ. Different nations organize their HQs in different ways, but within each nation the pattern is always the same. Thus, the US system, for example, splits the staff into: S1 – personnel, S2 – intelligence, S3 – operations, S4– logistics, communications and electronics, chemical, etc., and at high echelons, S5 – civil–military relations. At many field levels of HQ there are also officers who join the staff to advise on their specialization. Thus, at a brigade HQ, for example, there will be a fire support officer, usually the commander of the artillery battalion in support of the brigade and an engineer officer, usually the commander of the supporting engineer company. There will also be an air liaison officer, although he will be an air force officer permanently with the HQ rather than from a particular air force unit.

All field HQs are mobile, although their degree of mobility depends upon their size and the distance from the FLOT. To facilitate moves and to cut down the numbers in any one location, many armies split their HQs. One typical system splits the HQ into three. The first element is the *main* headquarters, which

Above: Temporary battalion HQ set up in a deserted building; British 15th Parachute Battalion on training in Wales.

Left: Special vehicles are used for HQs, such as this British Sultan with raised passenger compartment roof and extra radios.

is where the commander and the principal elements of his staff are located, and from which the battle is both commanded and controlled. The second element is the *rear* HQ, where the logistics (S4 and S5) staff are located and from which the formation (division, corps, etc.) is supplied and supported. The third element is the *step-up* or *alternate* HQ, which has communications and is lightly manned, and which takes over if the main HQ is destroyed or if a move takes place. Some commanders also use a *tactical* HQ, a very small group, but with good communications, which can deploy to a particular area for a specific operation in order to enable the commander to keep close touch in a critical phase of a battle.

Communications

Communications are now absolutely fundamental to military C^3, whether at the highest level or the lowest. Within a platoon, for example, in a mechanized infantry unit, there will be radio links:
- From the platoon HQ back to the company HQ.
- From the platoon HQ to the tank platoon with which the platoon is operating.
- From the platoon HQ to each squad/section.
- Between each dismounted group and its IFV/APC.
- From the mortar fire observer back to the mortar position.

In most cases these work on a common frequency on a radio 'net', where all the stations can talk to each other. Thus, when dismounted, the platoon could have its own net, with platoon HQ, each of the dismounted squads/sections and each of the empty IFV/APCs all on the same frequency. The set at platoon HQ talking to the company HQ would be on the company net, and the mortar observer on the mortar platoon net, and so on. It will, of course, be appreciated that there is a large number of radio nets in a mechanized battalion. However, the system is very flexible and the company commander, if he so wished, could have all the squads/sections on the company net for a particular operation or phase of an operation.

The problem of the overcrowding of the frequency band is a very real one. Within a brigade there is a very large number of nets. First, there are the three mechanized infantry battalions with all their nets, as just described. Then, to these must be added the nets within the tank battalion, the artillery battalion, the aviation unit, the engineer company and the logistics units supporting the brigade. Then, at divisional level there is a whole host of further nets at the HQ and within the divisional artillery, engineer and aviation units, and so on, plus the radio nets of army group-controlled units allocated to the division for a particular operation, such as nuclear artillery, heavy mortars, chemical units and engineers.

The problem is exacerbated by the fact

Above right: Field HQs are making increasing use of satellites for both strategic and tactical communications.

Right: Such a concentration of vehicles and VHF radio antennas is the unmistakable sign of a field headquarters.

Land-Based Communications and Their Military Use			
Waveband	Frequencies	Characteristics	Military Use
High Frequency (HF) (Shortwave)	1.5-30 MHz	a) Transmission follows two paths (Diagram 1). The first is Ground Wave which follows the Earth's surface. Range decreases as frequency rises but typically a 1kW transmitter at 5MHz would have a range of 500km (310.7 miles) b) Second is Sky Wave which is reflected by the ionosphere and can then be reflected again. Great distances can be spanned at moderate power and cost, but there is a minimum distance known as the 'Skip Distance'.	For a long time the HF band was used for Army tactical communication, but the great majority of such users now use the VHF band, although often with HF as an alternative 'stand-by'. b) HF is capable of long range, but is really susceptible to intercept and jamming.
Very High Frequency (VHF)	30-300 MHz	Transmission is virtually line-of-sight. Communications are very clear, but rebroadcast stations are often needed to give area coverage.	a) Used by most armies for tactical nets, i.e. at brigade, battalion, company and platoon level, often with on-line security. b) Can be jammed but more difficult than with HF.
Ultra High Frequency (UHF)	300-3,000 MHz	a) Both follow line-of-sight paths and where two stations cannot see each other one or more relays may be needed.	a) Used by most armies for higher level communications (brigade and rearwards) to provide a grid system with a high traffic capacity.
Super High Frequency (SHF) (Microwave)	3,000 MHz-30 GHz	b) Because of the great extent of the bands and the comparative lack of users, systems can use very wide band widths to handle a great deal of traffic.	b) Also used for satellite communication.

that each net demands at least one working frequency, plus, usually, at least three alternatives. Then, of course, in war in the forward areas there will be the enemy nets to be considered as well, while in peace there is a host of civilian users. Most of these military nets work in the Very High Frequency (VHF) band and there is no escaping that this is very crowded. Technical steps to ease the problems have, of course, been taken. Modern technology enables radios to be set up precisely on frequency and not 'wander' while in use and the width within the frequency band taken up by each user (known as 'bandwidth') has been squeezed down, so that more users can be accommodated. These, in turn, enable lower powers to be used, which makes it possible for another net to use the same frequency some distance away without interference between the two.

The problem has again been worsened by the increasing use of security measures. Many radios are today fitted with encryption devices which are permanently operating; i.e. whatever is said over that radio is secure and a hostile agency listening in could not make any sense of what was heard. However, such a device takes up greater bandwidth than a non-secure system. A recent develop-

ment is the 'frequency-hopper', which obtains its security by sending out tiny bursts of transmission, split between a number of frequencies in a pattern understood only by the transmitter and receiver, and which, to any unauthorized listener is totally random. This takes up a lot of frequencies, and although the time spent on any one frequency is microscopic and might not be detected by a distant user, there is considerable effect on other stations close to the transmitter.

In all this the allocation of frequencies is a mammoth problem which is so complicated that it has to be done with the assistance of computers. However, while this may seem like a communicator's technical difficulty, the effects, if things go wrong, would be felt by many users and would seriously affect the course of a battle. This is because every element on the battlefield is now virtually totally dependent upon radio communications, and if those communications are lost because of interference problems they will just not be able to complete their tasks. Cynics even say that were war to come in Central Europe there would be no need for jammers since the many thousands of radio nets on both sides would cause such gross interference problems that few radios, if any, would

be able to function properly.

In the past 30 years radio communications in the forward areas have used voice almost exclusively (before that technological limitations dictated that the Morse code had to be used quite often). While voice is excellent for passing commands and rapid information, it is not ideal for passing a lot of data, such as, for example, in an artillery fire order. This is not only because there is a possiblity of misunderstandings, but also because the passage of such information is fairly lengthy and the longer a radio transmits the easier it is for an enemy to detect it and to pinpoint its location. (Also, of course, one user passing a lengthy message prevents others from using the net.) However, today there is increasing use of information transfer using data entry devices. Typically, these are very small (about the size of a pocket calculator, or, possibly, the size of a computer keyboard), ruggedized, and consist of a keyboard, a display screen, a data store and a connection to the radio. The data is fed into the device 'off-line' (i.e. when not connected to the radio) and only when he is ready does the operator contact the distant station and pass the data, which is done in a very short burst, much faster than is possible by voice.

Right: Soviet Army BTR-50PU (Model 2) HQ vehicle. The vehicle is fitted with mapboards, extra radios, a navigation system and an on-board generator.

Soviet Army Principles

Different armies use their own principles for the provision of tactical communications, but those applied by the Soviet Army are fairly typical.

- Responsibility for establishing command communications is from the higher to the lower HQ. Thus, for example, at divisional level, the divisional signal battalion is responsible for setting up communications to the subordinate regimental HQs.
- Lateral communications for liaison are established from right to left. This would apply, for example, between the right-hand division of one army group and the left-hand division of another army group on its left.
- Communications between a HQ and a unit supporting it are the responsibility of the supporting unit. Thus, an artillery battalion supporting a motorized infantry regiment would be responsible for providing the link from its own HQ to the motor rifle regimental HQ.
- Radio is the primary means of tactical communications, especially when in contact with the enemy. However, messengers (using motor-cycles, field cars or helicopters) are also used, especially when security is involved and for bulky items.
- Command radio nets are designed to provide communications with HQs two-down for particular tactical operations. Thus, for example, a division HQ might control an infantry battalion directly in an attack.
- Wire (cable) is used extensively in the defence and when preparing for assault operations.
- Security is of paramount importance and operating procedures are meticulously followed.

Higher Level Systems

Although there are radio nets at all levels up to army group, particularly for the exercise of command in fast-moving tactical operations, at levels of brigade and beyond the information flow is such that the single channel available on a voice radio net can no longer cope. This leads to the use of microwave systems, which use frequencies in the Ultra High Frequency (UHF) and Super High Frequency (SHF) bands, thus allowing them to use many channels over one link; i.e.

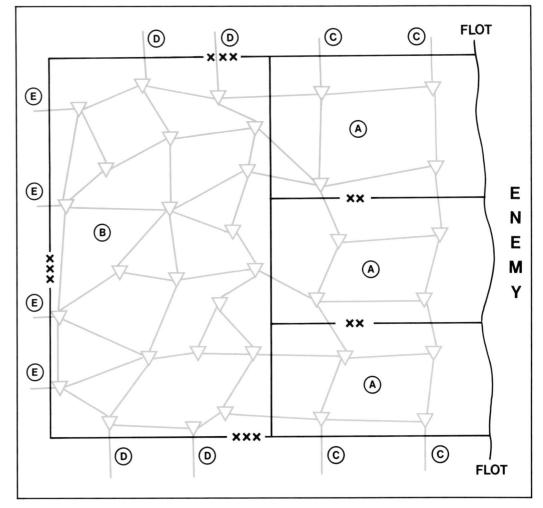

Above: **US Army Mobile Subscriber Equipment (MSE) System: the Corps System.** This diagram shows schematically a possible layout of MSE in a US Army corps area. The corps signal brigade has 22 Node Centres (NC) (shown with a blue triangle), and each division has four NCs. Shown here are three divisions, each with four NCs (A) forming a grid within the divisional area. Behind the divisions is the corps area (B) with its 22 NCs, themselves forming a grid and linked to the divisional NCs to form a corps-wide grid. The flanking divisions are connected to NCs in adjacent divisions (C) of the neighbouring corps while in the corps area there are MSE links to neighbouring corps (D) and rearward links to the army group communications system (E). The links between NCs are provided by microwave radios as shown by the blue lines. Having laid down the grid as shown here, the users can operate within the system as shown opposite.

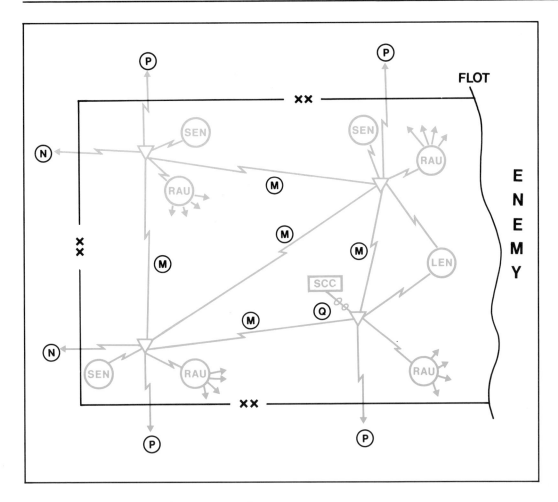

Above: US Army MSE: a Divisional Element. This diagram is a schematic illustration of some of the major elements of MSE within a division. The four Node Centres (NC) (blue triangles) are joined by microwave links (M) and there are also links back to the corps system (N) and to adjacent divisions (P). Within the division there are two methods by which a user can utilize the system. First of all a mobile user equipped with the necessary radio can call into any of the Radio Access Units (RAU) which are linked by microwave into the main MSE system. The user can then use his telephone to talk to any other user anywhere on the system, which is exactly the same facility as provided by the civilian 'cellnet' cellular telephone systems.

Other users, such as divisional and brigade HQs, use 'extension nodes' which are connected to a Node Centre by a microwave link. Depending on the size of the user and the facilities required he will use either a Large Entry Node (LEN) or a Small Entry Node (SEN). These entry nodes provide facilities for telephone, telegraph, data and facsimile communications.

Finally, there is a need for command and control of this complex system, which is provided by the divisional System Control Centre (SCC) which is linked to an NC by cable (Q).

It should be noted that both these diagrams show MSE and its equipment in general terms only. In reality, there would be many more RAUs, SENs and LENs in a divisional area than shown here, and there would be more inter-NC microwave links than shown.

using one link many voice conversations (or even more telegraph links) can take place simultaneously, as happens, for example, on civilian telecommunications systems.

At the frequencies used by these microwave links, the stations need to be within sight of each other, which often requires the use of relays to link two distant stations. Such systems used to follow the chain-of-command in a hierarchical fashion; i.e. from brigade to division to army corps, and so on. However, modern systems, such as the US Army's MSE, French Rita and British Ptarmigan, take a different approach. In these systems, a grid of *trunk nodes* is established across the area, which is quite independent of the chain-of-command. The HQs and units requiring communications then move within the grid and when they need to communicate they link into the nearest trunk node. These systems require computer control so that HQs and units can be identified and located within the grid and telephone calls, data and telegraph messages automatically routed to them.

Such a system offers a number of significant advantages. In the first place, the grid is totally independent of the chain-of-command and thus enemy EW cannot identify HQs by obtaining the

outline of the system. Secondly, the grid can be extended or contracted, or moved forward or rearwards according to the overall tactical situation, but is independent of the situation in any one area. Thirdly, the HQs and units using the system are much less limited in their choice of sites than they were with previous communications systems. Fourthly, the system is much more robust, since it can absorb a considerable amount of damage before user communications are affected.

Automation

As stated earlier, automated systems are playing an increasingly important role in military command and control, in order to cope with the sheer scale of the task. This is achieved by automated data processing (ADP) systems using computers. The earliest systems simply automated a manual task, typically one involving processing a lot of figures (known as 'number crunching'). One such task, for example, was the calculation of fire orders for guns, based on the required range, the direction of the target, type of ammunition, barrel wear, weather conditions, and so on. Traditionally this was done using tables and mechanical calculators, but it can be done very much faster and much more easily using a purpose-designed electronic computer, which also saves the use of valuable manpower in what are essentially routine arithmetical tests. Also in that first generation,

Above: A British Military Policeman uses the special deskset which gives him access to the versatile and efficient Ptarmigan field communications system.

Left: A staff officer operates a Wavell terminal in a field HQ; this British computer system revolutionizes staff work.

The output from Wavell is displayed as a series of messages, known as 'formats'. In other words, there is a standard layout for the displays; for example, the locations of 'Own Troops', which lists in a predetermined layout the known current locations of all friendly units. However, the essential map displays are still maintained manually.

The next generation of ADP systems will take the process a lot further. They will not only handle the collation, evaluation and exchange operations much faster but will also be able to display the information graphically on maps. This will really speed up staff procedures, eliminating the time-consuming process of marking and updating maps.

But yet further systems are already in the design stage which will have even more revolutionary impact. These are 'expert' systems, which start to assist with the decision-making processes, analysing situations, giving early warning of dangerous build-ups and presenting possible alternative solutions to the commanders and staffs. Needless to say, such possibilities are regarded with some concern in the more conservative armies!

The Electronic Warfare Battlefield

Because it is unseen, many people grossly underestimate or even totally ignore the battle which takes place daily in peacetime in the electromagnetic spectrum, and which would be even more intense in war. The electromagnetic spectrum extends from the audio-frequencies (i.e. those which can be heard by the human ear – roughly from 1–5kHz), through the radio bands and up through infra-red, visible light and ultra-violet to X- and Gamma-rays. There are military applications in most of these bands, and if there is a military application then there is inevitably a military counter-measure.

In today's ground and air forces there are very few equipments which do not have some electronic components, used either to obtain external information, to transmit information, or to control or operate the equipments in some way. All of these can be a source of information to the enemy or can be interfered with to either neutralize or destroy the equipment, unless very specific measures are taken to protect them.

The Soviets have developed their capabilities in this area into an integrated

puters began to be used to collate, sort and display information at headquarters, which again can be done more quickly by a machine.

The great majority of these first generation field ADP systems operated on their own, in what is known as the 'stand-alone mode'. However, it was quickly realized that, as was already being done in civilian applications, computers could be linked together to pass information and to interact with each other.

A typical system is the British Army's Wavell, an automated system for staffs at brigade, division and corps headquarters levels. Prior to the introduction of Wavell all information coming into an HQ was written laboriously by hand, summarized

and then recorded on a log sheet, before being transferred to a map or a 'state board'. All this was slow and involved nothing more complicated than pencils, paper and transparent covers for maps. Requests for situation reports required manual sorting of information and probably a number of radio transmissions, as well. Wavell, however, is an automated system, based on powerful computers at all major field HQs in 1 (British) Corps, which are linked to each other over the Ptarmigan communications system. Information is fed into the system manually, but is then collated, evaluated and processed automatically, and each computer in the system updates all the others.

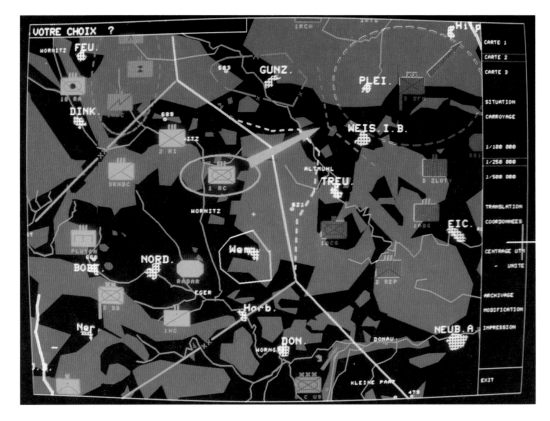

Above: A computer-generated tactical graphical display projected onto a large screen in a French system. Such displays promise to revolutionize the way army tactical headquarters operate.

system which they term Radio-Electronic Combat (REC), which combines signal intelligence, direction-finding (DF), jamming, deception and physical action to destroy the enemy's communications systems. Its purpose is to limit, delay or neutralize enemy command and control systems while simultaneously protecting their own. There is at least one REC battalion in each field army, consisting of a radio intercept company, a radio direction-finding company, and a radar intercept and direction-finding company. Its tasks are to monitor clear-text radio links, to provide direction-finding for targeting radio transmitters, to detect and locate enemy radars, command posts and communications centres, and to monitor tactical communications.

Numerous ECM techniques are available, depending upon the target and the desired effect. Thus, radars can be jammed using spot noise (i.e. transmitting 'noise' on the precise frequency of the hostile radar), pulses (i.e. intermittent jamming), chaff (strips of metal foil cut to the same length as the wavelength of the radar and dropped by aircraft or artillery shells in a cloud) and decoys. Missile guidance systems can be disrupted using electronic jamming or decoyed so that the missile is expended without hitting the target. Radio communications can also be disrupted by noise jamming, although in many instances greater long-term benefit is gained by listening-in (monitoring) to gain information.

For each of these electronic counter-measures (ECM) there is an electronic counter-counter-measure (ECCM), or if there is not one currently, one will soon be developed. Then a new technique will be developed to overcome that, and so on. In the field of passing written messages over radio, for example, there has been a constant battle to outwit the enemy. Once it was appreciated that such links could be monitored, the first step was to encode Morse messages using simple substitution 'paper' codes (i.e. replacing one letter/figure by another). These developed into 'one-time letter pads', but even these proved vulnerable. So, cypher machines were developed, which 'scrambled' the text into an apparently random series of letters and numbers; these became very sophisticated, but even the famous German 'Enigma' machine was broken in the end by the British intelligence services. Enigma and similar machines were mechanical and their combinations finite. But in the last 20 years electronic devices have appeared whose combinations are, to all intents and purposes, infinite. These are thought to be totally secure – but so, too, was Enigma! That German machine was overcome when the British deployed huge

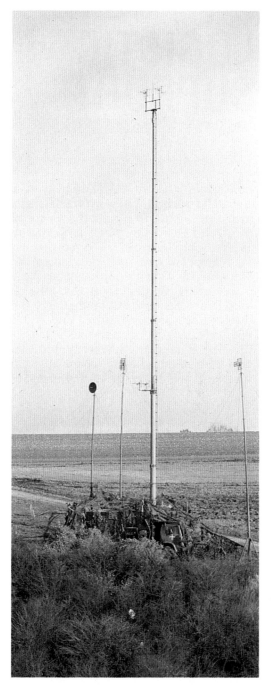

Above: Trunk 'node' in the British Army's Ptarmigan system. Many such nodes provide great survivability and flexibility.

resources of highly intelligent men and women, together with sufficient money and equipment to solve the problem. Could not the same ruthless application of today's people and technology overcome today's machines?

This is not an esoteric, distant matter, which applies to the staffs in the rear areas or the home country. The fact is that EW, ECM and ECCM all are battlefield subjects, with direct impact on the successful outcome of engagements at every level.

LOGISTIC SUPPORT

Tactics is the art of placing the required amount of men and equipment at the right place and the right time to overcome the enemy. This involves fighting men and militarily 'glamorous' equipment, and is exciting. Much less exciting, at least at first glance, is the requirement for logistic support, which ensures that those men and their equipment reach the place on the battlefield at the time required by the tactical commander, that the men are properly armed and equipped, adequately fed, and medically fit, that the equipment is serviceable, and that ammunition is there for the guns and fuel is available to drive the vehicles.

Furthermore, systems must exist to treat, evacuate and heal human casualties, and to extract and repair a vast range of equipment. Logistic support in its widest sense also embraces the multitude of tasks involved in keeping a modern army in the field. These range from control of refugees, burying the dead, guarding prisoners-of-war and water supply to such mundane activities as laundry and the provision of mobile baths.

Thus, while tactical maps tend to show just the front-line troops, the whole area behind the FLOT is, in fact, full of logistic units involved in a plethora of tasks in support of those fighting units. There is much talk, most of it ill-informed, about 'teeth-to-tail' ratios, by which is meant the ratio of front-line, fighting troops to the logistic support troops not immediately involved in the fighting. Such talk usually arises to make disparaging comments about the logistic troops, whose numbers are considered to have swollen out of all proportion to the task. As will be shown, this is not the case.

Modern armies place immense and ever-increasing loads on their logistic systems. For example, in just one area, that of artillery, both NATO and the Warsaw Pact have increased the calibre of their standard shells in the past years – the former from 105mm to 155mm, the latter from 122mm to 152mm. This means that the volume occupied by each shell and its charge is greater, and, of course, they weigh more, all of which increases the load on the logistic system. But, in addition, the latest guns also have a much greater rate of fire, thus requiring many more shells in a given time. Added to this is the fact that most guns, at least in theatres such as Central Europe, are now mounted on tracked, self-propelled chassis, which not only require greater fuel supplies and need more maintenance than the wheeled tractors of the previous generation, but they can also get into positions which are far more difficult for the replenishment vehicles to reach. Further, since the whole equipment (chassis, ammunition, gun and ancilliaries) is much more complex, more

spares are needed and more technicians to repair and maintain them. Finally, since the tracked SPs are heavier, they need larger recovery vehicles to cope with breakdowns and stronger bridges to cross rivers.

This is not the end of the story, however, since many artillery arms are now deploying multiple rocket systems. Such rockets are large, the rate of fire high and virtually all are mounted on self-propelled chassis. Further, air defence weaponry is also increasing rapidly (both in numbers and in firepower), the engineers have mine-laying systems which can lay many more mines at a much higher rate, army aviation units (both helicopters and fixed-wing) are deploying forward in ever-increasing numbers and so on, all of which require yet further support from the hard-pressed logisticians! Two examples will make the point.

MLRS

The US Multiple-Launch Rocket System (MLRS) is being fielded by the US, French, British, Italian and West German armies. This artillery rocket system fires a round which is 3.96m (13 ft) long, 227mm (8.94 in) in diameter and weighs 272kg (600 lb). Its maximum rate of fire is 12 rounds per minute per launcher, although it is highly unlikely that this would be sustained for more than a very

brief period. For the artillery and the operations staff MLRS is a superb system – quick to respond, very accurate, and capable of delivering a variety of highly lethal payloads. For the logistician, responsible for producing reloads at the launcher sites, it is a major headache. Indeed, so heavy is the logistics commitment to MLRS that each battery has its own integral supply platoon and special supply regiments are being formed in most of the armies involved in order to meet the requirement.

The rockets are resupplied in a standard launch pod container, which is also the storage container, which houses six rockets, each in a fibreglass tube rigidly mounted in an aluminium cage. The standard launch pod is 4.166m (13.7 ft) long, 1.051m (3.45 ft) wide and 0.837m (2.75 ft) high, and weighs 2,270kg (5,000 lb).

Each battery consists of nine launchers and, in the US Army, these are supported by a supply platoon with no less than 18 reload vehicles, each towing a trailer. The vehicle is the Oshkosh M985 Heavy Expanded Mobility Tactical Truck (HEMTT), an 8×8 vehicle with a

Below: US Army logistics supply vehicles arriving by ship on an exercise.

Above left: Ammunition being moved by a tactical fork-lift truck. Huge quantities will have to be moved in any conflict.

Left: A Leopard armoured recovery vehicle. Modern armies need large numbers of logistic support vehicles of all types to maintain and sustain them.

2,454kg (5,400 lb) capacity vehicle-mounted crane. This tows a Heavy Expanded Mobility Ammunition Trailer (HEMAT). Each truck and trailer combination carries a total of eight standard pods, for a total in the platoon of 288 pods or 1,728 rockets. At the firing position the HEMTT is parked near the launcher, a standard pod is raised by the vehicle-mounted crane, rotated through 180° and transferred to the twin-boom loader system mounted on the launcher vehicle, which then pulls the pod forward into the firing position.

Medium Artillery Ammunition Supply

On the field artillery side as well, the resupply requirement is growing steadily. The British Army is to introduce a new system called DROPS, an entire system devoted solely to the resupply of field artillery. In the US Army a new system has recently been introduced: the M992 Field Artillery Ammunition Support Vehicle (FAASV). Designed to support the M109A2/A3, the requirement must first be looked at.

The maximum rate of fire for the M109 A2 is four rounds per minute for three minutes. The sustained rate varies with the charge used: normally it is one round per minute, but at charge eight (the maximum) it is one round per minute for one hour followed by one round every three minutes thereafter. It is improbable that a gun would fire throughout the day, because not only does the crew need to rest but, in any event, guns must move regularly to avoid being located by the enemy and destroyed by counter-battery

fire. However, it seems reasonable to assume that in a typical battlefield day one gun might fire some 300 rounds, which in a six-gun battery amounts to 1,800 rounds. Each gun has 34 rounds on-board for a battery total of 204, leaving 1,596 to be brought forward to the guns by the resupply system.

The M992 is based upon the chassis of a standard M109 155mm SP howitzer, but the turret is replaced by a high, fully-enclosed superstructure. It has a crew of two. The M992 version, which supports M109 155mm batteries, carries 93 155mm projectiles, 99 propellant charges and 104 fuses. The XM1050 is under development to support 203mm (8 in) howitzers and this carries 48 projectiles, 53 charges and 56 fuses.

The concept of the FAASV is to supply the guns actually in their firing positions and to automate, as far as is possible, the current slow, manpower-intensive and vulnerable system, which is actually the major limitation in the current fire-support situation. M992 is estimated to enhance crew protection by some 50 per cent and work output by 15 per cent.

The projectiles are loaded into the honeycomb stacking racks in the divisional supply area, together with the fuses and propellants. The FAASV then moves to the gun position, where it parks immediately behind the gun. The shells are removed from the racks by the powered stacker and are then assembled and fixed before being passed by a conveyor belt direct to the gun vehicle at a rate of six rounds per minute (which is twice the sustained fire rate of the M109). The M992 rear door opens vertically and

Above: Soviet tank transporters on the move; such vehicles save track wear, but are themselves complex and expensive.

the M109 door sideways providing any crew members in the open between the two vehicles some limited protection against artillery fragments, but, of course, neither vehicles has any NBC protection during the reloading process.

The Soviet Supply System

The Soviet Army's logistics concept is based upon each division carrying with it on wheels some three to five days' consumption of all the supplies it needs. This covers everything from ammunition and petrol, to clothing, food and medical stores, and would be on a large scale. A conservative estimate of consumption over this three to five day period for a division is as follows:

	(tonnes)
Fuel and lubricants of all types	450
Ammunition for all weapons	550
Food	25
Other stores, spares, etc	50
	TOTAL 1,075

Right: British Army DROPS system is designed to bring palletized ammunition direct to gun positions, but rounds still have to be unpacked and passed to guns.

As the standard resupply truck in a division has a carrying capacity of five tonnes and tows a trailer with a similar capacity, this represents some 108 vehicles. In fact a Soviet divisional transport battalion includes some 200 cargo-carrying trucks and 100 fuel bowsers, with a further 30 trucks and 15 bowsers in each tank, motor rifle and artillery regiment's transport company, for a total of some 350 trucks and 175 bowsers in the division, and possibly many more.

For ammunition, the Soviet Army bases all its calculations upon a 'Unit of Fire' (UF), which is different for each weapon, but is frequently based on the ammunition carrying capacity of a self-propelled gun or of a tank. Thus, for example, the UF of a T-62 tank is 40

Above: The M109 Artillery Delivery System in use with the US Army enables the M109 to remain operational for longer periods in the field.

rounds of 115mm ammunition, while that of a 2S1 SP is also (by chance) 40 rounds of 122mm. Thus, for the artillery, one UF would be held on the SP itself, a further one UF on artillery battalion and regiment transport and a further one-half UF on divisional supply transport. In a tank division with 72 2S1s, this means that some $72 \times 1.5 \times 40 = 4{,}320$ rounds of 122mm ammunition would be held on wheeled transport within the division.

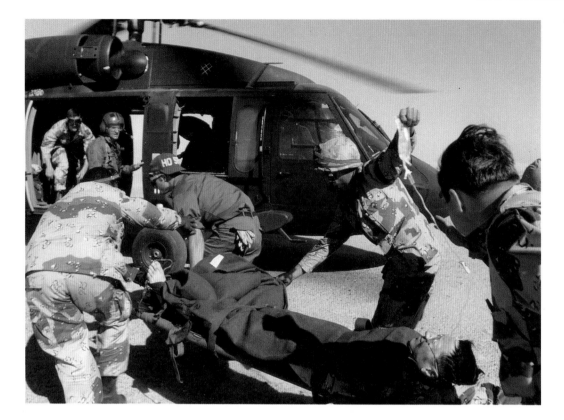

would be used, if they were available.

Thereafter the responsibility for taking casualties further to the rear lies with the next superior formation; i.e. regiments collect from battalions, divisions from regiments, etc. Treatment is kept to the essential minimum at each stage, although emergency surgery can be carried out at regimental medical posts (the first echelon with qualified doctors) and divisional medical stations.

The divisional medical station is operated by the division's own medical battalion, composed of some 35 officers and 135 soldiers. Located some 20km (12 miles) behind the FLOT, the medical station can process about 400 patients per day. From here casualties needing further treatment are taken back to field hospitals operated by medical units under the control of Army or Front.

Left: US soldiers on exercise in Egypt evacuate a casualty. Medical services are very necessary but require considerable manpower, resources and transport.

Right: Surgeons in a field hospital. All armies design their evacuation systems to get casualties to a field hospital as quickly and as comfortably as possible.

Below: British Army Saxon field ambulance, belonging to a unit in the UK Mobile Force (Land), on exercise in Denmark.

Medical

The scale of casualties in a modern war will be very high. The worst situation, which will be appalling beyond any previous human experience, will arise if nuclear weapons are used on a wide scale. Even chemical weapons will cause numerous casualties if proper protection is not available, and the recently-ended Iran/ Iraq War shows that these weapons may well be used if they are available. However, it would be an error to assume that if such weapons of 'mass destruction' are not used the casualties may somehow be bearable. The inescapable fact is that the effectiveness of virtually every type of weapon has increased dramatically in the past 30 years and thus even conventional war will involve massive casualties. It will be the task of the medical services to try to cope with this.

All armies have medical services and attempt to recover the wounded, move them back to the rear areas and try to heal their wounds. Some armies have very sophisticated systems, with very expensive and highly capable facilities, and large resources devoted to moving casualties.

Obviously, the Soviet Army, too, makes provision for medical treatment of casualties, although possibly not on the lavish scale of most Western armies. There is a trained medical orderly with each company and a medical officer with each battalion, known as a 'feldsher', who runs the battalion medical point. The feldsher is a warrant officer, who is

not a qualified doctor, but who is nevertheless highly trained to carry out minor surgery and treat minor ailments. He has one field ambulance at his disposal to recover casualties from companies, although, as with other armies, the Soviets would use any rearward-bound vehicle (such as an empty resupply truck returning for a new load) to send wounded men back. Helicopters, too,

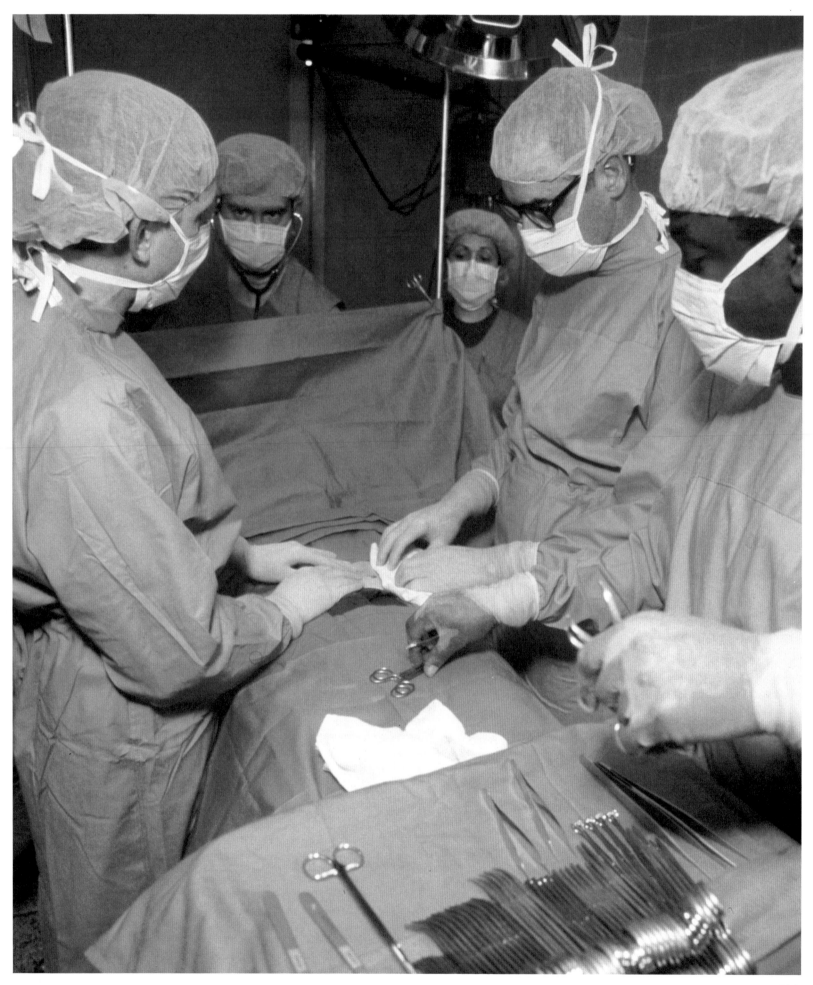

Food

All soldiers must eat and the size of the modern problem for the logistician is enormous. The US Army is well-known for the sophistication of its rations and excellent feeding arrangements in battle, but even the much less demanding Soviet soldier has a major requirement.

When in combat Soviet soldiers' field rations are normally fresh, with food being cooked under company arrangements on trailer-mounted field kitchens and delivered to the men at night in sealed containers. Each man carries an emergency ration pack which may only be consumed with the personal authority of the divisional commander. Ration scales are of the order of 2.27kg (5 lb) of fresh rations per man per day, or 1.14kg (2.5 lb) of dry rations, both of which include bread cooked in divisional bakeries. Thus, in a battle week of (say) five days fresh rations and two days dry rations consumption will amount to 13.6kg (30 lb) per man and thus 149,700kg (330,000 lb) for an 11,000-

strong division. This is 149 tonnes (147 tons) or 37 4-ton truck loads, a by no means insignificant figure.

Fuels

Perhaps the largest single problem for logistic supply chains is the provision of fuels and lubricants for the massive numbers of aircraft, vehicles, boats and generators in a modern army. The problem is exacerbated by the fact that, even after years of attempts to 'standardize', different types and grades of fuel are still used; thus, even at its most simple, at least two types of aircraft fuel will be required, plus petrol for some vehicles and generators, and diesel fuel for others. Further, the usage rates in modern combat are likely to be very high, while few, if any, military engines are designed with fuel economy as a major consideration.

Measures are, of course, taken to try to reduce the scale of the problem. For example, fuel tanks are made as large as possible and auxiliary fuel tanks are used in some cases. The Soviet Army even

Above: Stores being loaded at a field storage depot for onward delivery by truck to a unit. A vast range of stores is needed to keep an army in the field.

uses disposable fuel drums to extend the range of its tanks. During the Second World War and for many years after, most armies relied on the famous, German-designed 'jerrican', which carried 20lit (4.5 gal) of fuel. It was robust and easy for one man to lift, but in today's warfare it is totally inadequate (and dangerous) to have men out in the open, involved in such a very time-consuming task. So, most armies now use tactical pipelines as far forward as possible, with the fuel delivery being by bowsers, fitted with metal or flexible tanks.

Bowsers fitted with metal tanks are dedicated to the role of fuel supply. A typical field bowser is the standard Soviet Army bowser, the Ural ATsG-5-375,

Above: Refuelling a truck in a US Army brigade supply area. Field armies' requirement for fuel is insatiable.

Right: British refuelling 'pod' on a Stalwart 6×6 amphibious truck. Most military vehicles now use diesel fuel.

which carries 5,000lit (1,100 Imp gal) and is fitted with hoses and pumps for direct transfer to recipient vehicles' fuel tanks. Other armies have developed portable systems which can be transferred from one vehicle to another as the need arises. Thus, the British Army's Demountable Bulk Fuel Dispensing Unit (DBFDU) consists of two 2,100lit (462 Imp gal) tanks mounted on a frame, which can be mounted on a 4-ton flatbed truck, typically the Bedford Mk 4×4. Pumps, hoses, fire extinguishers and other ancilliaries are mounted on the frame, and fuel can be delivered at a rate of 455lit (100 Imp gal) per minute.

TACTICAL NUCLEAR WEAPONS

Hanging over any future battlefield in general war is the threat of escalation to nuclear war – in the military vernacular, that 'it will go nuclear'. Nuclear weapons lie in two general categories; strategic and tactical. At the 'higher' end lie the strategic weapons: warheads with massive yields and great accuracy, poised on the end of missiles sitting in underground silos, submarine launch tubes or (in their latest form) on road or rail launchers, and intended solely for use against the homeland of the enemy. At the other, 'lower', end lie the tactical weapons, with yields only a fraction of those of the strategic weapons, intended for use on the battlefield.

All the predictions about nuclear warfare are just that: predictions. Nuclear weapons have been used just twice – at Hiroshima and Nagasaki – and then against unprotected, (indeed, totally unsuspecting) civilians. Nuclear weapons have never been used against the military forces of another nation which possesses similar weapons. Thus, the considerable number of tests which took place up till the signing of the Test Ban Treaty have resulted in a large volume of data which is used as the basis of predictions of what might happen. The actual effects of any one nuclear weapon can be forecast with considerable accuracy, but the effect of large numbers – and especially of their non-physical effects on morale and the cohesion of forces – has never been put to the test.

Nuclear weapons are the most powerful military weapons ever to have been deployed and the possibility of their use

Below: A nuclear ground-burst, photographed at a height of 3,700m (12,000 ft) and a distance of 80km (50 miles).

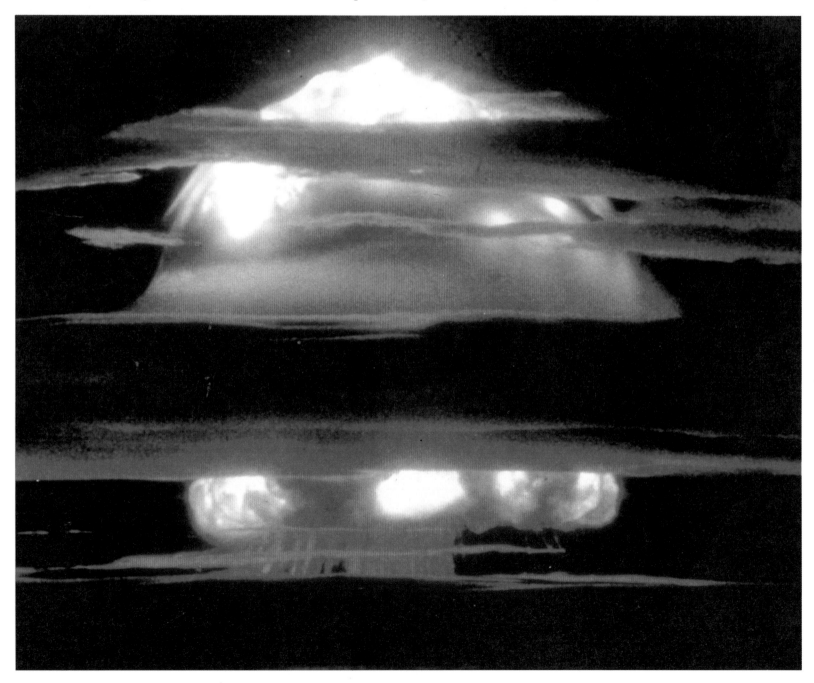

gives rise to considerable debate and concern. There are those who believe that a war could be fought with tactical nuclear weapons without escalation to strategic nuclear weapons necessarily taking place.

Others believe that as soon as one nuclear weapon has been used a 'threshold' is crossed from which there is no drawing back and which, once passed, leads automatically and probably very rapidly to all-out nuclear war. Within the military forces nuclear weapons are regarded as the ultimate and their first use, regardless of type or size, is stringently controlled and, in every case that they are deployed, release can only be given by the very highest political authority.

Nuclear Weapons' Effects

The effects of nuclear weapons are, of course, well-known. However, it is worth a reminder that the immediate effects of a nuclear explosion are blast, thermal radiation (heat), initial nuclear radiation and electromagnetic pulses (EMP). All these effects are directly proportional to the yield (or explosive size) of the weapon. This yield is indicated by a comparison with conventional high-explosive (TNT); thus, a nuclear weapon with a 20kT (kiloton) yield has an explosive effect equivalent to that of 20,000 tons of TNT, while a 1MT (megaton) explosion is equivalent to 1,000,000 tons of TNT, and so on.

The effects of any one particular nuclear explosion depend upon the height at which it takes place and, in particular, whether the fireball touches the ground or not. If the fireball just touches the ground it is a 'ground (or surface) burst', while if the warhead penetrates the ground before exploding and the centre of the fireball is beneath the surface, it is a 'subsurface' burst. Also there are two types of air burst: a 'normal air burst', where the centre of the explosion is below 30,480m (100,000 ft) and the fireball does not touch the ground, and a 'high-altitude air burst', where the explosion takes place above 100,000 ft. (The fifth type of explosion – an 'underwater burst' – does not concern us here.) The importance of these definitions is that the height of burst significantly affects the military consequences of the explosion.

The air burst puts nearly all the shock energy into air blast, while the thermal and initial radiation travel considerable distances, particularly in clear weather. There is, however, little residual radiation. In a surface and subsurface burst the earth will absorb much of the initial radiation and shock energy, thus reduc-

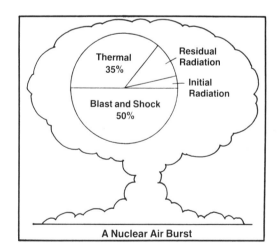

A Nuclear Air Burst

Top: Sukhoi Su-29 Flanker is the prime tactical strike aircraft currently in service with the Soviet Air Force.

Above: French ASMP missile on the centre station of this Mirage 2000N is a Mach 3 'fire-and-forget' nuclear missile.

ing their effect further from the centre, but in doing so the earth's surface will be pulverized and thrown up into the air, and the radioactive particles will be dispersed downwind as 'secondary radiation'. There will also be a considerable area of radioactive ground around the area of the burst.

All nuclear weapons emit electromagnetic pulses (EMP), whose primary effect is upon electronic devices (e.g. radios, microwave systems, wires (cables), telephone exchanges, etc.) lacking the appropriate electronic protection. In the case of most tactical nuclear weapons the EMP effects would be short range, and, in fact, the physical damage from the blast wave or thermal radiation would probably be more immediate and more significant. However, if it was decided that it was necessary to do so, a nuclear weapon could be exploded in the upper atmosphere – say, about 21,330m (70,000 ft) – which maximizes the EMP effect. However, such a nuclear explosion would have an equal effect upon its user's unprotected electronic devices.

Types of Weapon

Battlefield commanders have three types of nuclear weapons delivery at their disposal: air-delivered bombs, tactical nuclear missiles and nuclear artillery. As far as is known all examples of a fourth type – the atomic demolition mine (ADM) – have been withdrawn.

Nuclear bombs can be delivered by a variety of aircraft and can be dropped with great precision. A typical nuclear bomb would have a yield variable between about 10kT and 100kT and would be delivered by a strike fighter, such as the USAF F-111, British Buccaneer, French Mirage or Soviet SU-24 'Fencer'.

The great majority of these weapons have variable yields, which enable their effects to be 'tailored' to the particular target. All Western weapons, and presumably Soviet ones as well, incorporate locking devices to ensure that they cannot be used without proper authorization. All US weapons, for example, incorporate the 'two-man rule', which means that a minimum of two fully-authorized men must be involved in any function where people come into contact with the weapons or codes concerning their release.

According to the *Nuclear Weapons Handbook* (published in the USA in 1984) US weapons also feature a Permissive Action Link (PAL) in the arming circuits, which can only be opened (unlocked) by the proper code. One of the many features of the latest PAL is that after a certain number of wrong numbers have been tried the control system of the weapon locks up and the entire device becomes unusable, needing return to the factory for repair.

The Use of Nuclear Weapons on the Battlefield

The Soviet Union classifies nuclear, chemical and biological weapons as 'weapons of mass destruction'. The USSR is a party to international agreements banning the use of biological agents and there may soon be a treaty banning the use of chemical agents as well. It is intended, therefore, to dwell only on the possession and use of nuclear weapons.

As in the West, the decision to initiate the use of nuclear weapons would be taken at the highest level of government, almost certainly by the President of the USSR himself, possibly in committee with the top members of the Communist Party. Nevertheless, planning for the use of nuclear weapons takes place in every exercise and all fire plans at divisional level and above allow for the possibility of incorporating nuclear strikes. In a major

offensive operation, once the war had crossed the nuclear threshold, the primary Soviet targets would be enemy nuclear delivery means; i.e. aircraft (including airfields), nuclear-capable artillery systems (guns, missiles and rockets), together with the associated command, control and communications systems, and storage sites. Thereafter, targets might include defensive positions, major tactical headquarters and their associated communications systems, reserves and concentrations of troops. Although each target would be attacked according to the tactical requirements, Soviet writings

Left: US Army Lance tactical nuclear missile. 2,133 missiles were manufactured for NATO between 1971 and 1980.

Below: The latest Soviet battlefield nuclear missile, the SS-21 'Scarab', is greatly superior to the FROG missiles it replaces.

suggest that the most common use would be of low airbursts, using relatively large yields.

Nuclear delivery means in the Soviet Army start with artillery available as divisional assets; i.e. 2-S5 152mm SP gun (27km, 2–5kT), 2-S3 152mm SP howitzer (27km, 1–5kT) and the SS-21 short-range missile (120km, 100kT). These are backed up by army assets, such as the 2-S7 203mm SP howitzer (18km, 2–5kT) and 2-S4 240mm SP mortar (12.7km, 2–5kT). These would be supplemented in the tactical battle by aircraft delivering nuclear weapons in low-level attacks, with yields varying from a few kilotons up to about 500kT.

NATO has a similar array of weapons. SP artillery includes the US M109 155mm (18km, 1.0kT) and M110 (16.8km, 0.5–10kT), and the US Lance (110km, 1–100kT selectable) and French Pluton (120km, 15–25kT). With the demise of the Pershing and GLCM missile systems as a result of the INF Treaty there are no further land-based nuclear systems, but there is a full range of nuclear-capable aircraft.

Any discussion of the actual tactical

Above: US M109 155mm howitzer can fire a very low yield (0.1kT approx) nuclear round to a range of 14,000m (45,930 ft).

use of nuclear weapons is inevitably entering unknown territory. It is worth recalling that in the 1930s the wonder weapon of the future was the heavy bomber and the only real example of its use was in the Spanish Civil War. As a result, virtually all air forces entered the Second World War believing in the forecasts of the pundits of those days. These predictions were that, firstly, 'the bomber will always get through' and, secondly, that the effect of bombing civilian targets sufficiently heavily would be that pressure from a suffering and panicking populace would be sufficient to compel that country to sue for surrender. Neither prediction proved to be correct.

Quite when and how such use would be initiated is naturally highly classified by both sides. However, it is possible to speculate on the possible impacts of the use of tactical nuclear weapons.

As soon as the use of such weapons appeared at all likely the forces involved would start to take precautions against nuclear attack. All armies and air forces are now equipped with NBC suits and respirators (gas masks), which are normally carried in packs by the individual soldiers and airmen. However, even the best of these suits is cumbersome to wear and adds to the problems of wearers, and thus the decision to actually don them is postponed as long as possible. Also, modern fighting vehicles such as MBTs, most SP guns, IFV/APC and command vehicles not only provide some physical protection but also incorporate NBC filtration, normally using an overpressure system. It is possible, therefore, that in some units and some armies as the threat of nuclear warfare increased there would be a concommitant increase in the reluctance to leave vehicles or shelters which afforded some degree of protection.

The first strike by tactical nuclear weapons would undoubtedly produce a strong psychological feeling of having entered a totally new era. In the areas affected by the strike there would be massive casualties and there would be three major tactical priorities. The first of these would be to continue operations to ensure that the enemy gained only minimal tactical advantage from his strike. The second would be to find out precisely what had happened, which units had been affected, whether the burst had been air or ground, what areas were contaminated and what further effects might be expected from these strikes. Next, and by no means the least of the priorities, would be to start rescue work, to recover casualties and to commence their treatment.

All armies have sophisticated reconnaissance and monitoring organizations. In the Soviet Army, for example, there are monitoring teams in all divisions. In a motor rifle division, there are nine teams in the chemical battalion, four in the reconnaissance battalion, four in the tank regiment and four in each of the motor rifle regiments. These are equipped with

Above: US Ground-Launched Cruise Missile (GLCM) in a tactical position. Fielding of this weapon led to the INF Treaty.

BRDM-2-RKh radiological/chemical reconnaissance vehicles, which carry special sensors and have a system of automatic dispensers for marking clear lanes. There is also a requirement to cleanse vehicles and soldiers who have been exposed to light doses of nuclear radiation and this would be done at special decontamination centres equipped with NBC washing facilities. Again, the Soviet Army has good equipment in the TMS-65 decontamination vehicle, which uses a redundant air-force turbojet mounted on a standard Ural-375 truck chassis. Special liquids stored on the vehicle are sprayed at high pressure through the jet to hose down tanks, IFVs/APCs and other affected vehicles. Less

powerful shower units are used for the soldiers themselves.

These drills and procedures are, however, one thing, and easy to practice in peace. Quite how units and individuals would react once the nuclear Rubicon had been crossed is another matter. Within the areas of the strikes the devastation would be severe. In the area immediately around each nuclear explosion there would be tremendous damage, with even the heaviest military vehicles thrown about, trees flattened, aircraft hangars (particularly the non-hardened type) flattened, buildings collapsed, aircraft on the ground thrown about and destroyed, and debris everywhere. Fires would be raging, bodies lying on the ground and dazed survivors staggering about. The damage and effects would diminish with distance from the centre of the explosion, and there would be increasing numbers of survivors, although they would be likely to be in a severe state of shock and suffering from various types

of wounds, both as a direct effect of the nuclear explosion and as an indirect effect, e.g. being hit by flying debris.

It is at this stage that the evacuation and medical facilities would be tested to the full as survivors are sent back. It is virtually certain that casualty numbers would be on a scale never before encountered and even the best prepared medical facilities will be very hard pressed to cope.

While the men on the ground try to rescue survivors and assess the damage in an immediate way, the headquarters' staffs would be trying to sort out the tactical impact of the nuclear strike and to take steps to restore the situation. For example, a defender would try to work out what the enemy hopes to achieve by the nuclear strike and to restore the defence to prevent a breakthrough. It is highly improbable that troops would be able to move into the area where the strikes had taken place so the defence around the rim of the affected areas

Above: Clear evidence that US GLCM missiles have been broken up in compliance with the INF Treaty.

Left: Many nuclear weapons still exist and decontamination vehicles, such as this Soviet TMS-65, are still needed.

would have to be reinforced. Such head-quarters' staffs would be desperately seeking information upon which to base their assessments, but they are almost certain to be hampered by two factors. The first is that of reconnaissance teams actually getting into the affected areas. The second is that, in the strike, many communications systems are likely to have been destroyed in whole or in part, either by physical damage or by EMP. Also, of course, the communications soldiers will be as affected by the nuclear attack as any others. It may thus take a little time before reasonable communications are restored.

What happens next can only be a matter for speculation. One possibility is that the initial strikes by either side could be a form of limited 'demonstration', to show that there is a determination to 'go nuclear' in an even bigger way if forced to do so. The strikes would thus be designed to bring about a military halt to the conflict while some form of political solution was found. Another possibility is that the use of tactical nuclear weapons by one side is, whatever the original intention, interpreted by the other as the start of all-out nuclear war, in which case strategic exchanges might begin and what was happening on the original battlefield become increasingly irrelevant.

CHEMICAL WARFARE

Chemical warfare has always aroused a particular horror among soldiers and civilians alike. This is understandable, even though in some ways many chemical agents are less horrific in their effects than flamethrowers and napalm, neither of which is the subject of any major international outcry. First used in the First World War on 22 April 1915, when 5,000 cylinders of chlorine gas were used by the Germans, chemical agents have been used more frequently since then than many people appreciate. None were used in the 1920s, but blister agents were used by the Italians under Marshal Badoglio in their campaign of conquest in Ethiopia in 1936.

Above: Gas was first used on 22 April 1915. Antidotes were soon in use; these machine-gunners are at the Somme in 1916.

Left: Gruinard Island, off the Scottish coast, is still contaminated as a result of Second World War biological warfare experiments.

GRUINARD ISLAND
M.O.D. PROPERTY
LANDING PROHIBITED

During the Second World War both the Allies and the Axis powers had large stocks of chemical agents, but both held back from using them. It is of interest that Hitler's Germany, even when *in extremis* and although possessing some very potent agents, did not use chemical warfare. On both sides there appears to have been a true case of mutual deterrence.

After the Second World War there were loud allegations by the Chinese that the UN forces were using chemical and biological agents in the Korean War (1950–53). Egypt used chemical weapons during her intervention in the civil war in the Yemen (1961–67) and the United States used defoliation agents (but not anti-personnel agents) during the Vietnam War.

Then, in 1984, at a fairly early stage in the bitterly fought Gulf War, the Iraqi Army used mustard gas and nerve agents against an Iranian Army assault towards Basra, after which such agents were used fairly frequently. There were many Iranian casualties at first, but when they started to take proper precautions against such weapons the casualty rate fell off. In one particularly horrific episode in March 1988 the Iranians operating in north Iraq threatened the vital Kirkuk oilfields and the Iraqis responded once again with mustard gas and nerve agents. The Iranian soldiers were by this time well protected, but the civilian Kurdish population around the town of Halabja was not, and they were in the downwind hazard area and were virtually eliminated. The Kurds were victims of chemical agents once again in August and September 1988, but this time deliberately, when the Iraqis drove into the mountains to put down their insurrection, bombarding several villages with chemical agents in the process.

In most of their chemical attacks the Iraqis used missiles and artillery shells to deliver the agents. However, in several instances they also used aircraft, which, in one case, involved spraying marshlands just before an Iranian first-light advance so that the dawn haze was, in fact, a lethal barrier.

The Iraqis used Soviet-supplied SS-12 Scaleboard missiles and bombs to deliver their chemical agents, but it appears that neither the USSR nor any other Warsaw Pact country actually delivered any chemical agents, as such, to Iraq. Rather, the Iraqis used their own industrial plants to produce the agents. This is not a very difficult task with today's technology, which is the reason for the Western alarm over the alleged chemical agent production plant in Libya. Although by no means deliberate acts in a war, the three industrial accidents at Bhopal in India, at Seveso in Italy, and the Swiss spillage into the Upper Rhine in 1986 all show the shocking potential of this type of warfare.

On several occasions the international community has sought to ban chemical weapons. In 1925 many nations ratified the Geneva Protocol which concerned the 'Prohibition of the Use in War of Asphyxiating, Poisonous or other Gases and of Bacteriological Methods of Warfare'. Unfortunately, it only banned the use, not the development or manufacture, of chemical and bacteriological weapons,

and there were no arrangements for verification. This protocol is still in force as is the 1972 'Convention on the Prohibition of the Development, Production and Stockpiling of Bacteriological (Biological) and Toxic Weapons and their Destruction'. Current negotiations to ban these weapons completely are continuing and are based on the 1925 and 1972 documents.

These moves to ban the use of these dreadful agents are well overdue, but until there is absolutely firm, guaranteed and universal agreement, accompanied by some form of verification, the possibility of their use remains. Thus, chemical warfare remains a contingency for which the military must be prepared.

Chemical Agents
Of the chemical weapons currently available, the lowest in the lethality scale are

Below: USAF C-123s spray defoliant chemicals in South Vietnam; May 1967.

incapacitating agents, such as CS gas, which cause mild choking, tears and discomfort. They are mainly used in riot control and anti-terrorist operations, but are also used in limited war to flush enemy soldiers out of bunkers, caves and tunnels. Their effects are totally combatted by respirators and protective clothing.

The next group is the oldest: *blister* and *choking* agents. Their development and use dates back to the First World War, but both have been used in the past ten years. Both are exceedingly unpleasant, but, like incapacitating agents, they can be countered quite simply by wearing protective clothing and respirators.

Psychological agents are based on hallucinogens such as lysergic acid (LSD). These are not lethal in their immediate effects and could be used to disorientate totally groups of soldiers so that their position could be overrun without a fight. Such agents were under serious consideration in the late 1970s but an effective antidote (administered in the form of an injection) has been developed. There are also some *toxins* whose effects are to induce symptoms of acute terror.

Possibly the best known of modern chemical agents are the *nerve agents*. Some stocks of the older persistent agents such as GA (Tebun), GB (Sarin) and GD (Soman) may still exist, but there are also more modern types such as the non-persistent GB2. NBC suits and respirators provide protection against such agents and there are also antidotes. One such is the Autoject, which is a self-administered device. The size of a large fountain-pen, it is used by pressing against the thigh, whereupon a needle is released which penetrates clothing and the skin to introduce an atropine-based nerve agent antidote into the body. A pill must also be taken as part of the treatment.

Storage problems for chemical weapons are well-known; indeed, the only known Second World War casualties from chemical agents occurred when an Allied ship carrying chemical shells caught fire and blew-up in an Italian port in 1943. US research has, however, found an answer to this problem with the binary shell, which contains two chemicals in separate compartments; apart they are harmless, they only become lethal when

Right: US Army soldier in full NBC suit and respirator; no part of his skin is exposed to any CW agent. He (and his rifle) are also covered in a generous application of decontaminating powder.

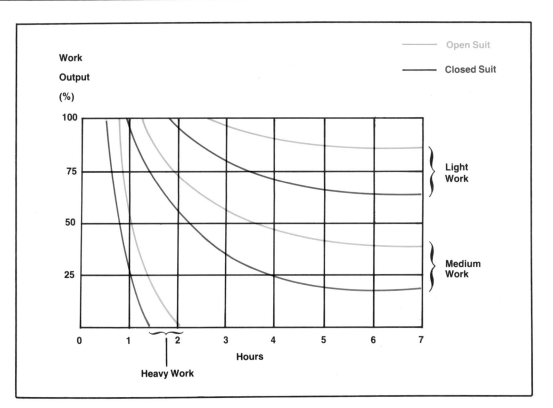

Right: **The Effect of Wearing NBC Suits.** Wearing Nuclear, Bacteriological and Chemical (NBC) suits inevitably has an effect on work output. Factors affecting soldiers' performance will include stress from the heat in the suits (accentuated by physical work), additional breathing stress through wearing the mask, reduced visibility and less manual dexterity. There may also be psychological stress from being under threat of NBC attack. The curves above show the reduction in work output which might be expected at various work levels when soldiers are wearing either complete NBC suits and respirators (closed suit), or a suit but no respirator (open suit).

the discs separating them are broken during flight to the target.

Combatting Chemical Agents

Since the first use of gas in 1915 most armies have taken extensive precautions against such attacks and throughout the Second World War virtually every soldier carried a respirator and some form of 'anti-gas' protective clothing. Since that war passive defensive measures have increased in scope and effectiveness, spurred on in the case of NATO by the massive Soviet chemical agent capability.

All soldiers now carry overclothing made of special material, an important consideration in the design of which is that the soldier is meant not just to survive in it, but he must also be able to continue to fight and operate his equipment. Thus, even when wearing the complete outfit, he must be able to march, run, handle and fire weapons, fly aircraft and talk to others (both directly and by radio or telephone), as well as eating, drinking and performing other bodily functions.

The widely used British 'Protective NBC Suit' is made of a charcoal-impregnated, non-woven material, which is flame-proof (thus giving some protection against nuclear flash) and impervious to liquids, although it is permeable to air and water vapour, thus making it relatively comfortable to wear. The suit comes in two parts – trousers and jacket with built-in hood – and can be put on very quickly over the normal combat clothing. Associated with the NBC suit are a pair of rubber gauntlets and rubber overboots. The outfit is completed with the Respirator.

The Soviet outfit is the OP-1 protective suit. This consists of a long, hooded coat-overall, the bottom of which is secured around the legs by straps, and a pair of long overboots (there are no separate trousers). There is also a pair of gloves. All these items are made from rubberized fabric and provide reasonable but not

complete protection. Additional protection can be provided by special undergarments. The standard protective mask, Model ShM, is unusual in that it has a rubber mask which completely covers the head; this gives good protection but can be uncomfortable. Separate filters are connected to the mask by a hose, but a new model with integral filters is being fielded.

Would Chemical Agents Be Used?

There have been great arguments over the past few years about the use of chemical agents. In the West the military saw a major build-up in Soviet chemical capability taking place at a time when the West was running down what little productive capacity remained. At the start of the 1990s there appears to be a general agreement, at least among the NATO and Warsaw Pact powers to do away with chemical weapons. However, such agreements do not appear to have been accepted by some other nations and there are at least a dozen with the potential to produce chemical agents, a relatively simple process, which can be set in train at short notice, as was demonstrated by Iraq. The fact is that chemical agents do

Above: An exercise NBC casualty is decontaminated prior to treatment.

Above left: Rapid decontamination of equipment is essential and many devices have been developed to achieve this.

exist and have been used as recently as 1988, causing great suffering to their enemies, but little opprobium to the user. It would thus be a foolhardy soldier who left his protective clothing behind in barracks, at least for the next decade!

TRAINING FOR WAR

Military forces have always needed to carry out training for war in peacetime, because without such training they will not be ready to fight in an efficient and coordinated manner when the need arises. Indeed, it might be argued that the aim of peacetime training is simply to win the first battle in the next war! Such military training is an area which encompasses a vast range of activities from individual soldiers firing their rifles, through pilots flying their aircraft at 600 knots at 200 ft, to generals practising the handling of army corps of 100,000 men. Today the range of training carried out is so vast, many of the techniques coming into use are so close to the limits of current technology and the expense so great that *training* has become a major activity in its own right.

The Training Cycle

It is virtually standard practice around the world that within an infantry battalion there is a recurring training cycle, the frequency depending upon the situation, with the individual soldier relearning his personal skills of firing his weapon (whether rifle, machine-gun, mortar,

rocket launcher, anti-tank missile or pistol), fieldcraft and camouflage, together with any particular skills such as vehicle driver, mechanic, radio or radar operator. Then, when all are thoroughly

Above: A soldier's training starts with individual skills; he must be able to fire any weapon he may use in battle.

Below: Next stage is sub-unit training, as for this Soviet officer and his men.

proficient in these individual skills, training at squad/section level can start, practising the men in working together as a tactical body and the squad leader in his command tasks.

Next comes platoon training, practising movement in APC/IFVs and building up to rehearsing attack and defence drills. Such training is partly in barracks, but most will be on training areas, tracts of land devoted to military use. Again, there will be a gradual build-up, starting by simply carrying weapons and equipment, and then to exercises with blank ammunition and pyrotechnics to add some realism, and finally exercises on 'live-firing' ranges where tactical exercises can take place using live ammunition, albeit under careful control.

Besides the infantry all the other parts of the army and air forces are going through similar cycles. Then, in the late summer, they all come together in task force/battle group, then brigade and then divisional exercises. Concurrent with all this is the training of headquarters staffs, who go through a similar cycle, practising their deployment drills and operating procedures. Sometimes, perhaps not every year, there are even larger exercises, perhaps involving the temporary mobilization of reserves or deployment overseas.

There are a number of military justifications for such training. Firstly, without training, individuals and units will not be ready for war. Secondly, such training demonstrates to a potential enemy that an attack would provoke a rapid, effective and timely response, which would prevent him from achieving his aim.

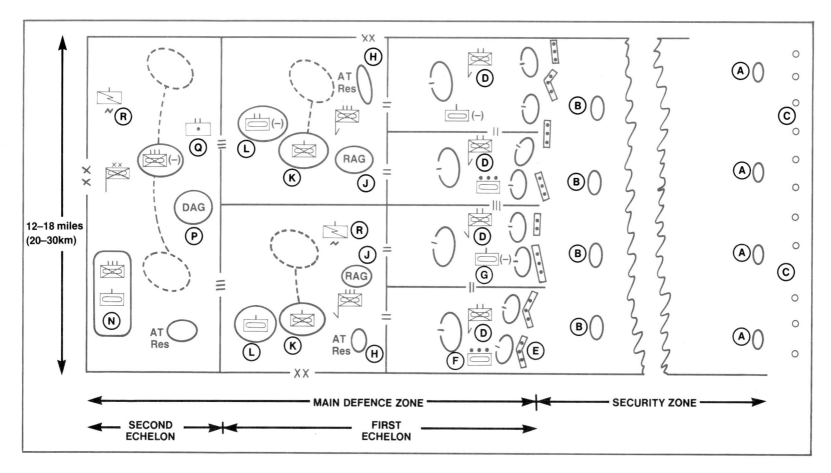

Above: **A Soviet Division in Defence.** Soviet tactics do not place much emphasis on defence, but it is of course practised. This diagram shows schematically how a Soviet motor rifle division might deploy in defence. The basic concept is one of defence in considerable depth, with the area divided into a Security Zone and a Main Defence Zone.

The Security Zone, normally some 16km (10 miles) deep, has two sets of outposts, the outer under divisional control (A) and the inner under control of the forward motor rifle regiments (B). A series of army-controlled reconnaissance troops (C) may be even further forward.

The Main Defence Zone is divided into First and Second Echelons, and could be some 16km (10 miles) deep. The position shown here has two motor rifle regiments forward, each with two battalions forward. The forward battalions (D) have two companies forward in the first echelon, with minefields across as much of the front as possible (E). Each of the forward regiments has placed a tank company forward, with one tank platoon (F) with one battalion, and the remainder of the tank company (G) with the other battalion. Each motor rifle regiment has an anti-tank reserve (H) and its Regimental Artillery Group (J). A motor rifle company (K) and a tank force (L) are

deployed to face the main threat axis, but alternative positions are planned (dotted lines).

Similarly, the divisional second echelon comprises a motor rifle regiment (M), less some detached units, with planned alternative positions, and a counter-attack force (N). The Divisional Artillery Group (P) and rocket battalion (SS-21) (Q) are under divisional control. Electronic Warfare units (R) are located in the divisional and regimental areas.

Thirdly, soldiers and units must practise in the environment in which they may have to fight. Thus, US Forces Command carries out training in Central America (such as the March 1988 Exercise Golden Pheasant in Honduras), while the British Royal Marines train every year in the Arctic conditions of Norway, which is where they would fight in war. Finally, modern warfare is extremely complicated and the higher the level (i.e. the more troops and units are involved) the more complex are the twin tasks of command and control, and thus the more they need to be practised.

Up till now, particularly in Central Europe (on both sides of the Iron Curtain), some spectacular exercises have taken place. The Warsaw Pact has held exercises involving hundreds of thousands of troops and tens of thousands of tanks at regular intervals, while NATO has held similar exercises, perhaps not quite as large, but nevertheless involving over 100,000 troops in some cases. Both the Warsaw Pact and NATO practise the mobilization of reserves and their movement, together with reinforcements of regular troops from, for example, training units, to their war positions. Such exercises enable headquarters and units to study their plans, to practise them under reasonably realistic conditions, and to learn lessons from mistakes and thus to improve their plans.

For many years in almost every nation such exercises have followed two fairly standard formats: Command Post Exercises (CPX) and Full Troops Exercises

(FTX). In a CPX staffs are exercised by setting up the selected headquarters together with a control element. Thus, as an example, if it is desired to exercise a division HQ, the HQ itself will be fully manned and deployed, with all its component parts (main, alternate and rear HQs), as if for war, but with a separate control organization to represent brigades (lower controls) and the corps HQ (higher control). These higher and lower controls feed in incidents, react to plans and orders from the divisional HQ and generally try to paint as realistic as possible a picture of the progress of a real war. For the staff being practised (the players) these exercises are fairly realistic, since they obtain responses over telephones, radios, and telegraphy just as they would in war, but the success of the

exercise depends upon a large and usually slow-reacting control organization. Also, even though only staff and communications troops take part in such CPXs they still involve a large number of troops and vehicles moving around the countryside and if realistic distances are used in order to practise the communications properly a large area is required.

The other type of exercise, the FTX, involves both HQs and units to deploy tactically in full strength and to react realistically to tactical situations generated by a control organization, which also includes an enemy. These exercises take up a lot of real estate and give valuable practice in controlling the complex organizations of modern war. However, it is also very difficult to maintain momentum evenly across all participants, so that everyone is kept reasonably busy for most of the time. The result is usually that some elements on the exercise work very hard all the time, while some are very bored for most of the time.

A further problem on such exercises is to give a degree of realism. Blank cartridges can be used to simulate rifle, machine-gun and tank gun fire, and in carefully rehearsed incidents additional 'effects' can be used to simulate incoming artillery fire and mine explosions, but control must be tight to maintain safety. Even so, the blank cartridge may give a reasonably satisfying 'bang' for the firer, but there is no indication of whether the shot was properly aimed and, if so, at what.

Above: Soviet Army on training. All armies are faced with the problem of devising realistic exercises which teach soldiers correct lessons.

Virtually all such exercises tend to be marred by accusations of 'cheating', with stories of troops walking unscathed through exercise minefields, of enemy vehicles driving over bridges which had been 'destroyed' by engineers, and so on. Umpire organizations are set up to try and judge who is successful and to seek to ensure that the exercise rules are followed, but they cannot be everywhere and even when they are present at an incident their judgement is almost invariably to the great dissatisfaction of most of the troops involved!

But such training has become less acceptable for a number of reasons. Firstly, the lack of realism due to slow and ponderous control organizations has caused increasing dissatisfaction, both at HQ level and at the fighting level. Secondly, the exercises have become increasingly expensive and there is a desire to obtain the maximum value for the maximum number of people, but at minimum cost. Thirdly, the space for troops to move around the countryside has become increasingly restricted, especially in Europe, and the population has become more resistant to the ever-

growing numbers of vehicles, especially those with tracks, churning up fields and tearing up roads and tracks.

However, it is no exaggeration to say that there is a revolution taking place in military training. New ideas, new technology and new methods are introducing new elements of realism and enabling both those undergoing the training and their assessors to obtain much greater value out of the activities. Further, these new methods are starting to reduce – although they can never fully replace – the massive exercises which cause such an impact on the civil population.

Tactical Engagement Simulation

As described earlier, traditional methods of simulating field combat on exercises have always been unsatisfactory. Blanks fired by rifles and machine-guns have added a degree of (sometimes not very realistic) noise but there has been no need for the firer to take proper aim, while the end-effect on the target has been a matter of judgement for an umpire – if one was available. Further, anti-tank weapons could only be pointed and even if, as in the case of tank guns, blanks were fired, the same problems arose – there was no adequate method of judging the success of the shot.

However, this is changing rapidly with the introduction of Tactical Engagement Simulation (TES), yet another product of modern technology. Virtually all TES uses a laser projector attached to a weapon, such as a rifle, machine-gun,

tank gun, etc., and when the trigger is pulled the laser fires a pulse in the direction of aim. All soldiers involved are fitted with TES harnesses, usually one over the body and a second, smaller harness on the helmet. These consist of a series of electronic sensors mounted on canvas straps and connected to a central microprocessor. When the soldier comes under 'fire' the sensor transmits the signal to the processor which decides whether the shot is a hit, a near-miss or a total miss. If it is a hit an audio signal is generated telling the soldier that he has been hit and he must then either lie on his back or use a key to deactivate his own laser projector to stop the tone, and is thus out of the exercise. If it is a near-miss or a total miss different audio tones indicate this to the target soldier so that he knows that he is under fire.

Left: One way to increase realism is to use laser-operated devices to indicate hits; this is the US MILES system.

Right: Live-firing in a tactical setting for a British paratrooper firing an LMG.

Below: As outdoor training becomes more difficult computerized simulations are being developed; realism grows every year.

Similar systems are used on APC/IFVs, trucks and tanks, except that in these cases many systems, instead of indicating a hit by an audio signal, are connected into the vehicle's electrical circuit and to pyrotechnic devices mounted on the vehicle roof, so that a valid 'hit' results in the vehicle actually being immobilized and a bang and smoke indicating the hit.

The basic TES have been used for some years, but the latest systems include new degrees of sophistication. For example, in the West German TALISSI system the soldier's harness includes a reflector, which sends back any received pulses to the transmitting projector. This enables the system to assess the range at which the engagement took place and to check that the soldier's sight was set to the correct range, whereupon the system software judges whether or not it was a valid 'kill'. Only if satisfied will the signal to the target sensors be given so that the soldier knows that he is 'dead'. The New Zealand OSCMAR system can also provide post-exercise analysis features; for example, each soldier's projector is given a unique identification code, so that when a target is 'hit' his microprocessor records the code of the firing laser. It also tells how active a part each soldier played (i.e. did he avoid being hit by sheltering behind a tree?). The Belgian Minidra also addresses a possible cheat by deactivating itself if the soldier removes his helmet for more than 20 seconds. This enables him to take off his helmet to go through a restricted doorway, but not to leave it off in order to reduce his vulnerability to enemy laser projectors!

Other devices now becoming available are mines working on the same principles, particularly above-ground devices such as the Claymore. Thus, when the Centronics Claymore simulator is activated, a pyrotechnic emits an explosive noise and smoke, while a projector activates all sensors within a realistic area; i.e. an arc of about 50m (164 ft) and 50°.

Indoor Facilities

The devices just described are all for outdoor use in field training. However, major progress is also being made in indoor simulators. In the 1970s weapons simulators came into widespread use, in which a firing engagement for an individual weapon could be simulated with a fair degree of realism.

These are particularly valuable for simulating missile engagements because not only is each live missile very expensive but providing targets for anti-tank and anti-aircraft missiles is both difficult and expensive. Other simulators are used

for skills such as tank driving and flying aircraft.

Modern technology is, however, bringing about major developments in this field as well. In the first place modern computers are making simulators much simpler and cheaper. For example, ten years ago a tank driving simulator consisted of a large table-mounted miniature model of a stretch of countryside, with a miniature television camera mounted on a gantry above it. The trainee sat in front

of a television screen and 'drove' the tank, with the camera moving across the model in response to his control inputs. Today, the model, the camera and the mechanical devices are no longer needed, since computer software can now be programmed with whatever countryside models the trainer requires, can generate excellent three-dimensional, coloured pictures, and can respond electronically to the driver's instructions.

Further than this, however, the US

Army is now testing systems in which such electronic firing simulators are linked to each other in a network to produce a combat simulation. Such combat can be one-on-one, e.g. one MBT against another MBT, or in combinations of brigade size, the only real limit being cost. Known as Simnet, the potential is enormous. For example, since the links between the simulators are electronic, there is no distance limitation. Thus, two M1 simulators fighting each other could be situated either side of a parade-ground in the same barracks, or one in California and the other in West Germany, linked by satellite.

An additional facility is that new ideas, techniques and even weapons systems can be tested in a known and realistic environment, using infinitely variable computer software rather than expensive hardware prototypes.

US Training Facilities

The US Army has developed the most sophisticated training apparatus in the world and is bringing the full benefits of modern technology to bear on the problem of realistic training. At the higher level a number of major training centres have been set up. Largest and most important of these is the National Training Center (NTC) at Fort Irwin, California, whose major facility is a training area of more than $2,590 \text{km}^2$ (1,000 square miles) where heavy units can train in mid- to high-intensity warfare against a Soviet enemy, represented by a highly skilled opposition force (OPFOR), which uses Soviet tactics and organizations, dresses in Soviet uniforms and uses a large range of Soviet weapons (plus some US systems altered to look like Soviet equipment). More than 300,000 soldiers have been through the NTC since it was set up in 1982 in some 200 battalion and brigade exercises. As presently established, the facilities of the NTC limit it to exercising brigades consisting of only two battalions, but by 1992 it will be capable of exercising every element of a full brigade; i.e. three battalions plus all the supporting elements. Counterpart of the NTC in Europe is the Combat Maneuver Training Center (CMTC) at Hohenfels in West Germany, which exercises 56 battalions per year on a four-day exercise with a live-firing element at the nearby Grafenwohr range area.

Similar training for non-mechanized battalions in mid- and low-intensity conflict is given at the Joint Readiness Training Center (JRTC) at Fort Chaffee, Arkansas.

For better staff training there is the Battle Command Training Program

(BCTP), located at Fort Leavenworth, Kansas, which gives NTC-type training for corps and divisional commanders and their staffs, against any type of enemy threat the US is likely to meet anywhere in the world. Commanders, their staffs and major subordinate commanders attend the BCTP initially for a five-day seminar, based on the AirLand Battle doctrine, which is intended to make them think their way through how they are going to fight. They then return to their base and prepare for the 'War-Fighter CPX', which is held at their home base using communications links to the BCTP computers between two and six months later. This CPX is as realistic as possible with today's technology and uses the

US army's 'Corps Battle Simulation' (CBS) system, which involves a VAX 8600 mainframe computer linked to 13 MICROVAXs and the joint exercise support system (JESS).

Above: In its search for realistic training the US Army has trained units in Soviet tactics and equipped them with real or simulated Soviet equipment.

Opposite: Some skills cannot be simulated on a computer; for example, the methods of deploying and crossing amphibious bridges can only be learned with real equipment.

Below: US Army M60 MBT crossing a medium-girder bridge in a unit training exercise.

THE CENTRAL EUROPEAN BATTLEFIELD

Europe has been the scene of the most devastating wars the Earth has ever known and over the past 1,000 years scarcely any European country has not known war and foreign occupation. Over most of recorded history there have been at least two major wars in every century

and Europe has been responsible for virtually all the major technical innovations in the science of warfare. Before looking at the nature of a future war in Central Europe it is worth taking a brief look at the past 200 years to see how warfare arrived at the form it has today.

The wars of the French Revolution and of the Napoleonic era engulfed the entire continent from 1792 to 1815 and also involved land and sea campaigns outside Europe, particularly in North America and India. Indeed, the period represented, to all intents, the first 'world' war, although, as was to happen again, the crucial battles all took place and the final decision was reached in Europe itself. The few technical advances were all designed with European warfare in mind and the leading exponents of tactics were all Europeans. Although in many ways the last of the 17th/18th century

wars, the Napoleonic wars introduced the concept of the 'nation in arms', at least in France, where conscription replaced the professionals and mercenaries of other armies.

There were a number of significant conflicts over the remainder of the 19th century, perhaps the most important of which did take place outside Europe. This was the American Civil War (1861–65), which was, in many respects, the first of the modern, post-Industrial Revolution wars and also took the concept of the 'nation in arms' one step further to the 'nation at war'. In the latter the entire

Below: The US Civil War was the first time in history when prosecution of the war became the state's prime business.

business of the state and its people became the prosecution of the war, and the national economies were totally integrated into the war effort. It was also the first war to use the steam railroad as a logistical weapon and the first to make major use of the electrical telegraph, although the latter had been used to a certain extent in the Crimean War (1853–56).

The Franco–Prussian War (1870–71) was the first European war of the modern era. It lasted just six months and ended in total French defeat, starting the Franco–German antipathy that was to last for a century and bring the continent to war twice more.

The First World War

The next occasion was the First World War (1914–18), which engulfed Europe even more comprehensively and disastrously than had the Napoleonic wars. Eight million died in a war in which the massive use of artillery, indirect fire and machine-guns demonstrated for the first time that weapons were more powerful than manpower. On the crucial Western Front both sides disappeared into trenches and protected themselves with barbed-wire and minefields. They then had to try to work out how to break the stalemate. The Germans tried gas, but it proved to be tricky to use, being very dependent upon just the right weather conditions, and once the threat was understood effective countermeasures were quickly devised. The British invented the tank, the armoured personnel

Above: The First World War brought Americans to fight in Europe for the first time.

carrier and the tracked self-propelled gun, and used them on numerous occasions, but never quite achieved the success in breaking the deadlock that was hoped for. This European war also saw the first large-scale use of aircraft in war and they, too, played a significant role in the fighting, but never brought

about the longed-for breakthrough.

The Germans attempted a final breakthrough in a series of assaults in the west between March and July 1918, for which new tactics had been devised and intense training carried out. However, despite being forced to retreat significant distances in some areas, the Allied forces eventually halted the German advance. Then, after the briefest of pauses, the British in the North started to counterattack, followed by the French and then the Americans. Between August and October 1918 the Allies swept forward in the mobile warfare for which they had so long prepared and in a series of stunning victories defeated the German Army. This period also saw a most significant development on the Allied side with the institution of the appointment of an Allied commander-in-chief, General Foch taking the post on 3 April 1918.

In the end attrition worked and the German will to fight evaporated as civilian morale collapsed, despite their successes in the east against Russia. However, while the horrors of over three years of trench warfare cast a long shadow over the history of the First World War, these two final phases (the German attack and the Allied counter-attack) must not be overlooked as they showed that mobile warfare was still possible and that the Allies in particular were very

Left: The devastation and casualties in the First World War were on a scale never before even dreamed of.

good at turning it to their advantage.

There had been large-scale conflicts before which lasted longer than the First World War, but even in the Napoleonic wars the fighting had been more sporadic and contact relatively intermittent, with opponents only meeting to fight a battle. In the 1914–18 War, however, and in particular on the Western Front, the contact and conflict were virtually continuous from August 1914 to November 1918.

When the war ended the victorious Allies in the west remained as occupation troops in Germany for some years; the Americans left in 1923, the British, French and Belgians a few years later. The inter-war years saw the major Euro-pean armies developing theories and equipment for armoured warfare, which they all were able to put into practice – with varying degrees of success – in 1939–40 at the start of the Second World War.

The Second World War

The Second World War (1939–45) started with a stunning series of German victories as they overran first Poland, then Denmark and Norway, followed by Belgium, Holland and France. Hitler's armies achieved in a few months what the Kaiser's armies had failed to do over a period of years. The Germans showed themselves to be very well trained, tactically flexible and masters of the craft of fighting. They showed that the integration of infantry, tanks, artillery and tactical airpower, coupled with an effective and rapidly responding command system could not be beaten by the French and British as they were then organized and trained.

Having decided not to attempt an amphibious assault across the English

Above: The physical damage caused during the Second World War was on an unprecedented scale. This is the village of St Aubin in France as British soldiers strive to clear the buildings of snipers, July 1944.

Above: US troops cross the Moselle river on 15 March 1945 on a pontoon bridge, as all normal bridges had been destroyed.

Left: The Soviet Army devotes vast resources to its obstacle crossing capabilities.

Channel, Hitler was able to turn his attention to what had always been his ultimate target – the Soviet Union; the other campaigns in Yugoslavia, Greece and North Africa were just 'sideshows' and of only peripheral importance to his goal. The attack started at precisely 0300 hours on 22 June 1941 along a 3,218km (2,000 mile) front. For some months progress was impressive and between June and November 1941 the Germans achieved one of the greatest sustained offensives in history. Soviet losses were some 3,000,000 (half of them prisoners), while the Germans had lost some 800,000. However, despite their losses, the Soviet armies had survived, and the Germans were widely stretched over the vastness of the steppes; German patrols had entered the outskirts of Moscow and glimpsed the golden spires of the Kremlin in the distance, but the Soviet Union was not conquered.

Throughout 1942 the battle in Eastern Europe swayed first one way and then another as the generals and troops on both sides gained experience in this new type of warfare. In February 1943 the Germans surrendered at Stalingrad and in July the greatest tank battle ever waged took place at Kursk, where the Germans lost 70,000 men, 3,000 tanks, 1,000 guns, 5,000 trucks and 1,400 aircraft, the Soviets slightly less. From then onwards the Soviets pressed the Germans inexorably back to their own frontiers, at first slowly and later with increasing rapidity.

In the west the Allies had been faced with a Continental Europe entirely occupied by the Axis powers, with the sole exception of the Iberian peninsula. They first drove the Axis powers out of North Africa, then took Sicily and invaded Italy, with the Italians themselves leaving the Axis in September 1943. The great D-day invasion of northern France took place in June 1944, followed by the invasion of southern France in August. From now onwards Europe was the scene of massive battles in the east, west and south as the Allies squeezed Hitler's forces between three great armies until they met in Germany. The Allied victory was total.

The Second World War was far more devastating for Europe than had been any previous conflict. Military casualties were twice those of the First World War, but civilian casualties, due to battles, bombing, starvation and the 'Holocaust' were on a vastly different scale. The war showed change in ground forces as mechanization increased the speed of movement, while tanks, when properly used, gave a striking capability which in its power and speed was unlike anything that had existed before. Tactical airpower had an immense impact on the way ground troops fought and moved. All weapons were 'better' than in the First World War, having more powerful warheads, greater accuracy, longer range and quicker reactions. Also, communications played an ever larger role in controlling these vast armies whose deployment was on a continental scale. One weapon that was available to both sides, but that was

never used, was gas, and there seems little doubt that this was a case of mutual deterrence, with each side uncertain as to what the other possessed and thus reluctant to be the first to use the weapon for fear of what the response might be.

It is the latter stages of the Second World War that are the most important guide to the future. The scale of the fighting and of individual battles between 1944 and 1945 was vast, covering enormous areas and involving huge forces made up of many nations. They provide what are probably the nearest indications of what a future war in Europe might be like.

Post-War Europe

The immediate post-war period found the countries of Europe shattered by five years of the most intensive warfare fought to that date and trying desperately to return to 'normality'. However, the wartime allies had divided Europe into four zones of occupation, which were, in effect, two zones: the three zones of the Western Allies who cooperated in almost every aspect of life and the Soviet zone which cooperated with the West on almost nothing. The Western alarm over Soviet intentions was heightened by the progressive collapse of the Eastern European democracies and their replacement by pro-Moscow Communist governments, and by the closure of access routes to West Berlin from 22 June 1948 to 12 May 1949.

So serious was the Soviet threat that the Western European nations signed the Brussels Treaty on 17 March 1948 and then joined with the North American nations to sign the North Atlantic Treaty on 4 April 1949. The original members of NATO were Belgium, Canada, Denmark, France, Iceland, Italy, Luxembourg, the Netherlands, Norway, Portugal, the United Kingdom and the United States. Greece and Turkey joined on 22 October 1951, and the recently-created Federal Republic of Germany in May 1955. Spain joined in 1983, but has yet to decide to join the integrated military command structure. France withdrew from the integrated NATO military command structure on 9 March 1966, but not from the Alliance itself, and from a nadir in the early 1970s military cooperation between France and the NATO allies has been increasingly close.

On the other side of the Iron Curtain Soviet hegemony was virtually complete by 1947, although Marshal Tito withdrew Yugoslavia from the Communist Bloc in June 1948. The Soviets took little additional action when NATO was origi-

nally formed, but when West Germany was rearmed and admitted to the Alliance they responded by forming the Warsaw Pact on 14 May 1955. The Pact comprised Albania, Bulgaria, Czechoslovakia, the German Democratic Republic (GDR or East Germany), Hungary, Poland and the Soviet Union. Yugoslavia declined to join and Albania subsequently left the Pact.

Since that time the NATO allies and the Warsaw Pact have faced each other across the breadth of Europe. There have been alarms, when higher than normal degrees of readiness were ordered by one or both sides, but the fact is that European peace has been maintained from 1945 until the present. During those years the two sides have fielded armed forces of unparalleled complexity and sophistication, and those countries with commitments outside NATO have nevertheless retained their highest capability, especially for land and air warfare for the Central European battlefield.

NATO versus the Warsaw Pact

It is no simple task to compare NATO and the Warsaw Pact and to measure their capability to deter each other. The military forces – land, air and sea – possessed by each side are clearly major elements in the equation, but there are others, too. For example, geography, economic strength, political stability, industrial and technological resources, and the availability of raw materials all play a role, as do the human resources, the social structure and its stability. In addition, differences in military strategy, the structure of the military commands and forces, the logistic system and leadership potential must be taken into account.

The Warsaw Pact countries, for example, make up one geographic entity; NATO does not. The Soviet leadership can send reinforcements from the USSR to any part of the Pact territory by road, train or air. The USA and Canada, and to a lesser extent the United Kingdom, must send their reinforcements across the

Above: US troops arrive in Europe to demonstrate national commitment to NATO.

Men	NATO	Warsaw Pact
Active ground forces	2,340	2,143
Ground force reserves	4,543	4,239
TOTAL IN WAR	**6,883**	**6,372**
Divisional Equivalents		
Manned in peacetime	105.3	101.6
Reservists	36	113
TOTAL IN WAR	**141.3**	**214.6**
Major Equipment		
Main Battle Tanks	22,200	53,000
IFV/APC	6,200	23,600
Artillery (including MRL)	10,600	36,000
Mortars (120mm and over)	2,900	8,300
Surface to Air Missiles		
Armed helicopters	2,400	12,400
	864	1,220
Land Combat Aircraft		
Bombers	350	888
Ground-attack Fighters	2,865	2,330
Air Defence Fighters	1,178	4,432

sea, an undertaking which will be progressively more hazardous as a war develops. Further, if SACEUR wishes to redeploy his men or equipment he must do so by air or sea, whereas the Warsaw Pact can communicate with all its fronts by land. In classical military parlance, the Warsaw Pact acts on interior lines, NATO on exterior lines.

The forces available to the two alliances can be calculated in a number of ways. Here it is intended to compare the forces and equipment available in a land battle assuming a short war. Thus, only regular troops and immediately mobilizable reservists are counted and the area concerned is restricted to that extending from the Atlantic to the Urals in the USSR. The figures therefore do include French and Spanish forces since, although not part of NATO's integrated military command, they are part of NATO's total military assets. The figures do not take account of the reductions promised by both sides in 1989/90.

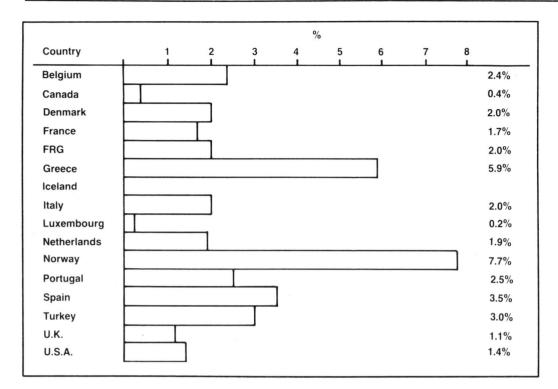

Country	%
Belgium	2.4%
Canada	0.4%
Denmark	2.0%
France	1.7%
FRG	2.0%
Greece	5.9%
Iceland	
Italy	2.0%
Luxembourg	0.2%
Netherlands	1.9%
Norway	7.7%
Portugal	2.5%
Spain	3.5%
Turkey	3.0%
U.K.	1.1%
U.S.A.	1.4%

Above: The chart shows mobilized troops as a proportion of the national population in NATO countries. Norway's figure is far greater than any other nation's.

Right: A future war would not only involve massive mechanized battles of manoeuvre, but also low-level infantry combat of a more traditional type.

brigades, two artillery regiments, 18 infantry battalions, four air defence regiments and numerous logistic units such as transport squadrons, field hospitals, supply companies and so on.

The Eastern Bloc countries also depend upon reserves. The USSR, for example, has several million reserves and

Reservists

One of the most salient points in this table is the importance of reservists to expand the standing military forces to a war footing. All countries mobilize at least some reserves in time of war, but none does better than Norway, whose reserves, once mobilized, bring the armed forces to a total of 285,000 or 7.7 per cent of the total population. To achieve the same ratio the United States would have to field a mobilized strength of 18 million and the UK 4 million.

The British Army depends especially heavily on reserves, of which there are two main types: the ex-regular soldier with a 'reserve liability' who is mobilized and posted as an individual reinforcement and the Territorial Army (TA), an organization some 75,000 strong, predominantly in formed units. The main field force is 1 (BR) Corps in Germany, which consists of some 55,000 regulars in peacetime. This is brought up to war strength by reinforcements from the UK, which include from the TA, two infantry

Right: French infantry deploy. France is a full member of NATO, but is not within the integrated military command structure.

uses the most recently demobilized primarily to bring their combat divisions to full strength. The Soviets have three categories of manning. Category A divisions are at between 75 per cent and full strength in peacetime and with full equipment of the latest type. Category B divisions are at 50–75 per cent strength in peacetime and with full combat equipment; it would take three days to man them to full strength. Category C divisions are at 20–50 per cent strength in peacetime and possess the greater part of their mobilization equipment, although much of it is probably of older types. These divisions would require seven days to man up to strength, but another 40–60 days to bring up to an acceptable standard of training. According to the London-based IISS it would take some 2,100,000 men to bring the Category B and C divisions up to full strength.

Assessing a War in Central Europe

These masses of forces could be used in a variety of ways, but it must be emphasized that nobody knows what the Third World War, should it ever occur, would be like. Some attempts have been made to discuss a possible future war in terms of developing a scenario, but this is always dangerous since the result is frequently more of a novel storyline than a serious prediction, and is always constrained by the need to tell a story. However, in order to give a 'feel' for what might happen, there now follows an examination of the various stages a possible future war in Europe might pass through and what might occur at various levels of command.

For clarity, attention is concentrated on the Central Front, but this is not to underrate the importance of the Northern and Southern Flanks, nor of the Atlantic.

Each possible stage of war is examined up to the crossing of the nuclear threshold. However, the war could, and, indeed, must be stopped far short of that.

War On the Central Front

If war was to break out it could be for a variety of reasons. These could range from a build-up of tension across a frontier, over territorial or ethnic disagreements, through escalating incidents at sea or in the air, to a war or incidents in some totally different area of the world (say, the Middle East), where Soviet and United States' interests clashed. Probably the most likely cause would be something totally unexpected and unpredictable: after all, who in 1981 would have been

believed if he had forecast that within months the United Kingdom and Argentina would have been locked in combat in the remote Falkland Islands?

Despite the strength of the Soviet Union's standing forces in peacetime and their present (1990) deployment in East Germany, Hungary, Czechoslovakia and Poland, they are not ready for a sudden and totally unexpected attack into Western Germany. This so-called 'cold-start scenario' is unreal and some preparation would be required, some of which would inevitably be seen. However, the problem for the threatened side is always not so much whether the signs are seen or not, but rather how to interpret them. As described in Chapter 15, the Israelis were taken by surprise by the Egyptian attack across the Suez Canal on 6 October 1973, despite their vaunted preparedness and despite a series of warning signs, such as a major Egyptian exercise, the evacuation of Soviet advisers and their families, and the sailing of Soviet ships from Egyptian ports.

NATO appears to have been taken equally by surprise by the Soviet invasion of Czechoslovakia in 1968, despite the build-up, both political (with a series of meetings between the Czech and Soviet leaderships), and militarily, with troop concentrations on the border.

NATO has explicitly stated that it is a defence organization and a pre-emptive strike by NATO on the Warsaw Pact, no matter what the provocation, is therefore out of the question. So, NATO will have to wait to be attacked and can only hope that it will obtain enough information and that it will be able to interpret the signs correctly.

Below: The United Kingdom has been totally committed to a continental defence, as was well demonstrated by these reinforcements arriving for the massive Exercise Lionheart in 1984.

Background to War

In theory a future war in Europe would start in an orderly way, with an incontravertible military threat and a series of graduated military and political responses, all accompanied by political consultations both within and between the two great alliances to try and avoid the catastrophe of war. However, wars and crises seldom follow the neat paths anticipated in peace and laid down with such authority by the planners. Nevertheless, as the crisis built up, the politicians and the military would be meeting to try to establish what was going on and endeavouring to see what could be done to prevent an escalation to war.

Every historically minded politician knows that in July and August 1914 a relatively minor and localized crisis was allowed to lead inexorably, but, with hindsight, avoidably, to the outbreak of the First World War. This was in part due to the fact that many political leaders were on their summer holidays, or in the case of the French at sea returning from a visit to Russia. It was also partly because those who were at their posts were rattled and indecisive. Finally, it was because the politicians found themselves the victims of the unyielding pressures of the military staffs' mobilization and deployment plans.

In those days the primary means of deployment were the railroads, supplemented in the case of the United Kingdom and

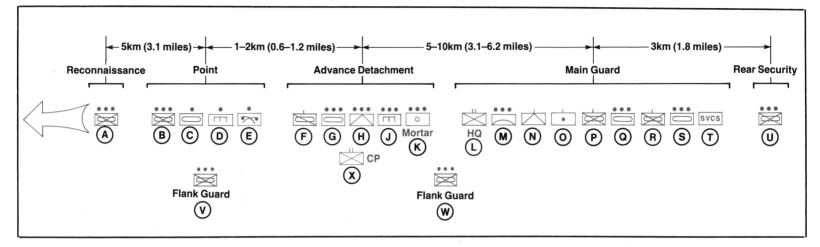

Above: A Soviet Motor Rifle Battalion Advancing: A Possible Deployment. In this situation a Soviet motor rifle battalion is advancing right to left, acting as the advance guard for a motor rifle division. An MR platoon (A) is well forward in the reconnaissance role, although there may be divisional reconnaissance troops even further forward.

Next is the 'Point', consisting of an MR platoon (B), tank section (C), engineer section (D) and chemical troops detachment (E).

The Advance Detachment is a reconnaissance company (F), a tank platoon (G), anti-tank platoon (H), engineer platoon (J) and a 120mm motor platoon (K).

The balance of the units are in the Main Guard. This includes battalion HQ (L), an air defence platoon (ZSV-23-4) (M), anti-tank company (N), artillery company (O), two MR companies (P) and (R), two tank platoons (Q) and (S), and the battalion's Rear Services (T).

One MR platoon serves as Rear Guard (U) and two more platoons as Flank Guards (V) and (W).

Command is exercised by the MR battalion commander at his Command Post (X), where he is accompanied by the artillery commander and, probably, the engineer commander as well. The CP will move well forward to be able to react quickly to any checks to the advance.

Note that distances are flexible and the composition of the elements will change to suit the tactical situation. At least a platoon of attack helicopters (HIND) will usually be placed under the battalion commander's orders.

France, by ships to move troops from England and North Africa to the Continent. The military staffs' timetables for the requisitioning of trains and the movement of men and material were considered unalterable. As a result, the politicians were brought under unremitting pressure to give the orders for mobilization by their general staffs and once one country mobilized the others had to follow suit within hours or else face, in the opinion of the staffs, almost certain defeat.

In the latter part of the 20th century aircraft have replaced trains, and it may well be that the aircraft timetable has replaced the railroad timetable of earlier times. Undoubtedly there will be too few aircraft for the tasks available – in both NATO and the Eastern Bloc countries – and staffs will be pressing the politicians for action, for decisions and for authority to mobilize and deploy. It is absolutely correct, and an inalienable aspect of life in both East and West, that the politicians make the crucial decisions affecting the safety and defence of the state, and these would be the most momentous decisions politicans have ever had to make. The pressures upon them are likely to be immense.

A further factor is that in both East and West there are not only national pressures but also alliance pressures to be taken into account. The USSR currently dominates the Warsaw Pact even more strongly than does the USA in NATO, but both would have to ensure that their partners proceeded at an equal pace, for in both alliances the members are interdependent and military plans are posited on the participation of all members; thus, there is no scope for one nation to opt out at the last minute.

The War Starts

Since NATO is committed not to react militarily until an act of aggression has actually taken place, our hypothetical war starts with the Soviet armed forces streaming onto Western European territory, with similar advances along a large number of axes. The Soviets ensure that these opening blows are as heavy as possible in order to derive the maximum initial advantage. The opening hours are characterized by heavy air strikes against critical targets, the most important of which, from the Soviet point of view, are the NATO nuclear delivery systems; i.e. strike airfields, nuclear artillery and rocket (e.g. Lance) deployment areas, and known nuclear weapon storage sites.

The Soviet land forces carry out a number of *desant* (envelopment) operations, in which helicopter-borne forces are sent deep into NATO territory to seize critical bridges and defiles. They are met at their landing areas by *Spetsnaz* (Soviet special forces) guides, who have infiltrated into NATO territory days, and in some cases weeks, earlier, disguised as long-distance truck drivers, tourists, visiting academics and the like. The highly trained Spetsnaz operate in small groups and, besides acting as guides, have many tasks of their own to conduct.

The Soviet forces drive as hard as they can to maintain the momentum. Commanders at every level are well forward, so that as soon as the advance is held up they can immediately take action to get it going again. Battalion commanders bring forward their second echelon companies, regimental commanders their second echelon battalions, and so on.

On the NATO side the progress of the first days of the battle depends upon how much warning they have received and how well they had been able to deploy, as a result. Those who have moved fast enough are in their planned defensive positions, with the infantry digging their positions as hard as they can go and engineers out in front using their mechanized minelayers to lay as many fields as they can before the enemy closes in. Forward of all these, reconnaissance troops, using light tanks, armoured cars and helicopters, are trying to find the advancing enemy and the direction of his thrusts.

In among all this the civilian population watch their televisions, listen to their radios, and telephone friends and people in authority trying to find out what is going on and asking what they should do. Some stay put, preferring the seeming certainty and familiarity of home, family and neighbours to the uncertainty of a trek to the West. Hordes of others, however, ignore the advice of the authorities and set out for the apparent safety of the Atlantic coast, although what they will do when they get there is not entirely clear. Thus, the roads, even the multilane autobahns, quickly fill up with refugees going West on one side and troops going to war on the other. Often the two moving masses pass each other in endless slow-moving columns heading in opposite directions like a German autobahn on a normal, sunny, summer weekend. But, at first occasionally, and thereafter with increasing frequency the two columns tangle, causing traffic blocks which rapidly become targets for attacking aircraft. Sometimes the military escape from these by simply sending tracked vehicles off across the fields, but most military vehicles are wheeled and their cross-country mobility, especially

when they are heavily loaded and the ground is soft, is very limited.

In the rear areas on both sides reinforcements pour in, in accordance with the plans so carefully made and so assiduously practised in peacetime. On the NATO side Dutch, Belgian and French reinforcements and reservists hasten to join their wartime units in the FRG, and in all continental countries reserve battalions and brigades form up, ready for their homeland defence tasks. In the United Kingdom the Territorial Army is called up once the political processes have been complied with, and the units form, some to go overseas to Germany, others to deploy to defend the home country. In the USA the regular units earmarked for NATO rush to the airfields to board aircraft and head for their deployment areas, picking up their war equipments, such as tanks, guns and vehicles, from huge depots as they arrive. Not only do the regular army and air force deploy from the USA, but also the reserves and the Army and Air Force National Guard.

Battle is Joined

The psychological effects of participating in what is clearly the opening phase of the Third World War are difficult to predict. The military are helped by the fact that, at least in the deployment phase, they are repeating well-practised drills and deploying through countryside they know reasonably well. At least for a while it seems like a slightly more realistic than usual exercise, but with extra pressure from above to deploy quickly.

The first engagements, however, come as a very rude and violent shock. As described elsewhere in this book, the effectiveness of modern weapons is much greater than those used in the Second World War. Further, the quantity of equipment on the Central Front and the means of concentrating heavy fire on a particular target will all combine to ensure that the effect is infinitely greater even than has been seen in recent wars in the Middle East and in Vietnam. Thus, an infantry company (of either side) which suddenly comes under fire from a regiment of artillery on the other side,

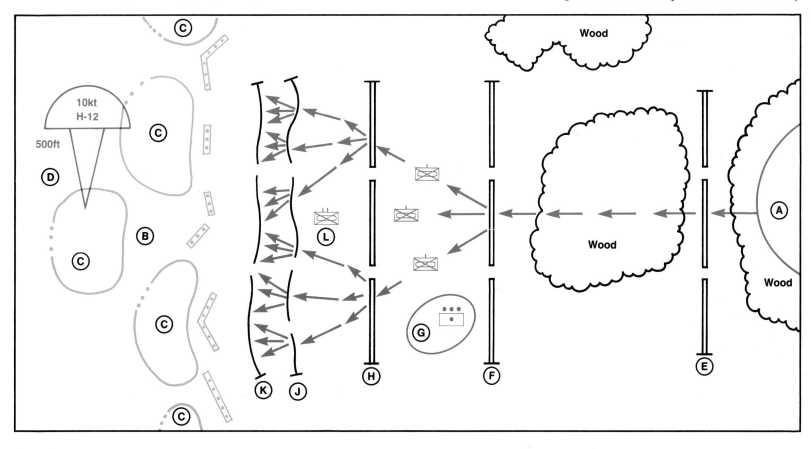

Above: **Soviet Motor Rifle Battalion Attacking Enemy Position from the March.** A Soviet motor rifle battalion at (A) detects a well dug-in enemy position at (B), consisting of platoon positions (C), each reinforced by tanks and anti-tank weapons and with minefields laid in front of the forward position. At H hour minus 12 minutes a 10 kT nuclear air burst (D) is exploded, fired by a divisional artillery 152mm howitzer. The motor rifle

battalion leaves the departure area (A), crosses the departure line (E) in column and at the 'line for deployment into company columns' (F) shakes out, with the lead company going left, the second company going right, battalion headquarters going straight on, and the third company moving slowly and centrally to act as the second echelon in the attack. The battalion mortars take up position just off the line of march (G).

At the 'line of deployment into platoon columns' (H), the two first echelon companies shake out yet again and then once more into section columns at the next line (J), finally crossing the 'line for going over to attack' (K) in line abreast. The attack is controlled by battalion headquarters (L) and engineers will be up with the leading vehicles to breach the minefields. Supporting fire will come from the Regimental Artillery Group.

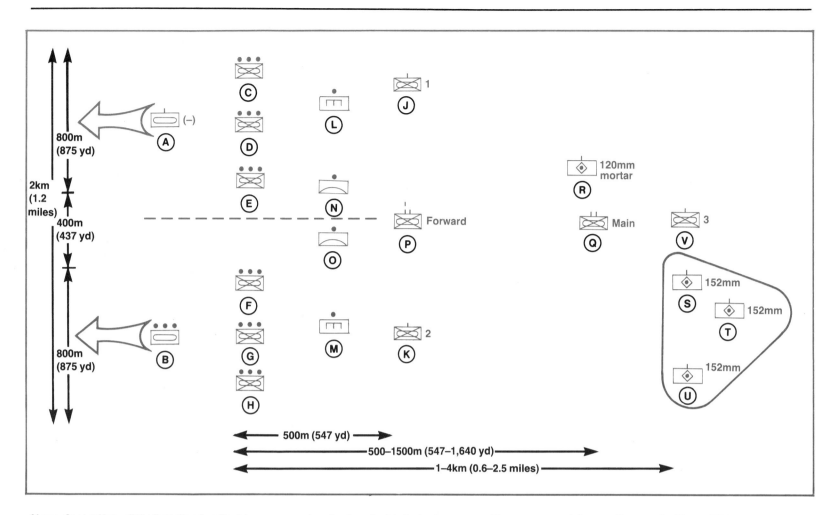

Above: Soviet Motor Rifle Battalion in a Rapid **Mounted Attack.** In this situation a motor rifle battalion has deployed from the line of march to carry out a quick attack and is attacking to the left of the diagram. The first echelon comprises a company of tanks and two motor rifle companies, with engineer and air defence sections under command. There is also an artillery battalion (18 152mm SP howitzers) and a heavy mortar company (six 120mm mortars).

Leading the attack is the tank company with company HQ and 2 tank platoons on the right (A) and the third platoon on the left (B). The two motor rifle companies in the first echelon have their platoons in line (C), (D), (E), (F), (G), (H), with company HQs about 500m behind them, (J), (K). Immediately behind the MR platoons are a section of engineers, (L), (M), ready to help to maintain the momentum of the attack should obstacles be met. There are also two sections of air

defence artillery, each with one ZSV-23-4.

The battalion forward command post (P) with the battalion commander and the artillery commander is well forward, keeping a tight grip on the battle, while the battalion main HQ (Q) is following. The 120mm mortar company (R) is deployed as are the companies of the 152mm howitzer battalion (S), (T), (U). The second echelon, the third company (V) is moving in column, awaiting orders to deploy if necessary.

Above: West German Marder IFV waits behind cover. NATO armies have successfully watched the borders for 40 years.

Left: Soldiers of a West German Panzer-grenadier battalion covering a road during NATO exercise 'Tartan Vandal'.

will suffer a devastating experience and casualties will be high.

Another factor which has an effect from early on is the pace of events. The Soviet land forces thrust as hard as possible for a breakthrough while the NATO forces are deploying and redeploying in repeated efforts to stop them. This, combined with the movement capabilities of modern equipment and with the many devices which enable movement, observation and fighting to be done in the hours of darkness, induces extreme fatigue within days of the outbreak of hostilities.

For the Eastern Bloc forces this is not so serious, as long as their concept of second and third echelon forces continues to work. In this system the force moves forward with layers (echelons) of balanced divisions and armies stretching back to the rear areas. Thus, when the leading division or army becomes bogged down, the next echelon simply passes through complete to break through whatever is holding up the advance and regain the monentum. Then, when that echelon is held up the next echelon passes through, and so on. The same can, of course, also be done when the forward units are tired. After six days, however, the NATO operational concept of

Follow-On Forces Attack (FOFA), in which they have concentrated air and artillery attacks on the second and third echelons, has temporarily frustrated the enemy.

For NATO, however, there are no second and third echelons. Some divisions have been held back in reserve, but there are quite insufficient resources of manpower and equipment to permit the regular replacement of units suffering from combat fatigue.

Whatever the neat diagrams that appear on commanders' maps in peacetime with their bold thrust lines or impregnable defences (depending which side they are on) the actual war proves to be extremely untidy. Some Soviet land thrusts have been very effective, penetrating deep into NATO defences, but others have been held, even turned back.

There are pockets of forces on both sides which have become cut off, surrounded by units of the other side. Many communications systems have worked well, but others have broken down and commanders no longer know where many units or formations are, what state they are in, or even, in some cases, whether they still exist.

While all this fighting is going on the logistics services have been conducting their own struggle. There is absolutely no doubt that the demands on the logistics services will be even greater than the most pessimistic peacetime forcecast. As the battles intensify, hard-pressed commanders have called for ever-increasing fire support from the artillery, who have the manpower, guns and launchers, as well as the desire to meet the requests. At first they carry out the fire missions, as the shells, rockets or missiles are available to enable them to do so. However, this ability rapidly diminishes, not through a lack of willingness, but because of the resupply situation. Nor are the logistics services reluctant to help, but their problem lies in getting the shells, rockets or missiles forward in time and in sufficient quantity. The roads have become increasingly crowded with both military and civilian vehicles and enemy

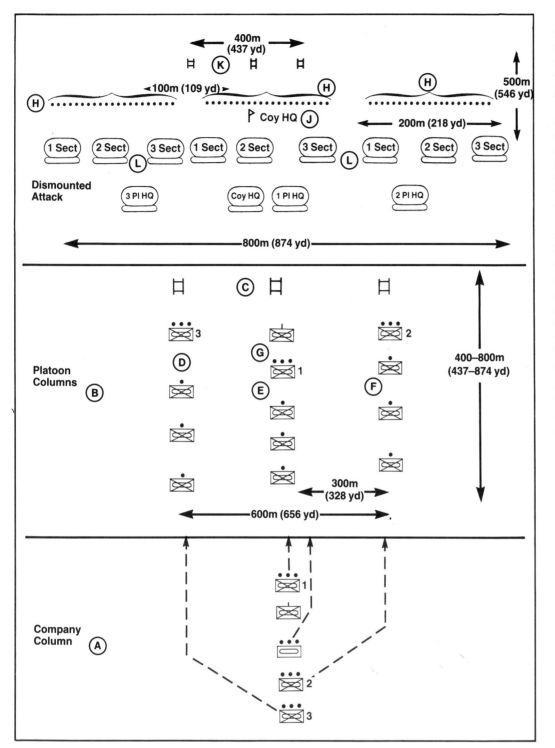

At the various levels of headquarters there is furious activity trying to control the battle. Much energy is devoted to the two apparently simple tasks of knowing where their own troops and the enemy are.

Headquarters' problems in this respect are made more severe by the rigid application of Murphy's Second Law, which dictates that they are overwhelmed with information about units which are irrelevant to their particular battle and quite unable to obtain information on some of the units that really matter to them.

Headquarters are often declared to be primary targets for each side's air and artillery strikes, but it is arguable that this might not necessarily be so, as in the case in our scenario. Throughout this conventional phase of the war there is an ever-present threat of the use of nuclear weapons and there is also much activity to try to prevent this from happening. This being so, both sides seem to have a tacit agreement that one of the best guarantees of keeping the situation under control, and particularly of ensuring that low-level units do not somehow take the initiative to use such weapons (assuming that the controls are such as to enable them to do so), is to maintain the proper command chain. So, to date no division, corps, army or front headquarters has been attacked.

The Pace Quickens

As the pace of the war quickens, several things happen. Firstly, the confusion increases and the two sides become ever more closely entwined, with commanders finding it increasingly difficult to discover where their own units are. The 'front' proves very difficult to identify and fighting is taking place in the most unlikely places, some of it far to the rear. Special forces such as the Soviet Spetsnaz cause chaos either by their physical presence or by rumours. One of their known modes of operation is to wear NATO uniforms and soon many soldiers and airmen wearing a strange uniform or driving an unrecognized vehicle (a not unlikely situation in a multi-national alliance, especially once reservists begin to deploy) are suspected of being a potential enemy.

Aircraft flying overhead at high speed and low altitude are visible from the ground for only a very brief period and thus the time available for recognition is extremely short. So, many units which have once been hit by an air attack prove very likely, whatever the orders, to fire first at any approaching aircraft with every available weapon, and to ask questions afterwards.

Above: **Soviet Motor Rifle Company in the Attack.**
A Motor Rifle company advances in Compan Column (A). On deployment to Platoon Column (B) the Tank Platoon moves into the lead (C), followed by the company in three platoon columns, with Platoon HQ leading (D), (E), (F). Company Headquarters (G) is well ahead to take control if resistance is encountered.

On deployment for a dismounted attack the platoon forms up in line (H) with Company Headquarters (J) also dismounted in the centre, with the tank platoon ahead (K). The empty IFVs follow behind (L) using their cannon to give supporting fire.

air attacks have not only severely damaged the roads and created obstacles in towns and villages, but have also increasingly prevented movement by day.

Similarly, the fuel consumption of the forward troops has been enormous and the logistics services have been under ever-greater pressure to produce more fuel. The same problems of crowded and damaged roads have applied. Over all this hangs the spectre of tanks unable to move because they have no fuel, of guns that have no shells and missile launchers with no missiles.

Associated with this is a lack of information from above as to what has happened so far in other parts of the battlefield, what is going on at the time and what is intended for the future. Inevitably, rumours have started to circulate among those with time to spare, and anxiety over families and friends has increased as time goes by and especially as refugees and local inhabitants appear increasingly distressed.

Some units are decimated through casualties, others become combat ineffective, but through exhaustion rather than actual losses due to wounds and death. At all levels and on both sides there are anxieties about what will happen next. Hanging over everyone is the fear of chemical weapons and of nuclear weapons not far behind.

More equipment is beginning to go wrong and it is becoming more difficult to carry out repairs for want of spare parts and/or tools. Supplies of stores and replacements from the rear have started to dry up, and some items have become totally unavailable.

A Field Headquarters

At a field headquarters of a mechanized infantry battle group, the atmosphere is one of grim determination coupled with extreme tiredness. The triumvirate of infantry, artillery and tank commanders feel that they have known each other all their lives, and they have a feeling of total interdependence and mutual trust beyond anything they knew in peace. They are very, very tired as they try to fight their battle, with two enemies, one in front and firing at them, and one (known collectively as 'them') behind, who give the battle group confusing orders, starve them of information and fail to deliver the ammunition and supplies they so desperately need.

The headquarters is depleted through casualties; some of these have been replaced but many simply left a gap which has to be filled by those who remain. They are short of one or two vehicles, as well, due to breakdowns and damage. Bathing has long since ceased apart from a perfunctory wash in the morning and the primary purpose of shaving would be to ensure an airtight seal on the respirator rather than for any other reason.

When the tactical situation permits there are visitors to the HQ from the subordinate HQs, seeking information, resupplies and reassurance. However, the air situation and the chaotic roads prevent the endless stream of visitors which characterize a peacetime exercise.

The keynote in every activity at the headquarters is 'unity of purpose', since

Above: Instead of the armoured warfare so widely predicted and prepared for, it may be that a future war could be fought by light, highly mobile infantry.

they have long since discovered that while they belong to different arms (infantry, armour, artillery) in peace, live in different barracks and even wear different badges, in war they have to act as one, because none can survive without the other.

If they have time to stop and reminisce after a week of fighting, perhaps they would concentrate first on the effectiveness of enemy artillery, whose volume of fire, accuracy and speed of response to any movement has come as a complete surprise, as well as causing a lot of casualties. In particular an attack on the fourth day using anti-tank minelets mixed with anti-personnel minelets has given them a traumatic experience, especially as pre-war technical intelligence said that the Soviets would not field such weapons for another five years. Also, it has taken them a few days to realize that one of the reasons for the rapid artillery attacks was that their radio nets were being monitored and their transmitters located. After that the amount of 'chatter' on the radios reduces dramatically.

Another surprise has been acting as spectators to a helicopters versus tanks engagement in which US Army AH-64s came in to blunt a Soviet Army attack. Having been warned of their arrival, the

battle group thought little of the helicopters' chances, but are proved wrong as the ugly aircraft taking shelter behind every dip and bush destroy one tank after another using their Hellfire missiles, before using their cannon on the accompanying BMP-1s. The battlefield ends up littered with burning tank and IFV hulks, with columns of black smoke adding to the general dirty atmosphere that covers the area.

During a short spell in reserve the battle group is sent off to clear a village, in which Spetsnaz have been reported. Trained in FIBUA (Fighting in Built-Up Areas) the battle group's infantry clears one house after another while the tanks remain outside covering the main exits. To their astonishment they find a few members of the civil population still sheltering in the cellars, eking out an existence on a dwindling store of food and hoping that the war will go away soon. Then they encounter the Spetsnaz and a nasty fight ensues which involves clearing each house room by room, and eliminating each member of the Soviet group one by one until there are none left. In the end it transpires that eight Spetsnaz have tied down a complete battalion for an entire day and caused 18 deaths and ten wounded.

The Air Battle

The war in the skies above the Central Front is as vicious as any ever fought. The battles start with each air force carrying out heavy attacks on the other's airfields, seeking to break up runways, make repair facilities unusable and destroy any aircraft on the ground. Some attacks are successful, others not. Some aircraft survive because they are in the air, others because they have deployed to field sites (although this can only apply to helicopters and the RAF Harrier) and a few because they have moved to operating sites on the autobahns. Thereafter the

demands for air support from the ground troops is insatiable and the aircraft fly all the hours they, their aircrews and ground crews are capable of. The process of attrition, however, is rapid. Ground defences take a heavy toll as the aircraft fly over the densest air defences ever known, bolstered almost inevitably by virtually every firearm the ground troops can bring to bear.

The weapons used by modern aircraft look awesome when demonstrated in ones and twos in peacetime, but dropped repeatedly and in large numbers in war, their effect is stunning. Bombs using fuel-air explosives, bombs containing large amounts of 'old-fashioned' high explosive or napalm, bombs dropping hundreds of deadly anti-personnel and anti-tank minelets, rockets, stand-off bombs, homing missiles – the range of weapons is great and they are all intended to attack targets on the ground. It is,

therefore, hardly surprising that ground troops begin to assume that any aircraft is hostile until proved friendly.

Politics

By this stage the politicians and civil service officials have also become very tired, a different sort of tiredness from the soldiers in the fighting units maybe, but their almost constant activities throughout the crisis and the war have taken their toll. At NATO headquarters outside Brussels the NATO Committee, the political body of ambassadors chaired by the Secretary-General, has been in

Below: Swedish soldiers fire Bofors RBS-70. Their country has remained firmly neutral in two wars, but such a stance requires constant vigilance and strength.

almost constant session, as, too, has the International Military Committee under its chairman, the senior military man in the Alliance. Their attention has been taken up by three major considerations.

First is the actuality of the current crisis as the red lines representing the progress of Warsaw Pact forces creep across the huge wall maps and reserves become fewer and fewer. The French armed forces have long since been committed, performing their vital role of counter-attack forces, amounting, in effect, to NATO's third echelon of defence. There have been reports of military disasters tempered by a few triumphs, but, above all, of a thin line being stretched ever thinner as losses mount and supplies become ever more difficult. The latter situation has arisen both because of the military situation and because peacetime calculations and budgetary considerations led to an underestimating of the requirements (sometimes deliberately so).

Second is the pressure to look for some way of bringing a halt to the hostilities, a field in which advice has not been lacking. It has come from the United Nations, where the representatives of the warring nations still meet in the same debating chambers and committee rooms.

It has also come from the national capitals of the Alliance, since even in war members are entitled to represent their individual national views, even though they have handed over actual command of the bulk of their military forces. It has also come from uninvolved countries, both because they genuinely want to stop the Europeans tearing each other apart yet again, and because they know that if the nuclear threshold were to be crossed, the damage and radiation would affect them, too. To be neutral or to declare a 'nuclear-free zone' does not put up any sort of barrier to nuclear fall-out!

That is the third and largest factor of all, because if Eastern Bloc progress continues any further there will be no choice but to use nuclear weapons. Successive SACEURs (Supreme Allied Commander Europe) have declared openly that the imbalance of forces is such that they would be able to hold the Warsaw Pact for about 14 to 21 days in a conventional war, but that thereafter they would have no choice but to use nuclear weapons.

So, as the days pass and the battles rage across Europe, on the Northern and Southern flanks and on the Atlantic, with NATO winning in some areas, holding its own in others, but losing in the crucial Central Front, the calculations start.

Above: Danish reconnaissance soldier maintains his watch during an exercise in Jutland. European nations will continue the watch for many years to come.

Officials prepare, Presidents and Prime Ministers consult, warnings are issued, deadlines are set and, in the military units the preparations start.

The Nuclear Equation

As the battles progress further, the reports coming into the higher headquarters of both NATO and the Eastern Bloc are increasingly urgent. On the Eastern Bloc side the generals are demanding one more push to break through the final NATO resistance, and on the NATO side the generals are demanding one last desperate stand to prevent that breakthrough. For both, their forces tired and over-extended, their equipment losses growing daily and their supply situation becoming ever more desperate, nuclear weapons appear to be the only way of averting military disaster.

Nobody, whether military, civil servant or politician, doubts the gravity of that decision, because the nuclear threshold is a crucial barrier, instantly recognizable, and which, once crossed, places everybody concerned in a new era. The decision-makers are faced with terrible choices. One is a massive tactical strike aimed at the destruction of such a large element of the opponent's forces that their military potential will end. Another choice is to launch just one or two nuclear weapons as a 'demonstration' of potential and determination, and a clear warning of the gravity of the situation. But, on one hand the large-scale tactical strike could be misinterpreted as a strategic strike leading to a massive strategic response, while on the other hand the 'warning shot' could be taken to be the preliminary to a strategic attack and invoke the same response, with the enemy getting his retaliation in first. There is also the possibility that, having been the victim of a 'demonstration', the enemy might consider that he, too, had to fire off an equal number of nuclear rounds to achieve some sort of parity of destruction before agreeing to consider a halt to hostilities.

But this is all unknown territory. Doubtless the two alliances have their plans, but the one thing certain about military plans made in peacetime is that they never quite fit the situation that arises in war.

Right: Nuclear war would be the terrible price to pay for failure to maintain the peace, crossing a threshold into an unknown and appalling territory.

A Conventional Possibility?

There are, of course, almost endless possibilities in the course a future war in Central Europe might follow. One obvious, but sometimes overlooked possibility is that the war would not cross the nuclear threshold at all. In other words, that in some way the two sides would deter each other from using nuclear weapons, just as in the Second World War all the major combatant nations (the USA, UK, USSR, Germany, Italy and Japan) possessed very deadly chemical weapons but never used them.

If the Soviet Union were to attack, one possible outcome, at least in the short-term, is that the NATO forces would eventually stop their advance by conventional means alone. If this were to occur the two sides might then face each other like two exhausted heavyweight boxers in the 14th round of a championship fight, spending most of the time sagging against each other, exchanging the occasional weak blow, but too tired to do anything more. Neither would be able to knock the other out (or even down), but both would remain determined, nevertheless, to see it through to the end of the final round. By the time such a stalemate was achieved the Eastern Bloc forces could be well inside the territories of the Federal Republic and Denmark, and possibly also of Holland, of Turkey and Greece in the south, and Norway in the north.

The death and destruction done up to this point would have been devastating, though only conventional weapons alone had been used. In the early stages air attacks would have concentrated on purely military targets such as airfields and troop concentrations, but they would then have switched to towns and villages as enemy forces took up position there. These attacks would have extended well into the rear areas on both sides as they attacked logistic supply lines, reserve troop concentrations and, in the case of NATO follow-up forces attacks (FOFA), the Warsaw Pact second and third echelons.

The latest weapons would cause not only blast damage but also start large-scale fires, which would sweep through entire districts. Artillery guns, mortars and rockets would also cause immense damage as they attacked any target where troops might be taking up position. Thus, farms, barns and woods would be swept with fire and destroyed.

Right: The conventional forces in NATO are currently strong and might bring an attack to a halt; but what then?

Wherever the front-line placed itself would be even more devastated in the sheer intensity of the fighting, as tank battles and mounted infantry attacks raged across the area. Although it is very difficult to make an objective assessment, the evidence of modern combat elsewhere (such as in the Middle East, for example) suggests that in a future European conventional war the fighting would cause a level of damage in weeks that in the Second World War took five years to achieve.

If it were to transpire that NATO did eventually hold the Eastern Bloc by such conventional means, it seems probable that the two sides would take up entrenched positions facing each other while they recovered from their exhaustion and tried to work out what to do next. In other words, it could be a repeat of the First World War, where NATO would find itself having lost a significant area and unable to push the Eastern Bloc forces out of it, and thus the enemy would find itself with its objectives only partially achieved, and unable to go forward, but unwilling to give up what had been gained.

There would then be a number of alternatives. One would be, as in the First World War, to batter away on the Central Front until attrition, a new weapons system or new tactics caused one side or the other to give way. Another would be, as in the Second World War, to gradually weaken the enemy on the flanks, before attacking his central fortress with multi-pronged attacks from several directions simultaneously. However, either of these courses would not dispel the ever-present threat of the use of nuclear weapons, since the third possible course would be to use nuclear weapons to break the stalemate. The fourth solution, therefore, would be to return to political negotiations.

Above right: Danish anti-tank detachment, part of the huge anti-tank defences fielded by NATO to counter the threat.

Right: German Leopard 1s. The consequences of battles between modern armoured forces, supported by highly efficient artillery and tactical air forces, in Central Europe would be worse than anything seen before. Damage would be on a scale and of a severity that can scarcely be imagined, without even one nuclear weapon being used.

LIMITED WAR OPERATIONS

For three generations the greatest apparent military threat has been that of a general war, in which the Western countries, centred on NATO, would find themselves pitted against the Communist bloc, under the control of the Soviet-dominated Warsaw Pact, in an all-out global war. The primary theatre in such a war, at least initially, would be Central Europe and it would involve an ever-present threat of escalation to nuclear war. However, such a war has so far been prevented, almost certainly due to the existence of the two alliances (NATO and the Warsaw Pact) and their mutual balance, and now appears an even more remote possibility than before.

What has happened, however, has been an unbroken series of wars. At one end of the scale of conflicts has been those between nations, such as between Iran and Iraq, Israel and Egypt, the United States and North Vietnam, China and North Vietnam and the United Kingdom and Argentina, to name but a few. At the other, lower, end of the scale, has been an equally unending series of protracted domestic conflicts, of which selected examples are those in South Africa, Nicaragua, Angola, Mozambique, Malaya, Cyprus, Algeria, Laos and Cambodia. As stated in the Introduction, at a conservative estimate some ten million people have died in these post–1945 wars, all of which took place in what is frequently but very mistakenly described as 'peacetime'.

Although fought at a high intensity on the battlefield, all these wars have been limited by mutual (usually implicit) agreement, although on occasions the limits have been very explicitly identified. In the Korean War, for example, fought between the United Nations forces on one side and the North Koreans and Communist China on the other, and which lasted from 1951 to 1953, the limit of operations for the United Nations forces was set at the Yalu River. However, General Douglas MacArthur, a

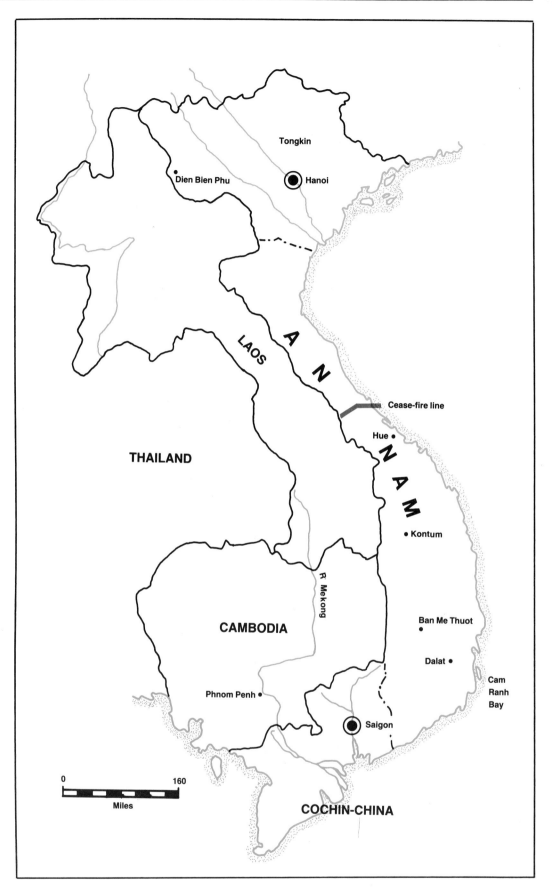

very successful American commander in the Second World War and by this stage the UN Commander in Korea, considered this to be unreasonable. He wanted to use conventional heavy bombers to attack Chinese bases in Manchuria and he

Above: From the Japanese invasion in 1941 until today Indochina has been the scene of constant conflict. Even now the end is not in sight and still foreign powers try to intervene, despite the stern and unhappy lessons of past involvements.

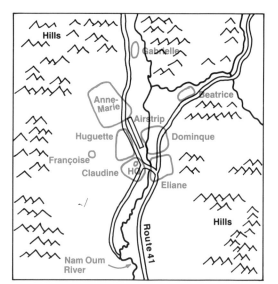

A March 1954: The French Defences

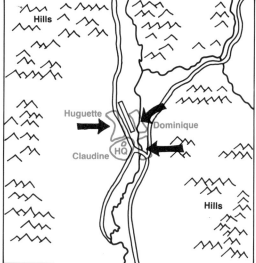

B Early April 1954: The Viet Minh take the outposts

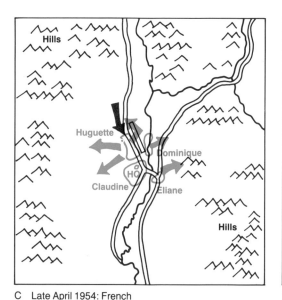

C Late April 1954: French counterattacks

D May 1954: The final positions fall

Left: **Battle of Dien Bien Phu.** The Battle of Dien Bien Phu was one of the most important battles of the 20th century and the first in which 'revolutionaries' took on a major army in pitched battle and defeated it. The French had set up camp at Dien Bien Phu in November 1953 with the aim of providing a base for operations against the Viet Minh. The commander, de Castries, set up a series of strong points (Map A) to protect the crucial airfield and its approaches. They were all girls' names, reputedly those of de Castries' former mistresses!

The Viet Minh, under General Vo Nguyen Giap assembled a massive force and attacked in March 1954, overrunning Beatrice (13 March), Gabrielle (15 March), Anne-Marie and Françoise (17 March). The totally unexpected deployment of Viet Minh anti-aircraft guns on the hills around Dien Bien Phu and the constantly contracting perimeter made air drops very difficult but nevertheless large numbers of men and a diminishing stream of supplies were dropped in.

By April it was clear that Dien Bien Phu must fall and some gallant French counter-attacks in late April (Map C) did little but to delay the inevitable by a few days. The Viet Minh combined heavy artillery bombardments with an almost medieval style of 'sapping', gradually but inexorably extending their trenchworks.

During the night of 6–7 May the last Viet Minh attack forced the French back into a central area around de Castries' HQ and at 1630 hours on 7 May the French ceased to resist (they did not surrender). The French garrison of some 11,000 men was captured and sent to prisoner-of-war camps and their defeat was total.

The defeat also made the French position in Indochina untenable and they relinquished their colonies shortly afterwards, but above all it showed that the old Western domination of the Third World was finished.

Below left: **A column of South African Ratel APCs. Fighting in southern Africa has been virtually continuous for 30 years.**

also wanted to unleash Chinese Nationalist forces on the mainland, both these actions being intended to distract the Chinese Communists from their attacks in Korea. The United States President, Harry Truman, was not, however, prepared to continue with a general who did not accept the limitations set by the political leadership and sacked him on 11 April 1951.

In other wars the limits have been less publicly set, but nonetheless clear. Thus, in the Falkland War in 1982 the British and Argentines confined their military actions to the Falklands Islands, South Georgia and the seas around them. In the Iran/Iraq War the limits were set for the first few years at the territorial borders of the two protagonists, but later they started to spread the conflict into international waters in the Persian Gulf and attacked neutral shipping. As a result a number of nations deployed warships to the area to protect shipping and to indicate to both countries that they had arrived at the limits of what others were prepared to accept.

The means, too, have been limited in the sense that nuclear weapons have never been used. The only known occasion when the use of atomic (not at that

Above: British 105mm Light Gun in the 1982 Falklands War. The war blew up out of nowhere in the space of a few weeks.

Left: Royal Marine Commandos stride the last mile into Port Stanley at the end of the Falklands War. Their faces show the strain of a short but violent campaign.

time nuclear) weapons was seriously considered was during the French war in Indochina (1947–54). In late 1953 a large element of the French Expeditionary Force became cut off in a remote northern valley at a village called Dien Bien Phu. Surrounded by the Viet Minh forces commanded by General Vo Nguyen Giap, it soon became clear that defeat was inevitable and in mid-March 1954 the French turned to the United States for help. Very careful consideration was given to the use of atomic bombs against the columns of Viet Minh troops and porters moving towards the battlefield, but the plan was dropped and the garrison eventually fell on 7 May 1954.

The other limitation accepted by most nations is that chemical and biological weapons should not be used; indeed, this is specifically banned by the protocol 'for the Prohibition of the Use In War of Asphyxiating, Poisonous or Other Gases and of Bacteriological methods of Warfare', which was signed in Geneva in 1925 and is still in effect. As far as is known biological weapons have not been used, but chemical weapons certainly have, as is described below.

Certain areas of the world are far more war-intensive than others. The Middle East has been the scene of almost constant conflict since 1949, as has South-East Asia. Other areas seem more liable to sporadic outbreaks of war, such as the Indian sub-continent and Africa, while Latin American countries are far more likely to suffer from internal strife than conflict between nations.

Colonial Wars

At the end of the Second World War the major empires still existed, but the granting of independence to India by the United Kingdom in 1947 signalled the start of the dissolution process. Many countries gained their independence with little fuss and certainly without conflict, but in numerous other cases wars, some of them quite lengthy, were involved. Unfortunately, the legacy of the colonial period in several areas is one of instability and continuing conflict. In Indo-China, for example, there has scarcely been a day free of war since the Viet Minh rose against the French in 1947.

There are few colonial territories of the 19th century type left. Hong Kong and Macau are both promised to be returned to China, and it would seem possible that an agreement on Gibraltar could be achieved within a few years. South Africa is, however, one major country left over from the colonial era whose future seems to involve continued strife unless the release of Nelson Mandela brings about a major change. The conflict there has been in progress for some years and is following the classical anti-colonial pattern, with the African National Congress (ANC) (now legalized) establishing itself politically and militarily abroad and carrying out small-scale, but high-publicity

attacks inside South Africa. As has been shown in other countries, this is the sort of campaign a group such as the ANC can keep up for many years at little overall cost; money will be forthcoming from foreign backers and there will never be a shortage of volunteers.

There was never any real question of the ANC taking on the South African Army, which is one of the largest, best equipped (despite sanctions) and most efficient in Africa. But in the 1950s and 1960s there were numerous guerrilla movements whose prospects of expelling the colonial power seemed very remote, as that power was backed by an equally efficient and highly trained army, and yet most of those guerrillas won in the end. The French were defeated in Vietnam in 1954 by a force described dismissively as 'little men in black pyjamas', and were forced to leave Algeria in 1962, a country which most Frenchmen had long considered to be, both legally and emotionally, an integral part of France. The Portu-

guese, too, who had been in their African territories for some 400 years, found their will to remain sapped by apparently endless and unwinnable wars in Angola (1961–74), Mozambique (1962–74) and Portuguese Guinea (1962–74). Even where the colonial power 'won', the outcome was frequently that they still left, as happened to the British in Malaya and in Cyprus.

So, the prospects for South Africa in the long term must be unsettled and unless Mandela's release initiates dialogue towards real change, the ANC campaign could last for many years. As the Russian Empire loosens its grip slightly under President Gorbachov's twin-track policies of *glasnost* and *peres-*

Below: Egyptian tanks on the move in the Sinai Desert. The Middle East remains a tinderbox, despite repeated attempts to find peace.

troika many of the nations are starting to seek some form of autonomy. The problem for the Russians is that the more autonomy they give to any one group the more that group will want until it has full independence, and the more independence one group gets the more other groups will want the same. Whether or not any of these national groups will want to take their cause as far as open rebellion

Above: Paratroops in the Radfan mountains in Aden in 1964; one of Britain's many post-Second World War campaigns.

is another question, but they may be encouraged by two factors. One is that the Soviet Army is made up of many disparate national groups, all mixed within each unit. Thus, any Soviet force deployed to put down an insurrection would inevitably contain many soldiers who might be sympathetic to the rebels. The second reason is that the Soviet Army, for all its might, could not defeat the Afghan Mujahideen.

The War in Afghanistan (1979–89)

One of the major preoccupations of Soviet Army officers in peacetime is the study of military history in order to learn lessons from past campaigns, which they then seek to apply to current and future problems. It is, therefore, astonishing that they should have made such a colossal error by invading Afghanistan in 1979, because there were two striking examples from history which should have told them that they would almost certainly lose.

In the first place the British, the predominant superpower of the 19th century and the rulers of India up to 1947, never truly conquered Afghanistan even though it was a constant problem. In the First Afghan War (1839–42) the British invaded the country and captured Kabul, but two years later the garrison was overcome. Having capitulated, the garrison was given safe conduct to India, but in the Khyber Pass the retreating column was annihilated, virtually all the 4,500 soldiers and 12,000 refugees being

Above: Dien Bien Phu, 14 March 1954. Viet Minh artillery, located in the heights in the background, shell French positions.

Left: Southern Angola, 13 June 1980. South African troops mop up after the largest cross-border operation to date.

massacred. A handful survived captivity and one man escaped back to India. A punitive expedition stormed into Afghanistan, and captured and sacked Kabul, but then returned to India as an occupation was considered 'too hazardous'.

The British returned to Afghanistan in the Second Afghan War (1878–80) and despite losing several battles managed to defeat the Afghans at the battle of Kandahar. Nevertheless, the expeditionary force then returned to India. Another war in 1919 again led to the defeat of the Afghan armies, but once more having restored the situation, the British avoided an occupation, despite a succession of campaigns on the North-West Frontier against Pathans raiding from Afghan territory.

Thus, the British experience, doubtless written off by the Soviets as dated, imperialist and irrelevant, was that Afghanistan was best contained from outside its borders. The occupation of 1839–41 and the annihilation of the garrison was a lesson never to be forgotten and the famous painting of the lone survivor sagging in the saddle of his exhausted horse became part of British imperial folklore.

The second historical lesson which the Soviets should have heeded was the very much more recent one of the USA in Vietnam. The USA had been dragged gradually but inexorably into the affairs of the countries of Indochina and, after the French defeat and withdrawal, found themselves propping up an increasingly unpopular and corrupt regime in South Vietnam. They eventually committed armed forces and quickly found themselves unpopular both within the country they were trying to 'save' and in the world community as a whole. In the end the USA was only too pleased to escape from Indochina and was quite unable to save the government in South Vietnam when the North Vietnamese invaded in 1975. Presumably this, too, was written off by the Soviets as an experience which could not apply to them.

By all rational reckonings the Soviets should have won and, like the USA in South Vietnam, they poured huge forces into Afghanistan. In 1986 their armed forces 'in country' were estimated to comprise: three motor rifle divisions and one independent motor rifle brigade, one airborne division, one air assault brigade, Spetsnaz units and numerous combat support troops. These were supported by an air army, whose equipment included 90 Sukhoi Su-25 'Frogfoot' ground attack aircraft and 45 MiG-23 'Flogger-B' attack fighters. There were also some 140 Mi-24 'Hind' attack helicopters and 130 trans-

port helicopters, a mixture of Mi-8 'Hip' and Mi-6 'Hook'. Unlike the United States in Vietnam whose home base had been some 8,000 miles from the conflict, the Soviet Forces in Afghanistan had a sanctuary and support base immediately over the border in their own country.

Against this was arrayed a rag-tag collection of resistance fighters, whose numbers were infinitesimal in comparison to the Soviet forces. These forces were known collectively in the West as 'Mujahideen', but this gave a very misleading picture of a united group under central command. Nothing could have been further from the truth as there were some 15–20 groups (sometimes perhaps more), with alliances being formed and broken throughout the war, a situation made the more complicated by the fact that the political elements across the Pakistan border in Peshawar often made alliances which bore little relation to those being effected by the field commanders in Afghanistan. Understanding the situation was made even more difficult for foreigners because frequently several different groups were operating under the same names. In 1987, for example, there were two groups called 'Hesb-i-Islami', while a military alliance called

'Islamic Unity' represented a different grouping from a political party which was also called 'Islamic Unity'.

These military groups fought with great bravery and dogged determination, but most Western observers agree that their use of minor tactics and camouflage was abysmal, and that they suffered unnecessary casualties due to poor understanding of what a conventional Western soldier would describe as 'basic military principles'. The Mujahideen were excellent at spontaneous skirmishing, an activity at which they are unequalled and for which their country's terrain is ideally suited. They are also extremely good at commando-style raids, using hit-and-run tactics against Soviet and Afghan government outposts. However, when they attempted more conventional style operations in larger units, their inherently individualistic characteristics precluded them from success. However, they do not need to be good at conventional tactics and large unit operations, as they are so outstanding at their own method of warfare, which they have used to great effect against British, Persian and Russian invaders over the centuries, and with such success against the Soviet invaders of the 1980s.

Throughout the war the Mujahideen received a considerable amount of

Above: Soviet Su-25 Frogfoot was deployed to Afghanistan, but to little effect.

Above left: Hind-A attack helicopters were widely used in the Afghan war.

Below left: Mujahideen with a shot-down Soviet Mil Mi-8 Hip transport helicopter.

weapons, equipment and other help from Western sources. It was on nothing like the scale of Soviet and Chinese assistance to the North Vietnamese, but was nevertheless substantial. Much of the support came in the form of infantry weapons, light anti-tank weapons, ammunition and mines, but towards the end included both British Blowpipe and US Stinger shoulder-launched, surface-to-air missiles. A certain amount of training assistance was also given by various groups, but most of those involved in this activity felt that the Afghans learnt little from it, simply because the West had nothing to teach them about the tactics they themselves were so good at. The Mujahideen also followed the practice of every successful guerilla movement and captured

as much military equipment as they could, in order to put it to use against its previous owners.

As for the Soviets, they fought a war using strategies and tactics more reminiscent of the French in Indochina than of the United States in Vietnam. They garrisoned the cities and towns and travelled between them either by air or in heavily protected vehicle convoys. Operations were carried out in the countryside, but in large, armoured columns with strong air and artillery support. Thus, like the French, they failed to control the villages and totally failed to come to terms with the people of the country, apart from dominating the increasingly resentful population in the towns. Like the Americans, the Soviet Army and Air Force took military forces which were equipped and trained for general war in Europe and used them to try and fight in a completely different situation.

Soviet deaths in Afghanistan, according to the figures published in *Pravda* in July 1989, totalled 13,833. The year-by-year breakdown of fatalities is as follows:

1979 –	86	1983 – 1,446	1987 – 1,215
1980 –	1,484	1984 – 2,343	1988 – 759
1981 –	1,298	1985 – 1,868	1989 – 53
1982 –	1,948	1986 – 1,333	

Of these, 13,310 died in action and the remainder as a result of wounds, disease or accidents.

Although small by comparison with the 46,226 US troops killed in action in Vietnam, this was still a very significant figure. Some Soviet troops suffered from alcoholism and drug addiction, and eventually, as the war became increasingly unpopular at home, began to show an increasing reluctance to fight unless it was unavoidable – all of which is distinctly reminiscent of the American experience in Vietnam. Nevertheless, the Soviets learned a vast amount from the experience, which was their first actual combat in 40 years, as opposed to suppressing civil unrest, as, for example, in

Above: Soviet troops and a light tank on the streets of Kabul, 25 December 1980. Ten years later all have returned home.

Above right: Government-armed village militia men in Afghanistan; they failed to defeat the Mujahideen.

Right: A war of long ago. Wounded men are loaded aboard a Huey; Vietnam, 1967.

East Berlin (June 1953), Hungary (November 1956) and Czechoslovakia (August–October 1968). Among the major lessons they learned were the importance of initiative and determination in commanders at platoon, company and battalion level, and in the use of helicopters to support combat troops. Also, many new weapons and techniques were developed and tested in action.

Above: The Gulf War finally involved the Superpowers. These Iranian towers were shelled by US warships, 19 October 1987.

Right: Chemical agents were used during the Gulf War and this Iranian cleric (left) is taking appropriate precautions during a 1988 visit to the troops.

However, despite the size and capability of the Soviet armed forces in Afghanistan, they were never prepared to commit sufficiently large numbers nor to exercise that degree of total ruthlessness which might have brought military success. The inescapable fact is that the Mujahideen, despite what a Westerner might describe as organizational and tactical limitations, simply wore out a huge Soviet Army. As with the United States' campaign in Vietnam, the Soviet national will to win evaporated, the cost in lives and resources became too great, and they packed their impedimenta and went home. The war lasted ten years, it cost many lives on both sides and it resulted in many thousands of wounded and maimed. The Soviet Army was never defeated in a major battle, but they failed to achieve their military and political

aims – and that means, by any definition, that they lost.

The Iran–Iraq War (1980–88)

The Iran–Iraq War is of considerable interest, having been one of the longest wars of this century, lasting just one month short of eight years (20 September 1980 to 20 August 1988) and thus of greater duration than either the First World War (4 years 3 months) or the Second World War (5 years 7 months). Although the standard of generalship was notably poor, the war produced some disturbing developments, not least of which was that it showed that nations could use chemical weapons on a large scale without incurring overwhelming international opprobrium. It also demonstrated that fanaticism is no substitute for

tactical skill, as tens of thousands of young Iranians died under the muzzles of late 20th century tactical weapons. It also introduced the first long-range missile exchange. While it is true that long-range missiles were used to bombard London in 1944, the British had no similar weapon with which to respond; the Iran–Iraq war, however, was the first conflict in which both combatants were able to bombard each other's cities with missiles.

The war produced not one general of note on either side as they both blundered on with one mistaken strategy after another, never continuing with any one strategy sufficiently long to achieve a breakthrough. With some 11 million tons of shipping either sunk or declared a constructive loss (virtually all to land-based missile or aircraft attack) this was

Above: United Arab Emirates platform in the Mubarak oilfield burns after an attack by Iranian gunboats on 18 April 1988, the first attack on U.A.E. property.

the most devastating assault on merchant shipping since the Battle of the Atlantic in the Second World War; indeed, the losses were only marginally less than those of the *entire* Allied and neutral shipping lost to all causes in the First World War (11,964,185 tons). Finally, it showed that the international community could not halt a war which two sides were determined to continue and it was only when both were so exhausted that they just could not go on that they were

181

prepared to accept United Nations intervention.

The ultimate tragedy of the war, however, was that after eight years of fighting, enormous suffering, the virtual bankrupting of both economies and probably well over one million deaths, both sides ended up almost precisely where they had started.

Iraq and Iran have disliked each other for many years, with their antipathy centring on two issues: Iranian support for the Kurds in the North and Iranian claims in the Shatt-el-Arab waterway in the South. A series of treaties concerning the use of the Shatt-el-Arab were concluded between 1847 and 1937, the last of which conferred rights of free navigation to both countries (and third nation vessels), but assigned actual sovereignty over the waterway to Iraq by setting the boundary at the low-water mark on the Iranian bank. The 1937 treaty endured until 19 April 1969, when the Iranians unilaterally abrogated it. Both countries massed troops on their borders and the Iranians sent two merchant ships under naval escort up to Abadan and Khorramshahr. On this occasion hostilities were avoided, but the situation led to armed clashes five months later in September 1969, followed by more in January 1970, February and March 1974, and again from January to March 1975.

The last series of incidents resulted in the Algiers Accord, which stopped the current round of fighting, and relocated

the border along the middle of the deepest navigable channel. However, it left the Iraqis feeling very resentful and they decided to bide their time. The Shah was overthrown in 1979 and replaced by Ayatollah Khomeini and shortly afterwards Iranian fanatics tried to prove their loyalty to the new regime by attempting to subvert the Iraqi population. The obvious mutual antipathy between Iraq's President Saddam Hussein and the Ayatollah Khomeini worsened an already bad situation. With Iran in turmoil, the prospects for a quick and easy victory must have looked good to the political and military leaders in Baghdad, and the Iraqis seized the opportunity, invading on 22 September 1980.

However, Iranian resistance was more united and far fiercer than expected, leading to a stalemate, with the Iranians launching successive attacks which the Iraqis were always able to repel, although each took its toll. In 1982 Iraq sought a return to the original positions, but the Iranians, scenting victory, demanded the replacement of the Iraqi regime and a virtual formal domination of Iraq by Iran. When Iraq withdrew to the pre-war frontiers in June 1982 in the apparent hope of a ceasefire the Iranians attempted twice (in July and November) to break through the Iraqi lines and march on Baghdad but were, in their turn, stopped.

It was during these battles that, in July 1982, the Iraqis first used chemical war-

fare, on this occasion non-lethal tear gas. Although this was the first use of chemical agents in this particular war, the Iraqis were by no means the first to use teargas, which has frequently been used to disperse civil riots and had been used on several occasions in combat; e.g. by the USA in tunnel-clearing operations in South Vietnam. The Iranians were taken by surprise and it proved an effective move. It may have been this success that led Iraq to acquire manufacturing and delivery capabilities for the more dangerous chemical agents that they were to use later.

With both sides now exhausted a stalemate ensued, and the appalling conditions for the troops of both sides were frequently described by independent observers as being reminiscent of the First World War, but with the addition of intense heat. During late 1982 the first rumours of Iraqi acquisition of Soviet-manufactured SS-12 Scaleboard missiles began to circulate. In fact, the Iraqis had acquired not only SS-12s from the USSR, but also empty aircraft bombs designed to carry CW agents. The bombs were

filled with chemical agents apparently made in Iraq from raw materials obtained outside the Warsaw Pact area and were fitted with fuses obtained from yet another source.

By 1983 Iraq was not winning the war it had started, its economy was in chaos, it had few, if any, friends on the international scene, both Superpowers were remaining very strictly neutral and armaments were proving ever more difficult to obtain. In early 1984 the Iranians mounted yet another attack, with some 100,000 men advancing across the marshes north of Basra, followed a few days later by a second attack. Faced with these severe threats the Iraqis carried out their first use of lethal CW agents and brought both attacks to a halt. These lethal agents, which certainly included mustard gas and may also have included a nerve gas, Tebun (also known as GA), were not expected by the Iranians, and their troops appear to have had no training or equipment to cope with such a situation. As a result they incurred massive casualties and the attacks failed.

Once again at a stalemate, the next

Above: Iraqi troops pose for the camera after advancing ten miles into Iranian territory, 27 September 1980.

Above left: A rather casually dressed UN fact-finding mission takes samples from an unexploded Iraqi chemical shell.

Opposite: A very dejected group of Iranian prisoners-of-war face journalists in Iraq in August 1980.

phase of the war was characterized by a series of attacks on ships and installations in the Gulf. In February 1986 the Iranians seized the Faw peninsula south of Basra in an amphibious assault, which was probably the most striking tactical undertaking of the war. This was a preliminary to another attack, but the Iraqis again used chemical weapons to halt them. Iraqi air and missile attacks on Iranian cities and oil terminals continued while the Iranians prepared for yet another assault on Basra, which they launched in December 1986. This developed into a major threat to Iraq and chemical weapons were used once more, but by this time the Iranians had issued protective devices to their troops and casualties were very much fewer than before. The Iraqis had to fight very hard indeed and incur very heavy casualties before they managed to bring the Iranian advance to a halt.

Yet again a stalemate followed. Both sides were tired of war, but unwilling to give up. Iraq was running out of men and unable to mount an attack which would settle the war, while in Iran there was a failure of public morale as the war seemed to drag on and casualties mounted inexorably without any apparent possibility of a solution. Once again both sides turned to the Gulf to attack shipping and oil terminals. Foreign powers deployed warships to protect international shipping in the Gulf and the situation there was contained, if not properly controlled.

The war dragged on into 1988 and the by now annual Iranian attack on Basra in February was noticeably weaker than in former years and soon came to a halt. However, attention then switched to the north where the Iranians, in conjunction with Kurdish guerrillas (who have been fighting the Iraqis for many years), achieved a considerable success in overrunning Iraqi positions near a major reservoir, which supplied most of northern Iraq with electricity, and threatened the crucial Kirkuk oilfields. Once more the Iraqis responded with chemical weapons, against which the Iranian troops were protected and suffered little, but the unfortunate Kurdish guerrillas and civilians suffered very badly and whole communities were simply exterminated.

By now, however, the Iranians were exhausted and feelers for a ceasefire were seized upon in Baghdad as a signal to launch a counter-attack in the South which pushed the Iranians back across the border, whereupon Iran agreed to the terms of the United Nations ceasefire. The Iraqis decided at this point to settle the Kurdish insurrection once and for all, which they did in August and September using chemical agents against unprotected villages.

Not surprisingly, Kurdish casualties were high and their resistance collapsed, while yet again foreign condemnation against this quite scandalous act was muted, to say the least.

Throughout the eight years of ground fighting neither side showed generalship of any distinction, while the soldiers fought doggedly and with considerable

Above: The Gulf War spread to involve international shipping. Here the Maltese tanker *Don Miguel* burns after an attack by Iranian gunboats, 27 May 1988.

Left: Yet another weapon brought into play by the Iranians was the floating mine. These were of a very old design, but their effect was still very deadly and several ships were damaged.

Above right: The town of Abadan burns, 25 October 1980. The picture was taken from the opposite bank of the Shatt-el-Arab waterway, over which the dispute was started.

Right: Iranian revolutionary guards and a young villager pose with the remains of an Iraqi shell, which, they claimed, had contained chemical agents. Chemical weapons have been used on many occasions since the Second World War; unfortunately they are relatively easy to make.

bravery (sometimes to the point of being foolhardy) in the most unpleasant conditions. Both sides proved to be very determined in defence, which meant that the other's attacks could never totally succeed. The Iranians showed considerable daring on occasions, but were hampered by equipment shortages and poor logistics, while the regime's distrust of the regular army and its encouragement of the revolutionary guards led to duplicated command chains, with all the friction and lack of coordination which inevitably follows.

On the Iraqi side military leaders at all levels proved somewhat inflexible, appearing to set greater store by the textbook solution and in the profligate use of modern weapons systems than in using imaginative tactics. Iraq was considerably better-off for aircraft than Iran throughout the war; the latter's primarily US air fleet, which had been purchased by the Shah, proving increasingly difficult to keep in the air due to a lack of spares. However, although Iraq used its aircraft frequently they somehow failed to take advantage of the opportunities offered, although they improved somewhat from 1985 onwards.

Above right: Trainee tank crew of the North Vietnamese Army with their Soviet T-54 tank in December 1984, prior to deployment to Kampuchea. They are members of an army which has been at war virtually without a break since 1941 and which has won some notable victories against those they saw as aggressors. Most notable of these victories was, of course, against the USA.

Below: Indian troops arrive in Sri Lanka on a peace-keeping mission in 1987, in an effort to end the Tamil secession. They withdrew in 1989, but the problems remain.

– One parachute division, with six parachute infantry battalions and supporting arms and services.
– One air-portable marine division.
– One light armoured division.
– One mountain division.
– One air-mobile division, with 241 helicopters.

Not part of the FAR is the Foreign Legion, still some 8,500 strong and composed of one armoured, one parachute and four infantry regiments. There are also 11 marine infantry regiments, although it should be noted that the term 'marine' is not used to describe amphibious troops as in America or Britain, but rather is a traditional name for units raised to serve overseas. Altogether this is a formidable force and one which France has used on numerous occasions.

In the United States the majority of intervention forces are in Forces Command (FORSCOM), but with some also in Special Operations Command. The command is large, to say the least, comprising over one million men and women:

Above: 'Tamil Tigers' (with blindfolds) after their arrest by Indian troops near Batticaloa, Sri Lanka, September 1987.

Right: US Army M-60 tank roars down a road in Honduras, during a 1985 exercise designed to show US deployment capability.

Intervention Forces

The types of military forces used for limited wars cover a wide spectrum. At the lowest level are the basically equipped, unsophisticated forces of Third World countries. At the other end are the highly trained and well-equipped forces of countries such as Israel and India, which are on a par with any force found in Europe. Also, as the campaigns in Vietnam and Afghanistan have shown, there is a requirement for intervention forces, where a major army becomes involved in a conflict in another nation's territory. Such intervention, incidentally, is by no means confined to the USA and the USSR. The Indians have recently sent forces to both Sri Lanka and the Maldives, Cuba long had forces (some 60,000 of them) in Angola, and Vietnam, so long the victim of foreign occupation, sent some 50,000 troops to Laos and a similar number to Cambodia, although the latter garrison has been partially withdrawn. South Africa has sent its

troops on regular forays into the territories of its northern neighbours and Syrian troops are in the Lebanon in large numbers.

One of the countries to have a force quite unequivocally designated for overseas intervention is France, with its Force Action Rapide (FAR), which is some 47,000 strong. Outline composition is:

	Regular	Reserve	National Guard
Armoured divisions	2	–	2
Mechanized divisions	4	–	2
Infantry divisions	3	–	5
Light divisions	1	–	1
Airborne divisions	1	–	–
Air assault divisions	1	–	–
Armoured brigades	1	–	–
Infantry brigades	1	3	18
Armoured cavalry regiments	1	–	4

A typical example of their potential occurred in 1988 when *Sandinista* troops crossed from Nicaragua into Honduras. Within days a US infantry brigade task force, consisting of four battalions, two from 82nd Airborne Division and two from 7th Infantry Division (Light) had deployed to Honduras on 'exercise'. Within 18 hours of the orders being given the lead troops were in the air and within just over 30 hours 2,950 soldiers and airmen and 904 tonnes (890 tons) of equipment were on the ground at the destination. Within 12 days there were no Nicaraguan troops in Honduras. It was a classic demonstration of the use of force as a deterrent.

COUNTER-TERRORIST OPERATIONS

Terrorism is by no means a new phenomenon and for many years numerous countries have been plagued by small bands of marauders who have preyed upon the rest of society for reasons which have varied from the political to the simply criminal. Such groups have gone under a multitude of names, ranging from bandits, dacoits, terrorists and insurgents to resistance and freedom fighters. Such fighters, however, tended in the past to carry out very localized campaigns, frequently confining their activities to one region of a country and rarely, if ever, operating outside the national borders, except to find sanctuary.

Terrorism

A number of European armies came across terrorism in relation to anti-colonial campaigns. These campaigns included the French in Indo-China (1947–54) and Algeria (1954–62); the Dutch in Indonesia (1945–49); the British in Palestine (1945–48), Malaya (1948–60), Cyprus (1952–59), Kenya (1952–56) and Northern Ireland (1969 to the present); and the Portuguese in Angola (1961–74), Guinea (1962–74), and Mozambique (1962–74). Even these, however, rarely spread outside the colonial territory concerned, although there have been exceptions, with the Algerian FLN and the IRA carrying out terrorist attacks in the metropolitan country. But, over the past 30 years or so terrorism has taken on a new dimension.

In the first place terrorists have started to attack outside their national frontiers, but in pursuit of a completely national aim. Thus, bewildered third parties have found themselves hosting terrorist acts in which they have no involvement whatsoever. For example, in April 1980 a

Right: British soldier on a street corner in Northern Ireland. The current phase of the conflict has lasted for over 20 years.

group of terrorists from the Democratic Revolutionary Movement for the Liberation of Arabistan took control of the Iranian Embassy in London. Their cause was regional autonomy for Arabistan, a region of Iran, and was one in which the British had absolutely no involvement at all, not even in the days of the British Empire. Similarly, aircraft hijackings have taken place, such as that of the Lufthansa Boeing 737 on 13 October 1977, involving groups of terrorists which have no particular reason to attack the airline's country of origin. Recently the Provisional IRA has carried out attacks against British servicemen in West Germany, the Netherlands and Belgium, countries which, again, have no involvement in the affairs of Northern Ireland. Thus, countries can find themselves involved suddenly and totally unexpectedly in having to deal with a terrorist incident, involving men and women fighting for causes of which the national authorities have the scantiest knowledge.

Secondly, terrorists have become infinitely more sophisticated in both their methods and their equipment. The days of the terrorist manufacturing a make-shift pistol from a piece of tubing, a household bolt and a spring are long since gone, as real firearms, explosives (such as the Czechoslovak Semtex) are only too easy to obtain. Further, terrorists make full use of modern electronics for tasks ranging from monitoring police radios to detonating bombs by remote control. Terrorists also use modern methods of travel, and the ease of entering and leaving countries makes international movement about the world in pursuit of their aims a relatively simple matter.

Counter-Terrorist Equipment

At first the military units involved in counter-terrorist operations used standard military equipment such as service rifles, supplemented from time-to-time by off-the-shelf commercial equipment. However, as the terrorist operations have become more widespread, their likelihood increased and their equipment and techniques become more sophisticated, so the counter-terrorist units have had to respond with increasingly specialized equipment of their own. For example, one frequently encountered situation is

with a small group of terrorists holed up in a known location, holding one or more hostages. In such a situation the hostages are threatened with death against a promise of some action by the authorities, such as free passage for the terrorist group or release of prisoners held from a previous operation. The initial priority for the authorities is to establish the number and location of the terrorists and their hostages.

Firstly, the terrorist discussions can be monitored within the place where they

are holed-up (a building, aircraft, vehicle, train or ship); there is a whole range of devices now available to do this. Secondly, the vast majority of terrorist hostage takers are part of a larger organization and need to make contact from time to time with others in their group, but outside the hostage location. Whether they use telephone or radio it would be surprising if the counter-terrorist organization, with all the technical means of the government now at their disposal, were unable to intercept and

Right: US and Lebanese troops survey the damage after the bombing of the US Marines in Beirut on 23 October 1983, in which no less than 240 young men died.

monitor what was being said.

Thermal-imaging (TI) techniques are particularly valuable for the surveillance of the terrorists, with their output either coupled to a telescope or to a television monitor. These devices can show the location of people through even quite substantial obstructions and can reveal detail not apparent to the naked eye; for example, people taking refuge in shadows or standing back from windows. This is a technology which was developed for military surveillance on the conventional battlefield, was then applied to counter-terrorist operations and is now being used in civil applications such as by fire services searching for bodies in ruined buildings in a civil disaster such as an earthquake.

A piece of technology which came in the reverse direction from the medical operating theatre to counter-terrorist use is the borescope. This is a tiny, flexible, fibre-optic device which can be placed inside a patient to see inside an artery or a vein. In military counter-terrorist use it can be inserted through a minute hole to see through a wall or inside a suspicious object, with the picture being presented either to an optical lens, a still camera or a television screen.

Counter-terrorist operations require weapons to be very accurate, highly reliable and easy-to-use, both in operation and in handling. In the past standard service rifles such as the 7.62mm FN FAL were just too large and unwieldy, and special weapons had to be obtained, one excellent example of which is the West German Heckler & Koch 9mm MP5 sub-machine gun. This weapon is used by many special forces units around the world as well as by police anti-terrorist squads (such as London's Metropolitan Police, for example).

One of the most popular versions is the MP5SD3, which is fitted with a silencer and a folding stock. This weighs just 3.4kg (7.5 lb), which, combined with an overall length of just 610mm (24 in), makes it easy to handle. It has a cyclic rate of fire of 800rpm, although the number of rounds fired in each burst is fixed at the time of manufacture (typically, three or five) and cannot be varied by the firer. There is, of course, a comprehensive range of accessories, the most important of which are a variety of sights.

Although most counter-terrorist actions will take place at short range, for which a 9mm Parabellum round as used in the MP5 is quite suitable, there may well be occasions when a more powerful or longer range round is needed. Fortunately, the new 5.56mm service rifles are now suitable for special forces operations, especially those using the new NATO standard M193 5.56mm × 45 round. Perhaps one of the best of the rifles is the SR88, made by Chartered Industries of Singapore, which is reported to have done exceptionally well in trials around the world and is being adopted by a number of special forces. With its butt folded, this rifle is 746mm (29.37 in) long and empty weight is 3.66kg (8.07 lb); a short-barrel carbine version is shorter and lighter still. Effective range is 400m (1,312 ft).

For 'special tasks' high accuracy sniper rifles may be required and for this the heavier, more powerful and longer range NATO 7.62mm × 51 round is still preferred by most counter-terrorist units. Typical of the current generation is the British Accuracy International Model PM sniper rifle, a substantial weapon weighing 6.5kg (14.3 lb) and 1,194mm (47 in) long. (One of its competitors, the Heckler & Koch PSG1, also a 7.62mm weapon, is even heavier and larger at 8.1kg (17.85 lb) and 1,210mm (46.7 in). The bolt-action PM uses a small integral bipod for first-round accuracy, with a stainless steel barrel mounted on an integral chassis to which all other components (stock, butt, magazine, trigger group, etc.) are attached. Almost any sight can be mounted on the universal rail machined into the top of the action. Effective range of this rifle is 1,000m (3,280 ft) and a silenced version is available.

Opposite, above and below: **The terrible price of failure; charred bodies and wrecked aircraft lie abandoned at 'Desert One' following the abortive Delta Force attempt to rescue 53 American hostages held in Tehran, 27 April 1980.**

Below: **US Delta and helicopter crews prepare for Operation Eagle Claw to rescue US hostages in Tehran, 1980.**

Counter-Terrorist Units and Operations

Countries faced with such a threat have taken a number of steps to counter the terrorists. In the first place incidents taking place within the national territory can be dealt with by the police or by specially trained counter-terrorist units within the police force. However, operations outside the national territory and against major incidents within the national territory must be dealt with by soldiers.

Many armies now have special units formed to undertake counter-terrorist operations. In Britain, for example, the Special Air Service (SAS) is an Army unit raised in the Second World War and which gained experience in counter-insurgency operations in Malaya and the Oman before returning to England, where, among other tasks, it has developed the counter-terrorist role. A second unit, the Special Boat Service (SBS) is part of the Royal Marines and specializes in sea-borne operations.

In the USA the joint-service Delta Force was raised by Colonel Charlie Beckwith (who had previously served with the British SAS) in 1977. The attempt to rescue the hostages held in the US Embassy in Tehran took place in April 1979 and proved to be dogged by ill-luck, culminating in a disastrous crash at the rendezvous deep in Iran – 'Desert One'. Since then this unit has gone on to become one of the Free World's major counter-terrorist groups.

The great majority of these special forces units are raised from volunteers from national armed forces and are under the command of the military authorities. The Federal Republic of Germany, however, has found a different solution. Germany's special counter-terrorist unit is formed from the Federal Border Police, the *Grenzschutzpolizei*, and is under the control of the Ministry of the Interior, Department P (Police Affairs); even if a soldier wishes to enrol he must first leave the Armed Forces and become a policeman. The unit is designated *GrenzSchutzGruppe-9* GSG-9) and was raised in the aftermath of the 1972 Munich Olympics when Arab terrorists and their Israeli hostages were all killed in a dramatic shoot-out at the Fuerstenfeldbruck airfield. GSG-9 showed its mettle in the Mogadishu rescue operation in 1977, when they released 87 hostages from a hijacked Lufthansa Boeing 737.

Counter-terrorist units exist in the armed forces of other Western countries and one of the most effective of these is in Israel, although the actual unit itself remains, not surprisingly, strictly anonymous. The Israelis set an example to other nations when an Air France airliner en route from Tel Aviv to Paris was hijacked on 27 June 1976 by a combined Arab/Baader Meinhoff terrorist team, led

Above: Terrorists often lose; Israeli hostages return in triumph following their release from Entebbe in 1976.

Below and above right: The Arab attack on Israeli athletes in Munich in 1972 forced the West Germans to move armed police into the Olympic Village (below) and into the athletes' hostel (above right).

by a German. The airliner was flown to Entebbe in Uganda where the non-Jews were released, except for the Air France crew, who insisted on staying with their passengers. A rescue mission was mounted by the Israelis, in which four Lockheed C-130 Hercules aircraft landed at Entebbe at 0001 hours on 4 July and after a gun battle with the terrorists (who were given substantial assistance by Idi Amin's Ugandan Army) rescued the majority of the hostages. Three hostages were killed in the cross-fire during the rescue and one, who had earlier been taken to hospital, was subsequently murdered; one Israeli soldier was killed, the greatly respected leader, Lieutenant Colonel Yoni Netanyahu. All four terrorists and some 20 Ugandan soldiers were killed.

The Soviet Union's special forces are the Spetsnaz (Spetsialnoye Nazranie), who are intended for special operations in war, but who have an obvious counter-terrorist role. It is believed that these highly trained troops were the first to fly into Prague, during the 1968 Czechoslovak uprising and may also have been the spearhead of the Soviet invasion of Afghanistan. Almost certainly the largest single group of special forces in the world, the Spetsnaz are reported to number some 30,000 in peacetime. There is also a Soviet hostage release unit, set up some years ago by the KGB.

Above: The hero of the Entebbe raid, Lieutenant Colonel 'Yoni' Netanyahu, was killed by a stray shot from a Ugandan soldier after the hostages had been freed.

Below: Training in counter-terrorist operations must be constant.

GLOSSARY

The US Army's M-728 Combat Engineering Tractor

AAM	Air-to-Air Missile	DBFDU	Demountable Bulk Fuel Dispensing Unit
AAMG	Anti-Aircraft Machine-Gun		
ABM	Anti-Ballistic Missile	DF	Direction Finding
ADAM	Area Denial Artillery Munition	DMZ	Demilitarized Zone
		ECCM	Electronic Counter-Counter-Measure
ADM	Atomic Demolition Mine		
ADP	Automated Data Processing	ECM	Electronic Counter-Measure
AFATDS	Advanced Field Artillery Tactical Data System	ELINT	Electronic Intelligence
		EMP	Electro Magnetic Pulses
AFV	Armoured Fighting Vehicle	ERA	Explosive Reactive Armour
AI	Airborne Intercept		
APC	Armoured Personnel Carrier	EW	Electronic Warfare
		FAASV	Field Artillery Ammunition Support Vehicle
APDS	Armour Piercing Discarding Sabot		
		FAC	Forward Air Controller
APFSDS	Armour Piercing Fin Stabilized Discarding Sabot	FACE	Field Artillery Computer Equipment
		FIBUA	Fighting In Built-Up Areas
ASARS	Advanced Synthetic-Aperture Radar System	FLOT	Front Line of Own Troops
		FOFA	Follow-On Forces Attack
ASAS	All Source Analysis System	FTX	Full Troops Exercise
		GEMSS	Ground-Emplaced Mine-Scattering System
ATCCS	Army Tactical Command and Control System		
		GLCM	Ground Launched Cruise Missile
ATGW	Anti-Tank Guided Weapon		
AVLB	Armoured Vehicle-Launched Bridge	GPS	Gunner's Primary Sight
		GSFG	Group of Soviet Forces, Germany
AWACS	Airborne Warning and Control System		
		HARM	High-speed Anti-Radar Missile
BAOR	British Army of the Rhine		
CBS	Corps Battle Simulation	HEAT	High-Explosive Anti-Tank (weapon)
CCVL	Close Combat Vehicle, Light		
		HEMAT	Heavy Expanded Mobility Ammunition Trailer
CENTAG	Central Army Group (of NATO)		
		HEMTT	Heavy Expanded Mobility Tactical Truck
CET	Combat Engineer Tractor		
CPX	Command Post Exercise	HESH	High-Explosive Squash-Head
CTOL	Conventional Take-Off and Landing		
		HF	High Frequency
DAACM	Direct Airfield Attack Combined Munition	HOBOS	Homing Bombing System
		IFF	Identification Friend or Foe

The TOW missile launcher in action

195

Index

Photographic Acknowledgments

Brian Trodd Publishing House Ltd has supplied the following photographs with the help of the organizations listed: BTPH 194; Dassault-Breguet 72 top; Department of Defense 74 top, 105, 129 top, 156 bottom, 176–177 top, 190–191; Embraer 89 top; FRO 195; Lockheed 94; MBB 72 bottom; McDonnell Douglas 89 bottom.

Popperfoto has supplied the following photographs: 175 bottom left and right, 178, 179 top, 180 bottom, 181, 182, 182–183, 183, 184, 184–185, 185 top and bottom, 186 top and bottom, 187 top, 191 top and bottom, 192 bottom, 193 top left and right.

TRH Pictures have supplied the following photographs with the help of the organizations and photographers listed: 8, 15, 36–37, 58–59, 59 top, 153 bottom, 169 top, 171, 176–177 bottom; R Adshead 18–19, 25, 117 bottom, 133 bottom, 148, 168, 188; Aerospatiale 135 bottom; Bell Corp 69; Bofors 164; British Aerospace 79 bottom, 88; British Army, 3rd Armoured Division 143 right; British Army of the Rhine 157; CIMSA 125 left; Y Debay 10 top, 19, 26, 30 top and bottom, 31, 33 bottom, 36, 41 top, 45, 65, top, 103, 111 bottom; Department of Defense 6, 7 top and bottom, 14–15, 20, 27, 35 top and bottom, 40, 43, 46 top, 52–53, 53 bottom, 58, 59 bottom, 61 bottom, 70, 71, 74 bottom, 75, 77, 79 top, 80 top, 86, 93, 96, 97, 98, 100, 104, 111 top, 120 top, 122, 127, 128, 130 top, 131, 134, 135 top, 136 top, 137, 138, 139 top and bottom, 141, 142, 143 left, 146, 149 top and bottom, 151 bottom, 153 top, 154–155, 163, 166–167, 177, 179 bottom, 180 top, 187 bottom, 189, 192 top, 193; Department of National Defence, Canada 21, 46 top, 115; Emerson Electric 14, 107; Euromissile 65 bottom right; General Dynamics 22, 38; GIAT 42–43; GKN 130 bottom; Guy Taylor 47, 48 top and bottom, 52, 136 bottom, 144 bottom; Hughes 73, 82, 101; Imperial War Museum 12-13, 140 top, 151 top, 152, 175 top; Indian Army 108 top; Lockheed 81; Martin Marietta 57 top; Matra 106 right; MBB 62 top, 91, 92; McDonnell Douglas 63, 66, 67 top; bottom left and right; Ministry of Defence 9, 41 bottom, 53 top, 56–57, 108 bottom, 109, 126 top, 172, 173; Multilift 129 bottom; NATO 11, 29; E Nevill 10 bottom, 16, 17, 23, 28–29, 34, 37, 39 top and bottom, 60, 64, 65 bottom left, 68–69, 80 bottom, 83, 85, 86–87, 87, 110, 112, 114–115, 116, 117 top, 119 top and bottom, 120 bottom, 123, 124, 125 right, 126 bottom, 132, 133 top, 140 bottom, 144 top, 147 left and top right, 156 top, 160, 161, 165; Raytheon 57 bottom; RCA 99; M Roberts 33 top, 61 top, 62–63, 76, 78, 84, 106 left, 112–113, 118, 169 bottom; Shorts 56; Tass 54–55; Thomson CSF 147 bottom right; Thorn EMI 102; United Nations 12, 95, 174; United States National Archives 150; VSEL 44, 49.

Front cover: M-48 tank of the US Army in Vietnam (DoD)

Back cover: 155mm artillery piece of the US Army (DoD)

Title page: An M113 APC and M41 light tank of the Danish Army on NATO exercise in Germany (TRH/E Nevill)